STRATEGIC ALLIANCES
Managing The Supply Chain

STRATEGIC ALLIANCES
Managing The Supply Chain

Tim Underhill

PennWell Books

PennWell Publishing Company
Tulsa, Oklahoma

Copyright © 1996 by
PennWell Publishing Company
1421 South Sheridan
P.O. Box 1260
Tulsa, Oklahoma 74101

ISBN 0-87814-615-6

Printed in the United States of America

1 2 3 4 5 99 98 97 96

ACKNOWLEDGMENTS

I would like to express my appreciation to all of the people and companies who supported my efforts in producing this material. My special thanks to those people who generously supplied me with specific examples and with whom I worked to develop this material at;

Amoco Production Company
Arby Construction
Chevron USA
Mobil Oil Company
Red Man Pipe & Supply
Wisconsin Electric Company
Wisconsin Gas
Wisconsin Natural Gas

While their support is greatly appreciated, all use and conclusions are mine alone

Additional thanks to my editor, Marla Patterson, who provided invaluable comments and help along the way.

Finally, I am grateful to my wife Kristen and daughter Lauren for their patience and understanding which make my work possible.

Tim Underhill
September 1996

CONTENTS

PREFACE

There are many types of strategic alliances and each alliance relationship takes on its own attributes and characteristics. The focus of this book is on alliances that involve supply chain partners—the customer (end user), the supplier (commodity/service provider), and manufacturer. It takes a realistic look at how these alliances work and bases the information in the book on actual industry successes and failures. It views the way companies have taken existing customer/supplier relationships, or built new ones, and moved these relationships from transaction-focused interactions into total-cost-focused alliances.

Tim Underhill's experience with alliances began in 1988 when he worked with Dow Chemicals, Monsanto, Hoechst-Celanese and a number of industrial distributors on partnering and supplier evaluation issues. Since that time as President of Underhill & Assoc. in Tulsa, OK, he has worked with numerous manufacturers, suppliers and end users in almost every aspect of alliances. It is these experiences around which this book was written. From 1994 to 1996 alone his experiences have included working through various aspects of alliances with such companies as

Utility Industry
> Arby Construction; Barr Engineering; Border States Electric; Burmeister Electric; Cooper Industries; Dueco Inc.; Consumer Power; United Illuminating; Northern States Power; Water Pro Supplies; Mueller Pipeliners; Priester Supply; Ryder Truck; Vanyo Inc.; WESCO; Westinghouse Electric Co.; Wisconsin Electric Co.; Wisconsin Gas; and Wisconsin Natural Gas.

Oil & Gas Industry:
> Amoco Oil; Chevron USA; Coastal Management Co.; Exxon USA; Gerhardts, Inc.; Mobil Oil; Oxy Chemical; Phillips Petroleum; Red Man Pipe & Supply; Reiley Electric; and Warren Petroleum.

Process Industries
> B&T Hydraulics; Bearing Distributors; Bearings, Inc.; Central States Industrial Supply; Haynes International; Ingersoll-Rand; Jimmie Jones-Airgas; Kirby Risk; Miller Brewing; Strong Tool; Target Specialty Products; Thrall Distribution; and Velon Valves.

The cumulative knowledge from these various experiences has resulted in the development of a number of common methods and tools used by companies, which are discussed in this book. It will provide many insights for companies and individuals in working through such various aspects of alliance as:

- *Discovery*: The identification of which suppliers can best meet the needs of the organization, while at the same time minimizing the costs, performance concerns and risks perceived by the various personnel associated with the alliance and the supplier, is the primary objective of discovery. To accomplish the discovery process companies have found it beneficial to break this process into three parts; commodity/service planning, supplier evaluations, and final selection. Discovery is a key ingredient to ensuring the long term success of an alliance.

- *Implementation*: Coming to terms on how the companies will work together to reduce each others costs and to share the risks and rewards is the objective of implementation. The implementation aspect of alliances also has three parts; setting joint objectives, building a joint operating structure, and managing the change. Of the three parts managing the change is the area companies struggle with the most. Alliance can impact almost every area within a company, failure to meet everyone's needs can result in a higher not a lower total cost.

- *Maintenance:* The maintenance aspect of alliances has the objective of keeping the alliance moving forward while also meeting the day to day needs of both companies after the initial "push" fades away. Anyone can "form" an alliance. But most companies find that unless total costs are continuously reduced the alliance has a tendency to end. As one Amoco manager put it, "a low maintenance alliance can easily become a no alliance relationship." Companies which make it through implementation find the need to go beyond the initial savings to continuously reduce costs and measure savings.

- *Measuring Total Cost*: The traditional relationships between customer and supplier were comparatively easy to measure; price, availability and a few performance issues. But most alliances are based on the principle of minimizing Total Cost. Yet in order to minimize Total Cost, companies must know how to measure the components: price, performance, systems/objectives and value added, and be able to tie these cost measures together into on comprehensive model.

- *Selling Alliances:* Suppliers are faced with their own "discovery" process of determining which customers to form alliances with and with which customers not to form alliances. But for the supplier the discovery process has a double amount of effort. In order to sell their abilities to the customer, they need to understand the cost drivers important to the various customer personnel. It is the use of a methodology for understanding these needs that most suppliers have found to be invaluable in securing alliances.

An alliance can either be a relationship that *drives cost out* of a company or *drives additional costs in*. For most companies alliances are new ventures. This book provides insights and ideas for making that venture a success.

CHAPTER 1

STRATEGIC ALLIANCES

INTRODUCTION

Changing market realities are forcing companies to restructure their business in dramatic ways. This need to change can come from such forces as competitive threats, stockholder expectations, or internal business requirements. The result is that companies are forced to "right size" or position the company more profitably.

In an attempt to get back to basics, some companies are reviewing their core competencies, selling company divisions, and outsourcing processes. Others are reorganizing their internal structures and processes to better meet the changing market realities. One of the most innovative solutions to arise from these new business models is the concept of strategic alliance.

> *A strategic alliance is a joint effort by two or more companies linked together in the supply chain to reduce the total cost of acquisition, possession, and disposal of goods and services for the benefit of all parties.*

In working with a number of industrial associations and companies Underhill and Associates has found that for many companies the purchases of goods and services can account for as much as 55% of each sales dollar. This presents a huge opportunity to reduce the cost of doing business. Additionally, as restructuring occurs many companies find a need to reduce the number of suppliers utilized and to have these suppliers perform tasks that once were performed internally. The result is that strategic alliances (alliances) are increasingly impacting not only company supply chains but entire industries as a company's supplier base is reduced by as much as ninety percent.

Typically a customer company that forms an alliance with its suppliers forces changes in relationships, expectations, and job descriptions for many positions in both companies. For the customer these positions can include such areas as purchasing, maintenance/operations, accounting, information systems, and the warehouse. The supplier could expect positions to be affected in the sales force, and areas of purchasing, accounting, information systems, and delivery.

How are these functions impacted? As an example, the customer's purchasing department would no longer use the "three bids and a buy" concept for many goods and services. Instead, they would look at the *total cost* for the goods or services. *Total cost* can include such hidden factors as the costs of acquisition, possession, and disposal. This means a change in the work requirements for the purchasing department as the customer, in developing new supplier relationships, works more closely with the remaining suppliers. This move toward enhanced efficiency eliminates errors and waste in all the organizational systems affected by the suppliers. These systems usually include

- determination of requirements
- identification and selection of suppliers
- all stages of acquisition
- storage
- process of payment
- installation and construction
- operations and maintenance
- disposal

This also requires the purchasing department to insure that the goods or services being purchased meet both the short-term and long-term needs of both the users and the company.

The supplier's perspective changes as well—the sales force no longer *sells* to its alliance customers. Its job becomes one of problem solving, supporting personnel, and training. Selling, in the traditional sense, is not needed since the supplier already has all the business. (Note: some selling for additional territories and product lines does still occur—however, it is usually minimized). The other departments and functions in both companies are now expected to work with each other in evaluating inventories, systems, processes, new technologies, training, work methodologies, equipment utilization, and a host of other opportunities to reduce the cost of operations for both companies.

Ultimately, the impact of an alliance does not stop at the boundaries of the partner companies. In a number of alliance ventures we found that as many as nine other suppliers get *cut off*—that is, they lose the opportunity to sell goods and services to the customer when that customer forms alliances with a few chosen suppliers. This affects not only the unchosen supplier's own business but the business of *its* suppliers as well.

With such far-reaching repercussions many managers question the final outcomes and whether it is really a smart move to form alliances. The answer to this concern is not a simple yes or no. Both the customer and supplier need to consider the cost/benefit tradeoffs. For now, consider the rewards that Underhill and Associates has identified as having been achieved by some companies.

- AT&T expects to cut its cost by as much as $1 billion annually by 1997 using alliances.
- Ford and Chrysler have dramatically reduced total operation costs using alliances.
- Using the alliance concepts, Amoco, Chevron, and Mobil have reduced their operational costs by as much as 10 to 20 percent with some of their suppliers.
- In the utility industry, companies such as Wisconsin Electric are using alliances to improve their position and rates as the market goes through deregulation.
- In the retail industry, Wal-Mart and other companies have worked with their suppliers to help reduce costs and to position Wal-Mart in a position of high profitability and lower prices.
- A recent Ernst & Young study estimates 85% of the companies in the electronics industry have a least one alliance in place.
- In the health care industry Columbia/HCA has used alliances to reduce cost by $ 200 million.

The reason so many companies and industries are moving into alliances is because companies can improve their competitive edge through increased sales, reduced operating costs, more streamlined systems, and by refocusing on core competencies. Additional studies by Arthur D. Little estimate that in some industries 80 percent of new technology in the United States is now obtained through alliances. Sharing research and development allows companies to reduce risks and costs, while at the same time reap the rewards of new technology.

While the results for many companies has been positive, *not all alliances work.* Failed alliances usually occur due to poor implementation, leading to unfulfilled expectations. The cost of failure is often high. Companies need to identify which costs can be affected and how to measure those costs. They also must determine the value associated with improvements and the primary barriers to overcome during implementation.

Total Cost of Acquisitions, Possession & Disposal

The first concept to understand with a strategic alliance is that each company in a supply chain affects some of the costs in the other company(s) beyond pricing. While price will always be a major component of total cost, other costs exist that can have an even greater impact on the bottom line. In the initial stages of forming an alliance, companies usually focus on four primary categories of cost in addition to price.

For hard goods this focus is usually on the processes of *ordering and invoicing, inventory* and *quality issues.* For service companies it most often revolves around *planning/scheduling of personnel, paper processes, equipment/consummables* and *quality issues.* Keep in mind that while these costs receive the most attention, they may represent only 30% of the costs which can be affected. To illustrate the impact this can have, consider the following examples:

Inventory Reduction

Many customers are looking at how they can safely get out of the inventory business. The operative word in this case is <u>safely</u>. Customers carry inventory primarily because it has been costly in the past to rely on suppliers to always have the required supplies available. Therefore the customer carries it *just in case.*

One of the major auto companies recently determined that it was spending 80 percent of its time pursuing less than 15 percent of its inventory items. The same was found at Miller Brewing which estimated that 80 percent of its time went into the purchase of maintenance, repair and operations (MRO) goods, even though those purchases amounted to 20 percent of its total expenditures. Such findings can lead to purchasing greater quantities than needed in an attempt to reduce processing costs and the odds of running short, which in turn leads to higher inventories.

In point of fact, Miller and other companies are finding that they have an inventory turnover ("turn") of just one per year for most MRO-type materials. This means the dollars invested in these items is equal to the expenditures expected to occur during the succeeding 365 days. Naturally, not all items have the same turn. Some items would be depleted in six weeks—others would last for six years. Also, some inventories such as direct materials may have better turns but the investment is is often larger.

The cost of carrying these excess supplies is high, ranging from 23 to 40 percent of the average value of a company's inventory. For example, take a company which has $10 million in inventory. The company must either borrow money to pay for the inventory or forego investment opportunities. Many companies use this cost of money as the value to calculate carrying cost, however the true carrying cost includes much more.

Most states impose a tax on inventory and most companies pay insurance on inventories. Add to this the cost of shrinkage and spoilage and the average annual cost to a company is between 15 and 25 percent of the amount invested in inventory. It is also a *hard cost*, meaning that dollars directly attributed to carrying inventory can be saved and have an immediate impact on profits. Other costs, such as the warehouse or storage rooms where inventory is kept or cost of employees to stock, manage, and move inventory, are *soft costs*. Consequently, the savings to a company would not actually accrue to the bottom line unless the company restructured or redeployed its assets. This soft cost can add an additional 8 to 15 percent to the annual hard costs of carrying inventory. So the yearly cost of carrying $10 million in inventory is somewhere between $2.3 and $4 million with hard costs averaging $2 million.

Companies are pursuing a number of inventory cost reduction approaches. These include:

- inventory *consignment* by the distributor/supplier
- dead and surplus inventory buy-backs by the supplier
- help in outsourcing surplus inventory to the supplier's other customers
- "just-in-time" delivery
- warehouse takeovers
- stock management by the supplier

- temporary consignment for projects (location trailers)
- standardization of inventory
- better planning of inventory needs/usage

Some companies are working with their suppliers to further reduce costs by having the manufacturer consign material at the customer's location, and having the distributor to manage it. Figure 1.1 illustrates the potential benefits of this approach. Using 20 percent as the cost of carrying inventory, each company's carrying costs are represented. All carrying costs are based on the end user's price.

Figure 1-1 The carrying costs comparisons based on ownership and management

The Cost to Carry $10,000,000 (valued at end users price)

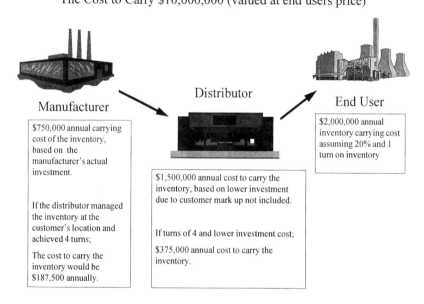

Manufacturer

$750,000 annual carrying cost of the inventory, based on the manufacturer's actual investment.

If the distributor managed the inventory at the customer's location and achieved 4 turns;

The cost to carry the inventory would be $187,500 annually.

Distributor

$1,500,000 annual cost to carry the inventory, based on lower investment due to customer mark up not included.

If turns of 4 and lower investment cost;

$375,000 annual cost to carry the inventory.

End User

$2,000,000 annual inventory carrying cost assuming 20% and 1 turn on inventory

For the end user, it is pretty straightforward. End users usually have turns on MRO inventories of approximately one. As such, the carrying cost is $2 million. If the distributor were to carry the same material for the customer (by consignment or "just-in-time" delivery), the cost would be approximately $1.5 million or $500,000 less. This initial ability to incur a lower carrying cost is based on the average distributor's cost of goods sold which is 75 percent of the customer's price; therefore, the average investment is 25 percent less. The customer's $10 million investment is only $7.5 million for the distributor. The manufacturer's cost to carry the same inventory would be $750,000, based on an inventory value of $3,750,000 because a manufacturer's inventory is often valued at one-half the selling price.

While this potential savings is impressive, the number of turns on inventory that can be achieved while maintaining high service levels is another factor in the true cost of carrying inventory. The average distributor has turns of approximately four while still maintaining a high service level. Therefore, the $10 million in inventory the customer keeps in order to insure that all service requirements are met is often reduced by the distributor to one quarter of that amount.

Granted, not all customers have an inventory turn of one—some are better. But there are also better distributors, some with turns as high as twelve. Yet, by using these averages, a distributor's costs go down to $375,000 annually. If the manufacturer consigns the inventory and the distributor manages it and achieves four turns the annual cost is $187,500.

But why would a customer use a distributor if the manufacturer can consign inventory for so much less? Remember the operative word—*safely*! Many manufacturers cannot spend a great deal of time servicing a single account, but a distributor can. The reason some companies have the manufacturer consign material and the distributor manage the inventory is due to total costs. Part of a distributor's core business is to manage inventory. Most do it better than the other companies on either side of the supply chain simply because it is part of their core competencies. Additionally, they carry inventory for many customers, so if an unusual usage occurs they can restock the customer quickly from their inventory. Distributors also represent multiple manufacturers. By going direct, a customer's supplier base would grow dramatically, increasing both ordering and invoicing costs and slowing the acquisition process, thereby leading to higher inventories. Thus most customers are using the distributor to save the $2 million in annual carrying costs to minimize service requirement risks and costs. Yet, keep in mind that to accomplish this the manufacturer or distributor would incur an additional cost between $187,500 and $375,000.

Why would companies accept these increased costs? Sometimes they do not, and often cannot unless the customer is willing to pay some additional amount (approximately a 2-4% increase in sales price) to save the $2,000,000. That is a nice return on investment for the customer and pays for the supplier's increased cost of doing business thereby minimizing the risk of the supplier cutting corners, which could result in lower service levels and higher costs.

Other times the supplier accepts the increased cost because of the reduced sales and inventory risks and the ability to plan better, which can reduce its cost of doing business. Keep in mind that while the example revolved around MRO goods, companies are also pursuing the same concept with direct materials.

Process Costs

The impact a supplier has on the customer's processes is often overlooked, and the actual cost of a process may not be known. This is particularly true when looking at the ordering and invoicing processes. For example, Wisconsin Electric Power Company (WEPCO) initially had 136 different suppliers of electrical parts for the transmission of electricity. In dealing with all of these suppliers, individual orders were running over 2000 per month, and consequently a comparatively large number of invoices were also being processed. Estimates obtained by Underhill & Associates from a number of companies and industries shows a company's average cost is approximately $110 from the point at which an order is received until an invoice is processed. This cost includes

- determination of goods and service needs
- needs determination for delivery
- entering the order into the computer
- checking on information to ensure correct product is bought
- phone time to receive three bids and a buy
- evaluation of bids
- physical receipt of goods
- matching freight bill, packing list with order
- processing receipt
- sending paperwork to accounts payable
- entering paperwork into computer
- matching for payment
- receipt of invoice
- matching invoice to receipt
- receiving payment authorization
- cutting the check
- mailing the check

Having learned the significance of such costs, WEPCO set out to reduce them. Like many companies WEPCO's first step in the process was to reduce its suppliers to only one. They are considering the following alternatives to reduce these process costs further:

- EDI for ordering and invoicing
- bar coding
- automated clearinghouse for payment
- electronic fund transfer for payment
- summary billing
- credit cards for purchasing
- consolidated ordering

To illustrate the impact such initiatives have, the following diagram depicts two processes from the time the buyer places the order through the receipt of the invoice on to the payment of the order and the costs a company incurs to process the paperwork. In this example, the average cost for processing paperwork is split evenly between the two primary segments of this process to illustrate how costs can be affected. Part A shows the yearly cost using the traditional method of ordering and invoicing. Part B shows the cost if only two alliance methods were used; consolidated ordering by a customer and summary billing by the supplier.

Figure 1.2 Processing costs and the impact alliances can have in reducing these costs)

A - Typical Processing Costs of $1,320,000

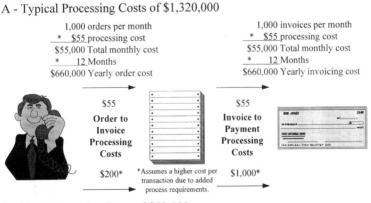

1,000 orders per month	1,000 invoices per month
* $55 processing cost	* $55 processing cost
$55,000 Total monthly cost	$55,000 Total monthly cost
* 12 Months	* 12 Months
$660,000 Yearly order cost	$660,000 Yearly invoicing cost

$55 — Order to Invoice Processing Costs

$55 — Invoice to Payment Processing Costs

$200*   *Assumes a higher cost per transaction due to added process requirements. $1,000*

B - New Processing Costs of $72,000 (Cost reduction occurs due to reduced transaction frequency)

25 consolidated orders per month	1 consolidated invoice per month
* $200 new processing cost	*$1,000 new processing cost
$5,000 Total monthly cost	$1,000 Total monthly cost
* 12 Months	* 12 Months
$60,000 Yearly order cost	$12,000 Yearly invoicing cost

Part A shows the processing costs that companies most often incur. Assuming a company places 1000 orders per month and incurs an average cost of $55 to determine order needs and place, expedite, and receive the order, the monthly cost comes to $55,000 or an annual cost of $660,000. The same costs occurs on the payment side, when a company matches the paper, enters it into the computer, corrects discrepancies, and cuts a check. The total annual processing costs comes to $1,320,000.

Part B shows the cost of ordering when purchasing from a single supplier. Instead of 1000 orders placed to many different suppliers only 25 orders are placed per month to one supplier, or one order per day. This consolidation requires more work. Consequently, the average cost to order climbs to $200 per order or a total monthly ordering cost of $5,000 and an annual cost of $60,000.

The supplier also uses a billing methodology called summary billing. Instead of billing each order, a bill for the entire month's purchases is supplied, complete with back up documentation. Naturally, a bill of this type requires more than $55 to process, so a $1000 cost is applied for a monthly cost of $1000 and a yearly cost of $12,000. The total processing cost comes to $72,000, or a $1,248,000 savings annually.

The numbers do not necessarily reflect the savings WEPCO is experiencing. This is due in part to different processing costs and different methods of processing paperwork with different suppliers. However, companies are saving millions in reduced processing costs impacted by their supplies. Several years ago Tenneco completed a study and found 139 steps in their process from receipt of the invoice to payment of the invoice. This represents only half of the equation just shown and yet, supplies a good example of why processing costs are so high. Suppliers can also affect other processing costs in an organization including planning, scheduling, production, maintenance, and repair. National Semiconductor has determined it will save $7 million a year in processing cost through enhanced supplier relationships.

But a word of caution should be made at this point. Changes in processing costs are usually soft costs, unlike many of the costs associated with carrying inventory which can have an immediate impact on a company's bottom line. Processing costs often take time to affect the bottom line and in some cases may never affect it. This may occur because companies fail to restructure or redeploy assets. A change in a process affects mostly people and overhead, such as office and warehouse space, computer usage, and other equipment requirements. In order that the benefits impact the company positively the company must redeploy those affected.

Outsourcing And Services

Many customers focus first on goods when setting up alliances. The reason is quite simple: hard goods are easier to define, measure, and compare against other similar goods. Yet, for companies outside of manufacturing, services can account for as much as half of the purchases. Services also tend to be approached differently from products because of the costs they affect. Unlike most products, with services the customer often has a choice of creating an internal supplier to perform the task or hiring a supplier to perform it. The types of services around which alliances are formed revolve around processes or operations such as

- mailroom
- credit
- accounting
- fleet management/repairs
- purchasing
- warehouse operations
- training
- computer maintenance/support
- engineering/technical support
- construction crews

This list is not exhaustive yet it makes an important distinction between products and services—the customer has the choice to furnish all, part, or none of the needed services. This often causes more internal strife than when dealing with hard goods because it can have a direct impact on the co-workers' job securities or an employee's departmental status and power.

The reason some services that were traditionally in-house operations are now outsourced is simple—even good companies cannot do everything well. Remember the old saying, "a jack-of-all-trades, but a master of none." Some companies are starting to understand the need to focus on core competencies. Ford Motor Company is a good example. They have focused on design and assembly as two of their core competencies. The actual manufacturing of most auto parts is outsourced because other companies can often manufacture parts better, faster, and less expensively.

Compare a typical company's accounts payable department to American Express and other credit card companies. Which company is more likely to process invoices more efficiently? Who can process the paperwork and make the payment in four days? Usually it is the credit card company, while the typical company struggles to pay invoices within 30 to 45 days. That is why companies like Shell Oil have outsourced part of their payable functions and divested their credit card processing activities.

Yet, efficiency is only one issue for a company to consider. If the service company can do it for less, do they do a good job or do they cut corners? This is more difficult to measure and may explain why many companies faced with a concern about outsourcing start with non-strategic operations (This concept will be discussed in more detail in Chapters 2 and 6).

Consider two potential services being offered today: outsourcing warehouse operations and purchasing. Which of the two would more likely be outsourced to a supplier? In most cases it is warehousing. With many companies having only one turn and warehouse operators having proven track records of between four and twelve with higher service levels it is becoming more common to outsource this operation. However, both can be outsourced. Companies like Tenneco are moving in the direction of becoming purchasing outsourcers. With strong buying power and more streamlined processes they are starting to make inroads. Fleet specialty companies now operate service bays for customers and Ryder Truck is taking over management of fleet operations for customers. Temporary employee companies are growing by expanding their offerings, in some cases operating a company's mailroom or managing secretarial services.

Why do companies turn over these activities to service companies? In many cases the service company offers an expertise that cannot be achieved in-house. This is particularly true for services that are in a constant state of change. For example, as training becomes more and more important to companies some have turned to universities to assess their needs and provide training. Training is one of the universities' core competencies. In other companies, it may be the computer system. With the explosion and rapid development of new software and hardware some companies find it costly to keep pace, and so are turning to companies which specialize in these areas.

When service alliances are formed, it does not mean everything must be turned over to the supplier. Some situations require this, while other companies may only need competent assistance in handling excesses. One example is the gas utility business. While some gas utility companies have completely outsourced certain construction activities, such as laying new lines or servicing existing lines, other gas utility companies consider this too strategic to their needsand keep their own crews to perform the work. Yet, they form alliances with construction companies to handle the excess work requirements.

Wisconsin Natural Gas (WNG) and Consumers Power (CP) have taken the philosophy of using an alliance to reduce variation costs; yet they keep part of this operation in-house. One of the biggest cost factors both companies hope to reduce is the variation of labor needs. If the lowest work requirement throughout the year is a need for 200 employees and the peak requirement is 300 employees, the variance cost can be high. Both WNG and CP must either pay for idle time or constantly hire, train, and then lay off additional workers. To avoid this cost both companies are considering an alliance company to manage their fluctuating needs. Since the construction company has other customers, it is easier for them to smooth out this variation. By sourcing with a single supplier the construction company can make better plans, resulting in lower prices and better service to the customer.

Quality Issues and the Supply Chain

The quality concept can apply to every aspect of a company's business including performance issues, duplicated efforts, misinformation, transfer of effort, and expenditures. Yet most companies focus primarily on deliveries when evaluating the quality their suppliers. However, while correct or on-time deliveries can affect a number of costs such as increased inventories, process costs, and down-time, many improvements that could potentially affect as many cost factors are overlooked.

Amoco Oil Company went beyond assessing the impact of its immediate supplier and started analyzing the entire supply chain. This included reviewing the costs of suppliers and the suppliers' suppliers. The following diagram represents the waste Amoco uncovered.

Figure 1.3 Primary tasks found in the typical tubular goods supply chain

Today's Typical Supply Chain

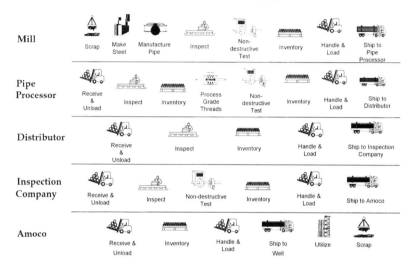

There are 33 steps represented in this diagram of which 23 are repeated steps. Amoco used the review information to work out a plan to eliminate some of these duplicated efforts. Their goal was to work with companies in the supply chain to eliminate 24 steps, reducing the process from 33 steps to 9. This can be seen in the next diagram.

Consider what this reduction means to Amoco. Since each company in the supply chain had to inventory the items where shown and since holding the inventory incurs costs, each company must add this cost to its pricing in order to be profitable. The same holds true for each handling, shipping, inspection, and testing step. Each time these steps are performed Amoco incurs a higher price, and for each step that could be eliminated costs could be reduced.

Figure 1.4 How the tubular supply chain could be improved through process step reduction

TOMORROW'S ALLIED SUPPLY CHAIN

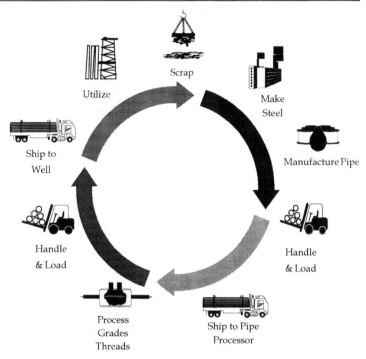

Scrap

Utilize

Make
Steel

Ship to
Well

Manufacture Pipe

Handle
& Load

Handle
& Load

Process
Grades
Threads

Ship to Pipe
Processor

Copyright Amoco Production Company

To date, more than 15 steps have been eliminated from Amoco's supply chain process, resulting in a better price to the customer and lower operating costs and higher profits for the companies involved. In order to accomplish this, Amoco worked closely with one company in each supply chain link. Instead of using multiple companies only one mill, pipe processor, distributor, and inspection company were utilized. The traditional approach could potentially have involved more than 100 different supply chain combinations. Now only one combination exists. This allows for better planning, scheduling, and communication.

Joint Effort

Each of the previous examples have looked at the common costs that companies are attempting to reduce. However, these common costs only represent a small proportion of the impact which can be made on total cost when companies work together. Most companies begin looking at these easier opportunities, yet even these costs require a joint effort to affect the bottom line. As companies dig deeper into the available opportunities, the work to exploit these savings grows greater.

Return for a moment to the inventory issue. In order to reduce the costs of carrying inventory the customer must feel comfortable that the supplier will have the right product at the right place at the right time. Yet this often fails to occur because a supplier's inventories may fluctuate dramatically—a factor of which the customer may be unaware. Changes in the customer's buying habits and requirements (perhaps due to shut-downs, expansions, non-repetitive projects, or other events) affect what the supplier should carry but these changes are often poorly communicated The two companies must communicate to understand each other's costs, needs, and goals if total cost is to be reduced. Reducing inventories will not achieve a lower total cost if the plant cannot operate because the needed products are not available.

The same holds true for reducing the cost of processes and quality. Only by working together can companies identify the costs that can be reduced without increasing other costs. The common costs that are the easiest to identify and reduce have been addressed thus far. Many more costs can be reduced but require increased effort to implement.

Figure 1.5 represents some of the obvious and not-so-obvious *cost drivers* that can be affected by an alliance relationship. The concept of cost drivers can be defined as *the consumption or expenditure of any resource or the limitations incurred on revenues (more on this subject in Chapter 2).* The obvious cost drivers provide a tangible target to attack and yet may represent only about 30 percent of potential cost reductions. The other 70 percent of the costs are usually hidden, take more effort to attain, and yet these hidden costs can be equally destructive to a company's bottom line.

Figure 1.5 The potential-cost iceberg. Most companies focus only on the costs they can see and miss many others.

The cost drivers represented in the figure are only a few. A more comprehensive list of possible cost drivers can be found in Appendix A. Also, keep in mind the Amoco supply chain example. Every cost a customer forces its suppliers to incur must somehow be paid for through increased prices or reduced services. This simply changes where and how the cost is incurred. To truly eliminate the cost companies must understand each other's cost drivers and work together to reduce internal waste and create greater efficiencies. This is the first step to successful alliances and mutual profitability.

Benefit of all Partners

Research by McKinsey & Company consultants found that two-thirds of alliances run into serious managerial or financial problems within the first two years and only 50 percent are judged to be successful. These results have lead to an average life expectancy of less than 3.5 years for most alliances. Why does this occur? The benefits are there. Allied Signal, Chevron, Mobil, WEPCO, Texas Instruments, Chrysler and Microsoft have found them to work. In many cases the savings can be in the tens of millions. And yet, half the alliances fail.

There are a host of reasons for those failures which will be discussed in greater detail in Chapter 4. For now, keep in mind that while failure is still quite common, improvements in the survival rates are being made.

The reason for improved survival rates is because companies are learning from both the successes and the failures of other companies. The graph below (Fig. 1.6) represents the learning curve that alliance companies are experiencing.

The first stage is the *explorer* stage. As the graph depicts, only a few of the first companies that attempted to form alliances succeeded. Estimates by Underhill and Associates place the initial failure rate at around 70 percent. This high failure rate is indicative of most new ideas—for example, Thomas Edison tried more than 1000 times before creating a light bulb that worked. The companies that succeeded found the balance for benefits and costs between the companies involved, developed sound implementation plans, and determined how to manage the ongoing concerns of both parties in the alliance.

Figure 1.6 Rate of alliance past and projected failure rates

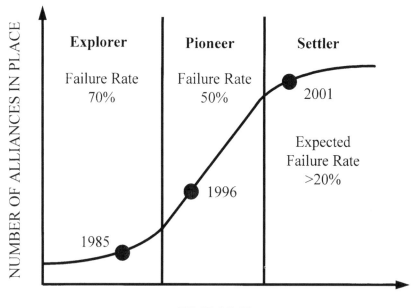

TIME LINE

The second stage is the *pioneer* stage. Once a number of companies were successful and gained an advantage from forming alliances, other companies started to follow their lead. From studying past successes companies could determine the factors that led to successful alliances. Others learned from suppliers who had successful alliances with those early explorers. The point on the graph labeled "1996" shows just the tip of expected growth. The growth of alliances in the near future is predicted to be phenomenal.

The settler stage will be the time when companies will create alliances because the risk seems lower. Yet, in reality, there will never be a guarantee of safety. Alliances do create aspects of risk, some of which can never be eliminated. As such, alliances are not for every company and every relationship.

Risks can range from an alliance partner who fails to perform to changes in management philosophy or key personnel. However, the biggest reason for failure tends to be that the alliance is not a win/win situation for both parties. A study by Harrigan Company consultants found that in only 45 percent of alliances are both partners happy. In 12 percent of the alliances both companies are unhappy. This infers that 55 percent of alliances include an unhappy or dissatisfied partner. The result, a failed attempt and often high costs to "get things back to normal" for approximately 55 percent of the alliance attempts.

Alliances must be created for the benefit of all parties. Too often alliances are misused and suppliers simply get beat up on price, or suppliers promise everything a customer requests in an attempt to get the business and then fails to supply all the promised services. Companies need to understand each other's cost drivers in order to work together to improve satisfaction for both companies.

The following example of the typical industrial distributor (supplier) illustrates the dilemma that can exist. Many companies use a distributor because they represent many manufacturers and can greatly reduce both risks and the cost of processing orders by carrying abundant inventory locally. The typical distributor has a Net Profit Before Tax (NPBT) of between 2 and 5 percent of sales. The actual percentage will vary from industry to industry, and some distributors have a 10 percent or better NPBT. The price they pay for goods is usually around 75 percent of the price they charge for these same goods. Consequently, distributors do not have a great deal of leeway to reduce the price of goods sold.

Figure 1.7 Price focus in alliance relationships can lead to higher total costs

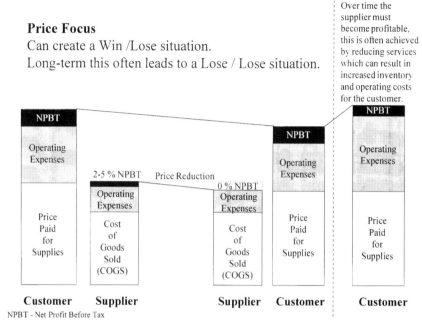

Price Focus

Can create a Win /Lose situation.

Long-term this often leads to a Lose / Lose situation.

Over time the supplier must become profitable. this is often achieved by reducing services which can result in increased inventory and operating costs for the customer.

NPBT - Net Profit Before Tax

Figure 1.7 shows the impact of focusing only on price. In order to be profitable, the supplier must reduce its overall costs. Sometimes larger orders and deliveries associated with going to a single source can result in lower operating cost because the supplier can get synergies from these significantly larger deliveries. Additionally, the supplier may be able to work deals with the manufacturers based on the additional volume. However, the reality in many cases is that the customer does not consolidate orders and requires increased services, resulting in higher operating costs for the supplier.

Manufacturers are also reluctant to provide significantly lower prices, with the end result being the relationship is unprofitable for the supplier. Suppliers feel forced to accept this because of the fear of losing the account to a competitor. Over time the supplier is forced to find ways to reduce its operating costs. The result is often reduced services, and unless the customer works with the supplier to reduce the supplier's operating expenses, the customer *pays* through its own operating cost being increased. Inventory goes up, poor performance increases inspection needs, down-time and delays result in higher costs and lost revenues, and both companies become unhappy.

GM experienced such events. After reducing costs over several years, they refocused on price. While some suppliers did reduce their prices to GM, these same suppliers could no longer afford to provide some services. Additionally, any new ideas or hard-to-get products were provided by the suppliers to GM's competitors first because it was more profitable for the suppliers. The result of such actions for some customers are production delays and escalating inventories, all of which can take their toll on the bottom line.

Figure 1.8 Total cost focus can reduce all costs if companies work together

Total Cost Focus
Can create a Win / Win relationship if companies understand each others costs and work to reduce each others costs.

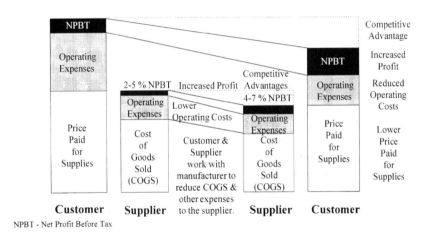

Figure 1.8 shows how working with suppliers can result in both reduced costs and better pricing for the customer. But in order to achieve a lower price, the supplier must be able to reduce its costs, and in many cases the customer must help achieve this goal if the alliance is to survive over the long term. Each partner must work to improve the profit potential of the other partner.

This improvement in profit can come in many forms such as
- reduced operating costs
- increased sales
  - other geographical areas
  - other products/services
  - 100 percent of business in product/services provided
- better planning

The most important point is that both companies can win. Through working together, suppliers can reduce operating costs, and by working together with the manufacturer they can potentially reduce the cost of goods sold (COGS) and other supply chain costs. Some suppliers are finding sound customer alliances not only improve their customer's profitability, but their own profitability as well.

But the key point to remember is that it takes a great deal of work. Simply giving one supplier all of the business is not enough. Understanding each other's costs, processes and the waste each company creates for the other is key if it is to be a win/win relationship.

Lessons from Total Quality

For years companies have attempted to implement the Total Quality Process, and while some companies have experienced a certain amount of success many have not. Research by Ernst and Young shows most companies quit after trying the process for several years, in part because management commitment was lacking and results were slow in coming. Studies by Underhill & Associates found that many companies could only impact one-third of the waste in their companies because external forces affect the other two-thirds.

This is where the concept of supply chain management comes into play. Research at Texas A & M University shows that 30 percent of a distributor's gross margin dollars are wasted. Based on the information above, that can amount to 7.5 percent of sales, more than most suppliers have as net profit before tax. Research also shows that one-third of this waste is created by the customer or end-user and that without the customer's help the supplier cannot eliminate this waste.

The customer has the same basic problem. Only one-third of the company's waste can be affected without working to correct problems either above or below in the supply chain.

Figure 1.9 Two-thirds of the waste occurring inside a company results directly from the actions of its trading partners.

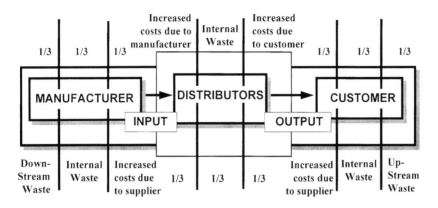

30% of a distributor's gross margin is wasted (approximately 7.5% of sales).
Customers and manufacturers each create 1/3 of this waste.
Attacking this waste through alliance efforts can triple a distributor's bottom line.
Both customers and manufacturers suffer the same impact.

Figure 1.9 depicts this unnecessary waste. By the customer, supplier, and manufacturer working together they can each reduce their overall costs to a far greater extent than working alone.

For example, WEPCO and Border States formed an alliance. The results over a nine-month period amounted to more than $3 million in savings to WEPCO on $10 million in sales. This amounts to a 30 percent savings from the previous year's costs! So what happened? Keep in mind that suppliers incur risk, primarily in terms of inventory. Too little inventory can cost the supplier as much or more than too much inventory. Both result in suppliers having to expend more effort to either source the material or get the customer to buy it.

If a customer buys the same material from five sources, then all five sources must maintain inventories to satisfy the possible demand for products. Failure to have the inventory on hand could cost sales, an expensive cost driver to the supplier.

When the customer moves to a single source the risk for the supplier diminishes. Now demand can be more certain and supply can better match the needs of the customer. The supplier can therefore experience both lower risk and lower costs assuming the customer works with the supplier. Further, the supplier now has more leverage to work with its manufacturers and secure better terms and methods for reducing costs.

DOW Chemicals used this leverage to their advantage several years ago when they picked a supplier of electrical parts who did not represent the manufacturer of choice. Together DOW and the supplier negotiated with the manufacturer and secured a method so that DOW could get a good price and have the products go through the supplier of choice.

Mobil experienced the same situation with some of its valves. Mobil and Red Man Pipe & Supply worked together with a manufacturer, which resulted in the manufacturer giving Red Man far better pricing than it had been able to secure in the past.

Companies attempting to achieve long-term viability of reduced costs must learn each other's processes and work together to reduce both companies' costs to grow both businesses. This growth will come from two directions—reduced costs and increased revenues. These two variables are starting to form the basis of measurement for a number of companies when evaluating the total cost concept of purchasing and selling. Jimmie Jones, a supplier of welding products, had a customer, a rail car manufacturer, that was experiencing high capacity at two plants. The supplier evaluated the customer's methods and suggested using argon shielding, rather than the carbon shielding the customer was using. The price was somewhat higher, but in this case, the change in products allowed the customer to increase production by $1 million in unit output, making the increase in price almost insignificant.

Naturally, this is not always the case. Sometimes the higher price is not worth the value it brings. Only by looking at the impact of all the cost drivers can the best decision be made. This will also require the customer to determine how to evaluate goods and services on a total cost basis. Total cost is not a new concept for most industries. What may be new are the tools companies have developed and are using to determine total cost. While a number of different models exist; the models named here incorporate the following three primary components and relate them to risks and costs:

- *Price:* the amount paid for the goods or services.
- *Performance Measures* : the added cost of doing business due to poor performance (+).
- *Added Value:* the reduction in costs and increase in revenues provided by other partner (-).

Together, these three components form the basis of total cost. A fourth component deals with assessing the supplier's ability to meet the objectives and system requirements a customer might have. It should be noted that the added-value piece of this model is somewhat counter-intuitive, because it makes added value a negative. However in terms of *cost*, it is a negative in that it reduces cost. Models depicting total cost are based on one overriding assumption; the company believes there are cost drivers other than price on which a supplier has an impact. Companies that understand these costs create models around the total cost to determine just how valuable a given supplier is to the needs of the customer.

This concept, and others such as "Total Life Cycle Costs" and "Total Systems Costs" look at all costs associated with a given product or service. Only through these total cost evaluations can a customer determine the impact a supplier has on the bottom line.

STAGES OF ALLIANCES

By studying both successful and failed alliances lessons can be learned about which factors make alliances work and which factors inhibit an alliance's success. Almost all alliances move through three stages: *Discovery*, *Implementation*, and *Maintenance*. The more successful alliances have much in common in terms of the time, resources, and methodologies used in each stage. Of particular interest is the time devoted to the Discovery stage by successful alliances in comparison to the time spent in the Implementation stage by less successful attempts.

Figure 1.10 The stages and main components of successful alliances

Stage 1 - Discovery

The Discovery stage deals with understanding which products or services are the best candidates around which to form alliances. This initial step is called *commodity/service planning*. The purpose for the customer is to determine, prior to selecting a supplier,

- which goods and services to group together
- which objectives and cost drivers are to be affected
- what risks, concerns and performance issues need to be taken into consideration
- the type of relationship desired

The purpose for the supplier would be to determine which customers to approach, on which cost drivers it could have an impact, and what concerns need to be addressed.

Once the commodity/service plan is put together the customer must then evaluate which supplier can best meet its needs. This requires the development of some method of measurement and some means to gather the information needed to compare suppliers. The most common method is for the customer to track performance and audit the supplier's capabilities. For the supplier, it would mean evaluating the potential relationship to ensure profitability, both in terms of increased sales and increased costs.

The final step in Discovery is selecting a sound alliance partner and determining which company can best help reduce costs, and improve profitability while minimizing the risk inherent in such a relationship.

Stage 2 - Implementation

The Implementation stage actually begins the alliance. Having evaluated each other and knowing what the other company can do and hopes to do, it is time to set the agreement and improvement objectives. These objectives should be set jointly by the alliance parties and with both parties committed to achieving them.

Once the objectives are set, the parties should determine how each will structure the alliance to allow them both to operate efficiently. Usually some form of joint management team is put in place to administer the contract and manage the alliance. Many structures also include joint improvement teams to work on specific cost drivers and improvement opportunities.

It is also necessary to manage the change in relationships. Many problems will surface and must be dealt with to avoid serious disruption to the alliance. It is essential that those people directly affected by an alliance understand the nature of an alliance, its goals, and its impact on all participants. It is also important to have a plan in place showing those involved how the companies will move from the traditional transaction-based relationship into a more total-cost-focused relationship. Both companies will need to work together in identifying and dismantling roadblocks to the alliance as it develops. This will create a supportive environment for the alliance.

Stage 3 - Maintenance

The Maintenance stage is really about keeping the alliance viable and healthy. In many situations the needs of the partners change. The alliance needs to be flexible and grow with the needs of the partners. As such, the agreement, objectives, and structure often change over time. And as personnel and business change so do the priorities of the alliance. New concerns and problems will surface which must be addressed if the alliance is to survive. And most importantly, the alliance must be evaluated in terms of total cost and any changes and progress communicated to personnel affected by the alliance. It is during this stage that the partners build trust and learn how to communicate better.

Time Frame

In order to set up alliances a certain amount of preparation work must be done. Many companies have rushed to get on the alliance band wagon. Unfortunately this approach is one of the prime reasons for failure. This can best be illustrated by the following analogy.

If a person wanted to build a house, a great deal of work would go into the development and planning stages.

- Plans have to be drawn showing the specific requirements.
- The site needs to be prepared and the land developed.
- Schedules and time frames need to be set.
- Crews must be hired.
- Financing must be secured.
- Permits obtained.
- Utilities brought in.

Failure to determine all of this in advance can create delays and drive up the costs. Much the same happens to companies that do not take the time to perform discovery well. Without knowing the concerns of those throughout the company who are to be impacted by the alliance, many problems develop. In order to develop plans and objectives, identify cost drivers and concerns, evaluate and select the best supplier, the process can take most companies 9 to 12 months, as shown in Figure 1.11. Yet, many companies fail to do all the research and jump into alliances in less than three months.

The results of moving so fast are delays, worsening relationships, frustration, and massive problems. To make it worse, management often forces the relationship on local operations, creating resentment and an inability to back up and reassess the situation. This is a recipe for disaster. Yet with a little extra planning many problems can be avoided, which can make all the difference between survival and failure.

Figure 1.11 Time frames of how companies move through the stages of alliance development

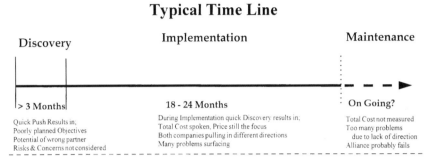

Typical Time Line

Discovery	Implementation	Maintenance

> 3 Months	18 - 24 Months	On Going?
Quick Push Results in;	During Implementation quick Discovery results in;	Total Cost not measured
Poorly planned Objectives	Total Cost spoken, Price still the focus	Too many problems
Potential of wrong partner	Both companies pulling in different directions	due to lack of direction
Risks & Concerns not considered	Many problems surfacing	Alliance probably fails

Proven Time Line

Discovery	Implementation	Maintenance

9 - 12 Months	6 Months	On Going
Needs assessment	Clear Goals & Direction	Total Cost is Measured and Improved
Leads to Purchasing Sales Plan	Leads to smooth implementation	Problems Barriers resolved quickly
Effective evaluation	Quicker Results	
Leads to Right Partner		

A Look Back and a Look Ahead

A study by McKinsey finds that alliances have been growing since the mid '80s at rate of about 30 percent per year. Many of these alliances have survived the problems they encountered and improved the profitability of the alliance companies. This strongly suggests alliances are not only doable, but also have the ability for long-term viability. And yet for every alliance that succeeds another one fails. Managers and executives must understand that alliances are neither for every company nor every situation.

Those companies succeeding at creating alliances have learned what total cost means to their companies, and how to measure it and apply it—and total cost will be different for each company. Measurements created during Discovery can also be used as part of the ongoing evaluation, but most often are used in conjunction with additional models.

Companies can learn from other companies how best to make alliances work and which pitfalls to avoid. Every company will do things differently, so the following information should be modified to meet your company's specific needs. The ideas presented are not meant to be taken as the only way to work through alliances. Rather, they are a composite of how many companies have been successful in making them work.

CHAPTER 2

DISCOVERY

PICKING THE RIGHT PARTNER

Discovery is the first stage in building an alliance and is the key in creating successful alliances. This stage is often passed over or minimized, resulting in poor planning, minimal direction, increased resistance, and ultimately, failure. In the discovery stage the personnel responsible for evaluating the product and service needs of the company (often referred to as a *commodity/service* team) do more than simply set up alliances. The commodity/service team identifies exactly what the product or service requirements are and then determines the supplier relationship or classification that best meets the needs of the users of these services or products. The team also determines the number of suppliers necessary to achieve the goals of the company without incurring unacceptable risk. More often than not, the relationship will not become an alliance. It might be an enhanced relationship—one in which the companies involved work more closely together than in past relationships—but not necessarily an alliance.

However, before looking at how to perform a strong discovery, it is important for companies to understand what the discovery stage is meant to accomplish. The first step is to determine the objectives for various commodities and services and the supplier relationships that best suit the needs of all areas/functions within the company. The commodity/service team is usually comprised of employees from those areas within the company which will be most affected.

The commodity/service team is also responsible for developing and implementing a supplier evaluation process to determine which supplier can best meet the needs of the company. Once the field is narrowed down to just a few of the most capable suppliers, a final selection is performed to pick the right supplier which can best meet the total requirements of the company at the lowest total cost.

Figure 2.1 Primary steps in the discovery process and possible supplier relationships

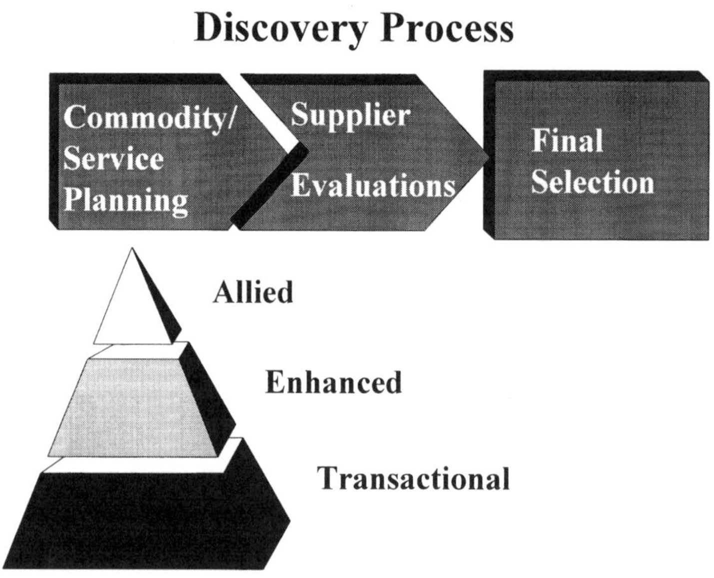

Discovery Process

The supplier relationship determined to be the most advantageous to the company should be determined based on the commodity/service plan.

These primary steps which the commodity/service team must perform are depicted in the figure above. The first step, commodity/service planning, has three primary objectives:

1. to understand the needs of the commodity/service users within the organization and the goals, concerns and objectives of the company management

2. to create commodity and service groups which can best meet the objectives of the company
3. to determine the supplier relationship that best meets the needs for that commodity/service group

From the determination of needs a company must then evaluate the supplier base to identify those suppliers with the ability to meet these needs. Keep in mind that up to this point the focus has been on *what is purchased* and not *from whom it is purchased.* Now the focus is switched and the commodity/service team must determine if there is a supplier that can help achieve the stated objectives. In order to evaluate a supplier in terms of its ability to meet the defined objectives, the company must determine

- the information needed to evaluate the supplier's ability to meet the company's objectives
- the importance of each piece of collected data to the overall evaluation of the supplier
- the methodology to collect this data
- the process by which the collected data can be compiled into an overall comparison of suppliers

Once the evaluations are complete, the commodity/service team must determine if there is one or more suppliers capable of reducing total costs while at the same time ensuring a minimum amount of risk. Initially there may not be such a supplier—however, the possibility of working with several suppliers in order to develop such a situation may exist. In this case, an alliance may not be formed, but an enhanced relationship may be formed which may develop into an alliance over time.

While the evaluations form the primary basis for selection of suppliers, there are other considerations in making the final selection:

- Current relationship and past history
- Innovation
- Perceived ability to meet future expectations

Most evaluations will take these factors into consideration. However, the commodity/service team must remember that it is building a relationship. Total cost includes future costs, which are driven up if the relationship does not last long-term.

COMMODITY/SERVICE PLANNING

Of all the steps in the discovery process commodity/service planning may be the most critical. This step drives the initial evaluation and selection of suppliers and continues to do this for the alliance itself once it is formed. It can also minimize the potential resistance to alliances if done properly. In effect, the commodity/service plan lays the foundation for building any relationship with suppliers.

Community/Service Evaluation Issues

There are two primary factors around which commodities and services are usually evaluated: *purchase volume* in dollars and the *added value /cost* impact. However, there are other issues that need to be addressed first. These issues come from both management and the area employees that will be involved with the alliance or relationship being formed. The most often cited issues include:

Level of concern to the company: Every company has products or services that it purchases or performs in-house which have either an operational or strategic importance to the company. Some of these products or services may be set aside and not included in a large commodity/service group. Instead they may need to be considered for a stand-alone relationship which can remain in its current status or in some enhanced format. For example, oil companies are starting to outsource the management and operations of secondary oil fields, but this is not an option on strategic fields.

Impact on customers, environment, safety: Some products or services may need to remain separate from a general alliance if their inclusion significantly increases the possibility of certain risks, such as

- products and services that can have an immediate and/or significant impact on a company's customers
- products and services that involve environmental and safety concerns

Utilities companies, for example, often choose to separate all products involved in nuclear operations from other alliance initiatives even if items are non-critical to safety concerns, to ensure a higher level of control.

Risk: When risks are encountered, such as concern over the possibility of plant or field stoppages due to supplier inability to perform, the customer needs to consider the cost/benefit trade-offs of changing the current relationships or reducing sources. Of course, there are always risks in any customer/supplier relationships; however, if the risks become significantly greater in changing the relationship, the expected return must be great enough to compensate for this increased risk. It is for this reason that many alliances are formed first around products/services that have low risk levels. Once these relationships are proven to work, other products/services can be developed with minimal added exposure to risk. Automotive companies used to produce the majority of the parts in their cars and trucks. Now many of the parts are purchased from other companies. The transfer started with small non-critical parts—now entire systems are purchased with a minimum of risk and lower total cost than could be done in-house.

Quality Issues: Performance and other issues of quality related to the supplier should be considered during the evaluation step. In terms of the commodity/service grouping, quality issues should also be a concern where certain standards are exacting in nature. The electronic industry is a good example. Companies such as Motorola can only use a limited number of suppliers if they are to reach their goal of reducing defects or errors from one or two in every hundred products to some stretch goal of one per million. In such programs the suppliers must supply products and services with an extremely high level of accuracy and reliability or the costs of doing business could escalate.

Impact on area performance measures: How a given area is evaluated internally and the impact a relationship can have on an area should also be of concern. Any change in relationships which has a negative result on one area's evaluation is likely to be resisted, even if overall it is advantageous to the company. In this case, the evaluation should change or the scope of the relationship should be limited. For example, if a construction company was chosen to supply all of a customer's construction needs at an estimated savings of $250,000 company-wide, the decision would be generally accepted by most people. However, if this savings included an increase in costs in one district of $25,000 due to some special requirements, the decision would be criticized by that area's management. If that district's internal budget/evaluation is negatively affected, that district might become a barrier which ultimately increases costs to the point where the alliance fails. The commodity/service team needs to identify these concerns and address them before they become a major issue.

Geographical Limits: Alliances can be formed around
- a specific plant or field
- a district, state, or region
- national or company-wide operations

The most common format is by district/state/region. This format is used as a means to minimize risk (for instance, if one supplier slips, a supplier in another area can pick up the ball) and to ensure that the market stays competitive (so that one supplier cannot dominate the customer— see Chapter 6). However, national alliances are becoming more prevalent. The reason for this is simple: increased volume can often result in significant price concessions and a willingness by suppliers to incur other cost transfers such as inventory buy-backs and service provisions.

The risk with national alliances is that location-specific service levels and performance can suffer. No two company locations have exactly the same service needs nor will a supplier's locations have exactly the same abilities. The operational costs for specific locations with a number of large alliances have increased dramatically. Saving $100,000 means little if increased costs and downtime have a much greater, but negative, effect on profits. Local suppliers often cannot match the price and asset transfer concessions of larger suppliers and instead focus on service and support to reduce a customer's total cost. Miller Brewing has chosen to use national alliances for its MRO supplies. Amoco, on the other hand, uses a mix of national, regional and local alliances to service its needs. Companies need to determine the geographical alliance size which can best meet their total needs.

Once the above issues have been considered by the commodity/service team when forming the commodity/service groups, the team can now focus on the two most common issues in determining the alliance scope:

- *Purchase volume:* As previously discussed, many alliances require a great deal of effort to actually lower costs. Unless purchase volume is high, it may not be worthwhile to expend the resources necessary to impact these costs. Also, without high volumes provided to the supplier, there may not be enough incentive to reduce prices.
- *Added value or decreased costs:* This aspect considers all of the cost drivers other than price. It includes any reductions or increases in other costs dealing with everything from operating efficiency to transactions and inventory, as well as improvements in revenues where applicable.

Figure 2.2 Primary commodity/service grouping factors

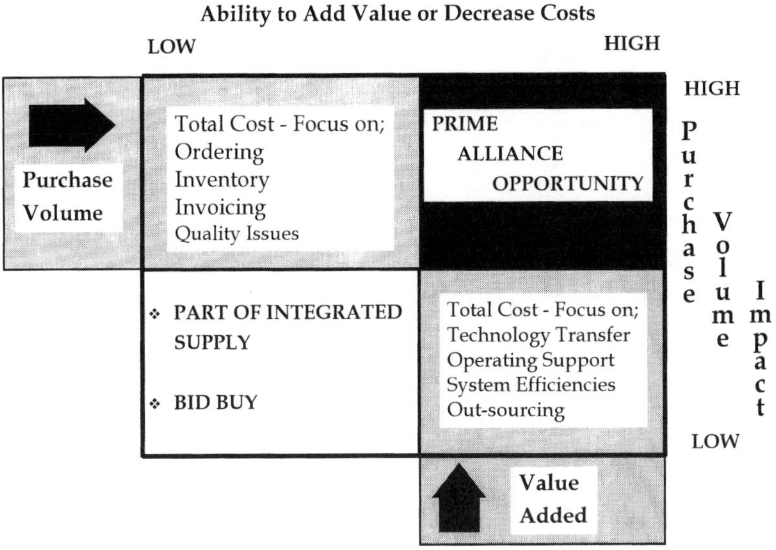

Ability to Add Value or Decrease Costs

	LOW		HIGH		

	Total Cost - Focus on; Ordering Inventory Invoicing Quality Issues	**PRIME ALLIANCE OPPORTUNITY**	HIGH P u r c h a s e	V o l u m e	I m p a c t
Purchase Volume					
	❖ PART OF INTEGRATED SUPPLY ❖ BID BUY	Total Cost - Focus on; Technology Transfer Operating Support System Efficiencies Out-sourcing			LOW

**Value
Added**

Figure 2.2 illustrates these two issues. The ideal alliance opportunity is where the dollar volume of purchases is sufficient to justify the time spent building and maintaining an alliance and where the value added beyond the price can dramatically improve the bottom line. Where volumes are high, but other cost drivers are slow, the focus is most usually placed on reduction in transactions and inventory costs. Where volume is low but other cost drivers are high, the focus shifts to operational support and efficiencies.

Cost Drivers

As stated in Chapter 1, the concept of cost drivers can be defined as *the consumption or expenditure of any resource or the limitations incurred on revenues*. To better illustrate the cost driver concept, consider the following examples;

Price

- *Amount actually paid* - this is a cost driver and in many alliances is the only one truly measured in the alliance
- *Price protection*-the supplier protects the customer from increases in price for a specified period of time—it is a cost driver in that it limits expenditures

System & Processes
- *Time* - the time people spend performing a task is the consumption of an intangible resource
- *Overhead* - the equipment, computers, supplies, buildings, furniture and other expenditures necessary to do a specific task are also cost drivers

Inventory
- *Carrying costs* - the expense of insurance, investment funds, and taxes
- *Overstock & dead stock* - investment in unnecessary inventory can be a large cost driver if the items become obsolete or unusable and do not result in a return on investment
- *Handling costs* - people, equipment, and storage facilities

Requirements
- *Overengineered* - can create unnecessary expenditures or constrain the output within the system
- *Underengineered* - can increase other expenditures such as maintenance costs and undue replacements and/or limit revenues

Operations
- *Maintenance costs* - time and material costs to keep systems operational
- *Operating efficiency* - limits on output or increased energy costs to produce revenues

Revenues
- *Down time* - inability to produce product
- *Improved output* - increased ability to produce product

Total Cost

Figure 2.3 is an example of how Chevron USA has separated the "Total Cost of Ownership" for some of its products. Total Cost of Ownership is Chevron's method for showing the impact that cost drivers can have on total cost. While price is often the major focus in products and services, this chart shows that over time it has less impact on overall profits than other factors. Imagine the advantage to Chevron if it paid 10 percent more for a product than the current price but this more expensive product also decreased maintenance costs and improved operational efficiency by 10 percent each. Is it worth paying the additional price? Obviously, yes. The same holds true if the life of the product were significantly improved as well. While most companies know that these differences exist and are important, the emphasis still remains on price. The result often is lower overall profit. When forming alliances, companies need to look at the total cost if they are to truly improve the bottom line.

Figure 2.3 Example of total cost breakdown

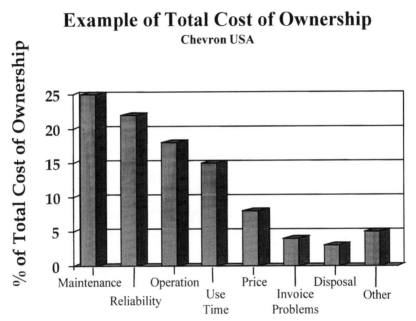

Example of Total Cost of Ownership
Chevron USA

The chart is based on data gathered on one commodity group

Copyright Chevron USA

Commodity/Service Groups

Initially, grouping commodities or services does not appear to be a difficult task. However, poorly considered groups lead to an increase in total cost instead of a reduction. Consider a situation where a company might hire a construction company or work crews to perform a service. Often these crews install materials of various types such as motors, seals, pipes, valves, electrical components, or other material. The construction company could be responsible for the acquisition of these materials or a hard goods supplier could provide them to the end user (customer). In forming alliances, a company needs to decide how to proceed by answering questions such as:

- If the purchasing is to be carried out by the contractor, will that provide the lowest total cost? In some cases the contractor gets as good as or better pricing for these products; in other cases, the price may be significantly higher.
- If the agreement is for cost plus on these products, what is the actual price paid on a comparison basis?
- What other costs are involved?
- Are scheduling costs reduced?
- Are invoicing and ordering costs eliminated?
- Is inventory cost minimized?
- If the hard goods supplier is given these goods how does this affect the overall cost of goods purchased?
- Can the supplier work with the construction company by providing the goods at the work location, but charge the customer?
- Does this increase or reduce the costs of scheduling, invoicing, ordering, and inventory?
- What products should this supplier be expected to provide?

Normally a company will have an abundance of large dollar items. It is these items around which most alliances are built. Yet much of the costs associated with purchasing products revolve around additional and smaller volume purchases. Should an electrical supplier be expected to provide the sales of fasteners, hand tools, and other items not traditionally purchased through the electrical supplier? Many companies are saying "Yes." This has created the concept of *one-stop shopping* or integrated supply.

The real challenge then becomes which goods and services should be included in a specific commodity group and which should be included in another grouping, or whether a change in buying habits of a particular product or service is needed. Also, it is important to keep in mind *what such groupings do to the customer's suppliers*. Expecting the supplier to acquire items for which it does not have expertise or strong purchasing power (which would allow the supplier to procure the items inexpensively), can place a tremendous burden on the supplier.

The purpose of commodity/service grouping is to take the objectives of the company and identify several alternatives for grouping these commodities and services and get responses back from users and suppliers on these groupings. However, this need for feedback is often ignored by many commodity/service teams. The benefit of skipping this step is less time and effort. The cost can be that the groupings created can drive the suppliers' costs up, for which the customer eventually pays. In the long run this may result in the loss of support and credibility of the users and a waste of the resources expended in creating the wrong group.

RELATIONSHIP DESIRED

Once the commodity/service group is established, the team must then decide on the supplier relationship which would be the most advantageous for their company. Keep in mind that alliances can be valuable but this is usually for only a limited number of suppliers and services. For example Miller Brewing is moving from 4000 suppliers to 250. Of the remaining suppliers, only 12 will be alliance partners. WEPCO started their reduction with 7,000 suppliers and is likely to have around 700 in the next few years. Only 15 to 20 suppliers will be alliance partners. Amoco had over 13,000 vendors in 1992—as of 1995 it was 6,500, or half the number with which they started, and the reductions are continuing. Less than one percent of those supplier relationships are alliances.

Alliance suppliers will be those few suppliers who supply the bulk of the goods and services or with whom it is advantageous to spend the time and effort to reduce other costs besides price. Mobil Oil recognized this need to shift purchases to fewer suppliers with closer relationships to Mobil. In 1994 Mobil determined that in one field 91 percent of its purchases came from 15 percent of its suppliers (Figure 2.4). The majority of the spot purchases were being made from the top 15 percent as well. Therefore, the cost of maintaining 85percent of its supplier base for 9percent of the purchases did not make good business sense. A change was in order.

Figure 2.4 Mobil Oil's current and future expenditures and supplier relationships

Relationship Structuring

Changing Focus on Relationships

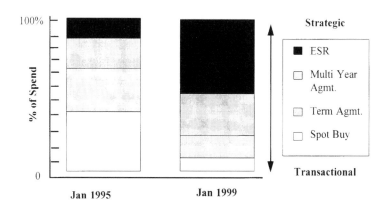

ESR - Enhanced Supplier Relationships, Mobil's term for alliances

Suppliers Vs Spend

In one division...

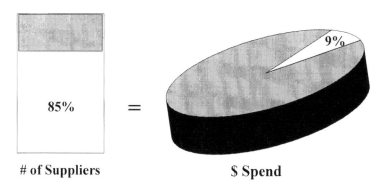

By 1999 Mobil Oil plans to shift more than half of its purchases to suppliers that qualify for *enhanced supplier relationships* (ESR). ESR is Mobil's term for a supplier alliance. The majority of the remaining purchases will come from some form of added-value relationship. Only a very small percentage will come from spot purchases.

Many companies are foreseeing the same trend. As Figure 2.5 shows, alliance partners are likely to be few. By providing the supplier the bulk of purchases made, transaction costs are minimized, the supplier's risks are reduced (inventory will be sold) and the elimination of buying variation allows the supplier to meet quality and service needs more easily. Enhanced supplier relationships are based on total cost but the synergies of working together usually involves little or no effort. The difference between alliance suppliers and enhanced relationships can be defined as weighing the cost drivers which can be affected against the amount of work or expense required to reduce the costs. Alliances uaually require more work but have a greater return potential for this effort than enhanced supplier relationships.

Figure 2.5 Supplier relationships and the purchases made through these relationships

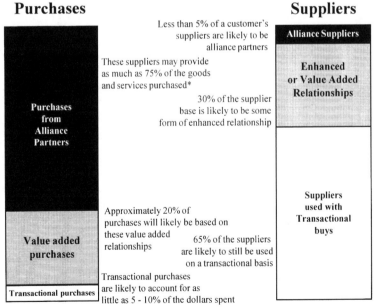

* Estimates reflect the added effect of integrated supply

Figure 2.5 is not meant to be viewed as representing the *best practice*; it is an example of how a customer's supplier base and purchases may be divided based on a composite profile of a number of customers actively involved in alliances. It shows the typical percentage distributions of the relationships a company is likely to have. Every company will be different but the main point is that only a few suppliers will actually be alliance partners. However, while a customer's allied suppliers will usually only represent at most five percent of the suppliers used, the purchasing which goes through these suppliers can often amount to as much as 75 percent of the actual purchases made. The same holds true on the sales side (discussed further in Chapter 5).

Over half the supplier base will likely remain "business-as-usual" suppliers with a relationship primarily based on price. But as customers increasingly rely on their suppliers and shift more demands for service on to their suppliers, additional purchases will be shifted to those suppliers who can provide these services. These service providers may be involved as either alliance relationships or enhanced supplier relationships, based on how much can be saved and the cost involved in reducing total cost.

The commodity/service team must first determine the level of supplier relationships which best matches the commodity/service group needs. This stratification of suppliers has also proliferated due to the ISO 9000 requirement for supplier evaluation. ISO 9000 is an international standard for a documented quality system and is being used by some companies and industries as baseline criteria in evaluating suppliers. Another method commonly used for differentiation of suppliers is the use of an evaluation performed by the customer. Based on various factors, the overall score determines the designated level of the supplier. Only those suppliers who receive scores meeting defined criteria would be considered for an alliance relationship. Normally, only one supplier of a given commodity/service group will be an alliance partner. However, there are exceptions when two suppliers of similar products and services both have scores which would place them in the allied relationship level. This becomes a problem if both suppliers want the same geographical areas of business. Sometimes, when the scope of the alliance is not for the entire company, two suppliers of the same commodities and services can both be allied; each is simply given a different operating area.

Levels of Supplier Relationships

Companies typically will create three levels of suppliers. These levels are *allied* suppliers, *enhanced* suppliers, and *transactional* suppliers.

Allied suppliers are those few suppliers who qualify as being exceptional by having top ratings in their evaluations and with whom the customer identifies a need and a return on the investment of the time spent reducing total cost. It must be remembered that suppliers can influence a number of cost drivers but the return will differ with each commodity/service group. Different types of alliances may be developed based on the cost drivers being considered.

Enhanced suppliers are suppliers the company will turn to first if the products and services needed cannot be purchased from the allied suppliers at the lowest total cost. Enhanced suppliers often perform three vital functions. First, they provide products and services that do not make economical sense to include in an alliance. This may be due to a lack of volume or inability to lower total cost. However, based on the company's evaluation, it would make sense to reduce the supplier base for this commodity or service even if they are not reduced to a single source. Frequently there are two or three suppliers in this classification. The second function may be as a back-up to an alliance partner. Some products and services may be bundled into an alliance commodity/service group which holds a high risk to the customer if the supplier fails to meet the customer's needs. As such, a number of customers use enhanced suppliers as an insurance policy to provide coverage if needed.

The third function for which enhanced suppliers are used is for a specific product need. They might, for example, provide a specialized product or service which no other supplier can provide. The use of performance factors or evaluations are usually minimal in this case because purchase volume is often limited.

Transactional suppliers are those who provide back-up and goods or services that do not make sense to include in any other groups. They may sell specialty items or services or be used occasionally when needed. The trend has been to minimize their use through using integrated suppliers. However, some of the time it may not make sense to use the integrated supply concept with these purchases.

Figure 2.6 shows how two companies in different industries, Amoco and WEPCO, have classified suppliers. It is not uncommon for the enhanced supplier group to be split into two classifications. For Amoco this additional classification was based on performance concerns. WEPCO created the nuclear classification to minimize risk and safety concerns.

Figure 2.6 Common supplier relationship classifications

	Amoco	WEPCO
Strategic Alliance Partners	Allied	Alliances
Enhanced Relationships	Certified	Nuclear
	Preferred	Special Agreements
Transactional Suppliers	Approved	Conditional
	All Others	

Types Of Alliances

Allied suppliers as a category can be separated into a number of different types of relationships. The difference among these alliances are the cost drivers on which the alliance is focused. The main types of alliances found in the market today are:

Single sourcing. Single sourcing is the easiest and most common form of alliance. In its simplest sense, single sourcing means giving all the business to a given supplier. In return, the end user receives a better price for all of the supplies purchased (Fig. 2.7).

Figure 2.7 Single Sourcing

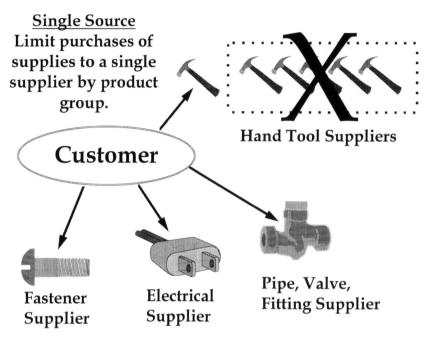

Single Source
Limit purchases of
supplies to a single
supplier by product
group.

Hand Tool Suppliers

Customer

Fastener
Supplier

Electrical
Supplier

Pipe, Valve,
Fitting Supplier

But single sourcing goes beyond these basic features. The fact that the customer purchases everything from one source often minimizes the risk of the inventory the supplier carries. A service company, such as a construction company or consulting firm, has inventory in terms of people and equipment. The greater the fluctuation involved for these companies, the more often new employees are taken on, trained, and then laid off. The same holds true for hard goods inventory. Both too much or too little can hurt the supplier.

The supply company, therefore, is often willing to reduce its price in exchange for this reduced risk. Other advantages exist for the customer such as a decrease in the number of orders placed, a decrease in the number of problems (every supplier comes with its own set of problems) and a better ability to plan. A decrease in the number of a company's suppliers can decrease the amount of cost incurred, such as in the number of transactions. This is why many companies are reducing their vendor base even if they are not forming alliances.

This trend toward vendor reductions has caused a perception problem about alliances. Many companies already have one-to-one relationships or contracts with specific suppliers. While advantageous to the customer, many of these relationships are not alliances. Alliances go beyond simply giving the business to a single supplier—they focus on working together for the mutual benefit of both parties.

Partnering. Partnering takes an active interest in reducing total cost aspects beyond price (Fig. 2.8). The cost drivers most customers focus on in a partnering relationship includes: transactional processes (invoicing, order processing, scheduling), "inventory" ownership (minimize investment tied up in goods, people and equipment) and quality issues (including delivery, paperwork and product concerns).

Figure 2.8 Partnering

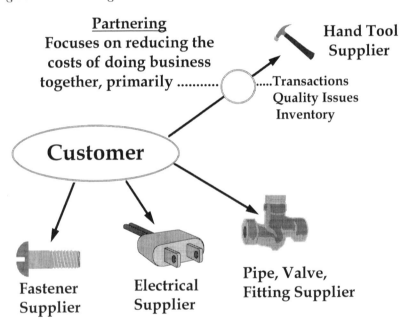

Partnering
Focuses on reducing the costs of doing business together, primarily ....

Hand Tool Supplier

.....Transactions
Quality Issues
Inventory

Customer

Fastener Supplier

Electrical Supplier

Pipe, Valve, Fitting Supplier

Integrated Supply. Integrated supply attempts to create a *one-stop shopping* relationship (explained in more detail in Chapter 6). Many companies like this shopping mall approach in that many products or services can be purchased with one call. For example, assume a company has a need for fasteners, valves, and an electric motor (Fig. 2.9). A call to the integrator will let that company place one order which may be filled by three separate companies behind the integrator. The integrator not only creates one invoice but may also send only one shipment. Companies considering the use of integrated supply need to look at the differences in total cost between using a one-stop shop and having separate relationships with several suppliers. If a company chooses to use an integrated supply relationship it is often more economical to focus on additional cost drivers such as standardization, safety issues, lead times and planning. Typically this occurs because the purchase volume is now large enough to justify working on these cost drivers when it might not have been so previously. The focus on these additional cost drivers is the first step to addressing costs beyond the typical 30 percent of costs previously mentioned. It goes beyond transactional costs but at the same time reduces these costs even further And it is this ability to focus on additional costs which created the name: "Integrated Supply." The supplier must become integrated into the customers business to achieve these cost savings.

Figure 2. 9 Integrated Supply

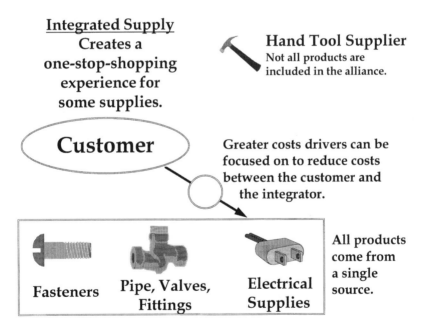

Supply Chain Management. While integrated supply has gained popularity among end users, supply chain management will likely be the next wave. Supply chain management, unlike most forms of alliances, affects primarily hard goods. The focus for this form of alliance is to go beyond the immediate link in the supply chain and involve multiple links or companies in reducing total channel costs (Fig. 2.10). The Amoco example in Chapter 1, where the company planned to reduce its supply chain steps from 33 to 9, is an excellent demonstration of supply chain management. Most companies practicing supply chain management involve the distributors and manufacturers to identify repetitive tasks, over/under-engineered applications, output efficiencies and new technologies.

Figure 2.10 Supply Chain Management

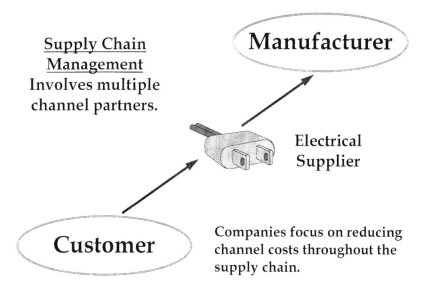

Supply Chain Management Involves multiple channel partners.

Manufacturer

Electrical Supplier

Customer

Companies focus on reducing channel costs throughout the supply chain.

Outsourcing. Outsourcing can have the greatest risk but, for many companies, can also have the greatest potential for return (Fig. 2.11). When outsourcing first started, it was primarily a question of dealing with manufacturers and whether a company should make parts or buy them. The automobile industry is a perfect example. Not so many years ago, the automakers made most of their own parts. Today, the vast majority of parts are outsourced—meaning *purchased*. Today the concept of outsourcing has expanded greatly and many companies are outsourcing processes such as purchasing and engineering.

Figure 2.11 Outsourcing

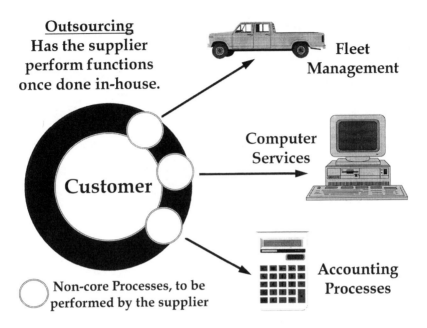

Outsourcing
Has the supplier
perform functions
once done in-house.

Fleet
Management

Computer
Services

Customer

Non-core Processes, to be
performed by the supplier

Accounting
Processes

When a company decides that an operation currently performed internally could be done more effectively, efficiently, and at a lower total cost by an outside entity, it becomes a candidate for outsourcing. As an example, Wisconsin Electric outsourced the management of their fleet to Ryder Truck. WEPCO did this because Ryder Truck is in the business of managing fleets, and could do a better job than could be done internally. So far, the results justify the decision. Some of the most commonly outsourced functions are:

- Accounting
- Warehouse operations
- Purchasing
- Engineering
- Maintenance
- Construction
- Credit
- Mail Room
- Fleet management and repair
- Computer support

As the use of outsourcing has increased so have the concerns of employees and unions because this type of alliance results in the most job reductions. The specifics of outsourcing will be discussed in greater detail in Chapter 6. Companies considering outsourcing need to be sure that the supplier has the capability to perform the function to the required degree at a lower total cost.

SUPPLIER EVALUATIONS

To effectively perform supplier evaluations, companies need to accomplish four primary steps. These steps are:
- identify informational needs
- determine weight or importance of each informational need
- determine the data to collect and then collect it
- score the supplier based on the data collected

When performing the supplier evaluations, the commodity/service team needs to keep the objectives, concerns and desired relationship in mind. Each different product/service requires the team to consider what is needed and how important it is in accomplishing the goals of the organization. The information gathered should be based on facts with examples provided where applicable.

Identify Informational Needs

Based on the typical cost drivers and concerns most companies have, the following criteria are the most common informational requirements.

Competitive pricing. Price is always going to be a primary concern. Many companies use a *market basket* comprised of typical goods and services with anticipated quantities to analyze the bid for the purchases they are expecting to make. The principle is to find which supplier has the lowest total price based on usage volumes for the categories of items.

Cost management. Cost management addresses what a supplier is doing to contain or reduce costs, including price. The focus of the cost management criteria includes the supplier's ability to identify, measure, and modify the cost drivers both within the supplier organization and with its trading partners.

Financial strength. This criterion is important to customers to ensure that the chosen supplier has the financial strength required to accomplish the objectives. It includes both growth and asset investments—for example, the abilities to acquire any technological equipment and processes which might advance the companies involved. In effect, it questions whether the supplier has the finances available to get those resources needed for improvement.

Company direction. This evaluates whether or not the supplier is headed in the same direction and has the same goals as the customer. If the supplier is headed in another direction, it is not likely that the desired objectives can be accomplished. For example, if a supplier stays focused on price while the customer is attempting to reduce other costs, little will be accomplished.

Management capability/stability. Alliances create mutually beneficial, long-term relationships, which both companies view as important. Changes in management, particularly top management, can disrupt the established continuity. This can result in increased effort to stabilize the relationship or even the collapse of the alliance. A number of companies have started assessing the risk involved in this possibility. Companies are also looking at the level of empowerment which can allow for quicker response to customer needs.

Total quality/improvement. Strategic alliances began as part of a tactical response to the demand for total quality. Companies found that when they attempted to improve certain processes, external forces interfered. Consequently, total quality has become an important criterion. If a supplier is not actively involved in improving its own processes and costs, how can that supplier be expected to help the customer? Additionally, without documented procedures, use of statistical methods for tracking performance, and effective team management skills, improvement opportunities may be substantially impaired.

Service capacity/location. The service capacity a supplier can provide can be crucial, particularly when minimizing inventory is a prime objective. How well does the supplier match up with the customer geographically? How quickly and easily can the customer's requirements be filled? For example, if a customer has an objective for "just-in-time" management of inventory but the supplier is located far away, the match may not be good unless the supplier has a great deal of logistic abilities. Special attention or requirements may be needed if the supplier is not within a reasonable delivery distance. One frequently implemented solution is to have the supplier move in and take over the customer's warehouse so that service capacity is no longer an issue and operating costs are reduced.

Product mix/quality. Companies planning to create an integrated supply relationship or one-stop shopping will need to identify a partner who can provide a very broad product or service mix. The quality of the product or service is important in identifying a suitable partner; not only in terms of how good or efficient they are, but also in terms of compatibility to existing products, systems, and knowledge. With products, any plans to implement supply chain management will also increase the need for evaluating brands and their manufacturers to determine their willingness to work with the supplier to reduce total channel costs.

Sales force/support. The sales force can play a major role in alliances and not just from the supplier's perspective of selling an alliance. An alliance is a closer relationship than many other forms of buyer/seller relationships. A number of companies entering into alliances have suggested there is no longer a need for the salesperson to call on them. Exxon, in starting one of their alliances, looked at eliminating the salesperson and hoped for an immediate cost savings. It is true that the traditional role of a salesperson is not always needed. However, many suppliers use the sales force as a liaison between the companies, and to provide technical support, introduce new technology, develop new systems, help identify problems/opportunities, and develop solutions.

For most customers the evaluation of the sales force emphasizes these issues. How does the supplier provide this support and ensure that improvements on total cost are made? While some suppliers do use their sales force, other suppliers use non-sales personnel. Barr Engineering utilizes its consulting engineers for selling as well as providing the day-to-day services for which it is known. The result is exceptional support at the service level. Customers must determine how to measure support if it is important to obtaining their objectives, and at what levels and within which functions this support is important.

Delivery system/adequate warehouse. This criterion evaluates the supplier to ensure that there is adequate rolling stock and a method for delivery of the product to where it is needed in a timely manner. This is another particularly critical issue for companies planning to reduce their inventory investment through reliance on the supplier. If the supplier does not have a good delivery system or the necessary resources to back that system up, some companies have found their total cost increases as their inventory decreases. When evaluating the

supplier on this issue companies need to pay close attention to
- whether the supplier is willing to consign or buy back items
- if the available stock is actually relevant to the company's needs
- the inventory management system used.

Volume alone does not provide the whole story. Most customers should not evaluate the supplier based on its having 100 widgets on hand. The customer should instead evaluate the supplier's ability to provide five widgets as needed. Having the additional 95 widgets increases the supplier's cost for which the customer pays. As such turns and service levels are of primary concern.

When evaluating service companies the same concerns exist, only now the inventory is not products, but equipment and people. Inventory management consists of the capacity to schedule these assets. Otherwise, the evaluation is based on the same factors—whether the supply company can get the *right product* to the *right place* at the *right time* and at the lowest total cost.

Computer capacities. Computer capacities, both for operating systems and for communications, are important to companies forming alliances. Increasingly, companies are looking to e-mail and the Internet for improving communications and sharing documents and information. This need becomes even greater in an alliance but it is the operational capacities of the computer that are most important.

What data can be tracked and reported? Do Electronic Data Interchange (EDI) and bar coding capabilities exist? Can the supplier/customer systems be tied together easily? How flexible is the system? Can it be reprogrammed to meet new needs? How efficient is its inventory management (people, equipment, and products)? Reliance on computers has grown and ineffective systems can slow down improvement efforts.

Purchasing systems/supply chain evaluations. For those companies interested in supply chain management, this is a major factor. It is harder to accomplish the goal of reducing all channel costs if the supplier is not actively working with its manufacturers to reduce costs on up the chain. Yet even companies interested in other forms of alliances find purchasing systems and supply chain evaluations important. Costs created up the chain are paid for down the chain by the customer. Poor performance by a manufacturer can increase inventories, create delivery problems, and require greater use of the supplier's time. These increase the price or performance costs for the customer.

Accounting systems. Accounting systems are evaluated by some companies but are not often considered a critical factor. The importance of accounting systems lies in a supplier's invoicing abilities and desire to improve these processes. The primary issues concern the supplier's abilities to accept credit cards (increasingly being used) and use of summary billing, electronic invoicing, and electronic receipt of funds. Usually the evaluation is a simple determination of whether the process capabilities exist that are important to the customer.

Experienced personnel/training. As companies shift burdens and responsibilities onto the supplier, concerns are often raised about the supplier's abilities to perform to the necessary degree. How the supplier assesses its employees' capabilities, the employees' experience, the training provided, and supplier's hiring practices must be evaluated. Some companies have requested interviews with the supplier's personnel who will service the customer's needs as part of the evaluation. As alliances become more prevalent in industry, potential new partners want to see active examples of cost savings and details of existing alliances. Positive past experience with alliances can be a major asset to suppliers.

Environmental issues. Depending on the industry, environmental and safety issues may also be evaluated. Typically, this has focused on whether programs addressing these issues are in place and on the supplier's past performance. If these factors are pursued to any depth, it is usually within service companies directly involved in environmental or high risk endeavors.

Performance. Almost every evaluation includes some form of assessment of a supplier's performance. The specific criteria may vary from company to company and among different industries; but when forming an alliance, poor performance is a major cost driver. It is so important in some industries that companies measure total cost solely on price and performance. The most common performance issues include
- on-time deliveries (early or late)
- shipment errors
- billing errors
- poor quality of product or service

- damaged orders
- missed completion dates
- accurate paperwork
- ability to expedite

The type of alliances being formed and their specific cost drivers often determine the criteria used to evaluate suppliers. Figure 2.12 indicates how often companies use a specific criterion based on the type of alliance being formed.

Figure 2.12 Alliance types and the criteria most often used in evaluating suppliers

Type of Alliance

CRITERIA	SS	P	IS	SCM	OS
Cost Management	R	S	F	F	F
Competitive Pricing	F	F	F	F	F
Financial Strength	S	S	F	F	F
Company Direction	R	S	F	F	F
Management Capability & Stability	R	S	F	F	F
Total Quality / Improvements	R	F	F	F	F
Service Ability / Location	F	S	S	S	S
Product Mix / Quality	S	S	S	F	F
Sales Force / Support	S	F	F	F	F
Delivery Systems / Adequate Warehouse	F	S	S	S	S
Computer Capabilities	R	S	F	F	F
Purchasing Systems / Supplier Evaluations	R	S	S	F	S
Accounting Systems	R	S	F	S	F
Experienced Personnel / Training	R	S	S	S	F
Environmental / Safety Issues	R	S	S	S	S
Performance Factors	S	F	F	F	F

R - Rarely used
S - Sometimes used
F - Frequently used

SS - Single Sourcing
P - Partnering
IS - Integrated Supply
SCM - Supply Chain Management
OS - Outsourcing

Weighing Informational Importance

Not every criterion the team uses to evaluate the supplier has equal importance when compared to the other criteria. The commodity/service team must determine, prior to the evaluation process, the relative importance of each criterion. The methods and means for accomplishing this are described further, later in this chapter.

Collecting Information

There are four methods most commonly used in collecting the information:

- *Tracking performance.* Suppliers are tracked on service issues such as on-time deliveries.
- *Surveys.* Questionnaires are sent to the supplier to be filled out and returned
- *Documentation evaluation.* Documents, such as financial statements, quality manuals, and procedures manuals are reviewed.
- *Site audits.* Similar to surveys but the customer completes the questionnaire on the supplier's premises based on actual observations and examples which provide a more in-depth assessment.

It is common for companies to track performance and initiate surveys in the initial stages of supplier evaluations. After the list is narrowed to a few suppliers, documentation evaluations and site audits may then be performed. Figure 2.13 shows the information most commonly gathered by these different methods.

Figure 2.13 The criteria and methods for collecting supplier evaluation information

Evaluation Methods

CRITERIA	TM	S	DE	SA
Cost Management		X		X
Competitive Pricing			X	
Financial Strength			X	
Company Direction		X	X	X
Management Capability & Stability		X		X
Total Quality / Improvements		X	X	X
Service Ability / Location		X		X
Product Mix / Quality		X		X
Sales Force / Support	X	X		X
Delivery Systems / Adequate Warehouse	X	X		X
Computer Capabilities		X		X
Purchasing Systems / Supplier Evaluations		X	X	X
Accounting Systems			X	X
Experienced Personnel / Training		X	X	X
Environmental / Safety Issues		X	X	X
Performance Factors	X	X	X	X

TM - tracking methods
S - surveys
DE - documentation evaluations
SA - site audits

Scoring The Information

Having gathered the information, the last step is to determine a score for the different types of information as well as assign an overall score to the supplier. This is shown in greater detail later in this chapter.

FINAL SELECTION

The final selection of a supplier for an alliance partner is usually based on a number of factors in addition to the evaluation results as shown in Figure 2.14. All of these factors are reviewed by management and internal users of the supplier to determine if the supplier would be a good match as an alliance partner.

Figure 2.14 The factors for final selection

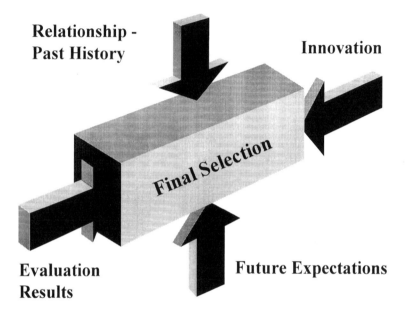

Relationship - Past History

Innovation

Final Selection

Evaluation Results

Future Expectations

Evaluation Results

The evaluations can provide useful information about current performance, operating systems, and company direction. While this information shows the strengths and weaknesses of a supplier, it cannot determine how good a partner they will actually be in an alliance— therefore a number of companies use the evaluations as a *weeding out* process. A minimum score is expected in order to be considered as a potential partner. Those suppliers meeting this minimum score are turned over to internal personnel for further scrutiny.

If no supplier receives the minimum score necessary, no alliance should be created. Commodity/service teams need to keep this in mind. Too often in the rush to set up an alliance, a supplier that did not meet the minimum score is selected because the supplier has the best score or even simply the lowest price. A minimum score is determined to assure adequate performance capabilities that will minimize the risk inherent in developing alliances. Remember, there is currently a 50 percent failure rate with alliances.

Relationship - Past History

A major point that is difficult for evaluations to accurately measure is the relationship between the company and supplier and their respective employees. Many times a single problem that was not handled well is held against the supplier for years, but the many times the supplier saved the day are quickly forgotten.

In an alliance the people within both companies must work together to minimize costs. The question is whether this is possible based on previous relationships between these companies as well as the relationships each department has had with other suppliers. If a company is accustomed to being coddled by the old supplier, and a new one is not likely to continue this service, dissatisfaction can result even in the case when the service did not add value. It is not uncommon for plant and field personnel to have a problem with a supplier because the supplier does not call on them every day, even though orders are placed once a week and a simple telephone call can handle any unusual circumstances. It is also possible for the reverse to occur, such as when the old supplier provided added-value support on technical problems but the alliance candidate does not or will not. In such a case the new supplier may not be a good match.

Innovation

Choosing a supply company as a partner brings the chance for both rewards and risks. The supplier's past innovations and future plans are now receiving more attention and are becoming a larger part of more evaluations. Innovation is addressed by these companies because of its importance to alliances. Innovative companies offer the greatest potential for returns to their alliance partners—poor innovations on the part of a partner may result in few gains.

A number of supply companies play the "me too" game. These suppliers state that they are capable of doing all the typical transactional cost savings other suppliers can do. Usually this is true; they *can* do them. However, when asked for new ideas on cost savings or improving output, nothing more is offered in terms of ideas or accomplishments in these areas with other customers.

The ability to find suppliers who are aggressive in identifying opportunities to improve is a key to achieving continuous cost improvements. Evaluation of internal improvements is the most common aspect, but equally important are cost savings achieved with other customers as well as with the supplier's own suppliers. (i. e., man-ufacturers/subcontractors).

Future Expectations

Companies, industries and market conditions change. When selecting an alliance partner, the company needs to choose one with whom it can grow and change. Too often, the emphasis is on the immediate return; however, the relationship can cost more than it saves if the wrong partner is chosen.Many potential alliance partners can offer immediate cost improvements, but their potential for future cost savings may be slight due to a number of factors. A partner whose total cost is least in both the short-term and long-term and who has the lowest potential risk is the best choice.

THE "HOW TO" OF DISCOVERY

Up to this point this chapter has explained the purpose of discovery and why it is important. The following two flow charts in Figures 2.15 and 2.16 demonstrate how discovery is performed. These charts were initially developed by Chevron USA as a method for initiating alliances. Modifications have been made based on the needs and concerns of other companies. Most of what companies must work through to create alliances is represented.

Naturally every company has its own unique concerns and methods. As a result each company will individualize the discovery process to meet those needs. The present method is not meant to be the only way to perform discovery—instead it is to be used as a guide for direction. The remainder of this chapter will touch on each step and explain its intent and the methods most often used in successful discovery. Two additional flow charts can be found in Chapter 3 which continue the methodology shown here for discovery through the implementation process.

Figure 2.15 The methodology for working through the discovery process, Part 1

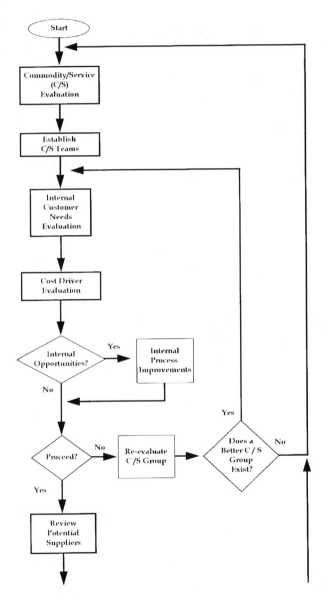

Modified from Chevron USA

Figure 2.16 The methodology for working through the discovery process, Part 2 continued in Figure 3.6

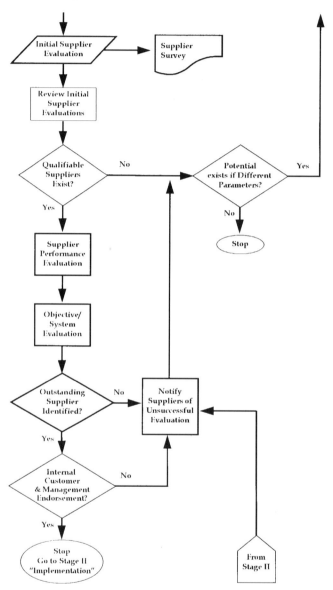

Modified from Chevron USA

Commodity/Service Evaluation

There are two primary goals to be accomplished in the commodity/service evaluation:

- develop logical commodity/service groups
- determine those functions within the company which will be affected by a given commodity group

In most companies it becomes the role of purchasing to develop these groups. The first step is to identify large, repetitive buying habits. This should include the identification of those areas responsible for generating requests for these commodities and services. If distinctly different areas have different buying habits, assimilation into a single commodity/service group may not be possible. For example; some electric utility companies will form several alliances around electrical supplies, such as a transmission/distribution group for supplies from the plant to the user, and an industrial group for needs inside the plant. Factories and plants that use different types of equipment might each have unique product and service needs, making placement under one alliance less favorable.

Purchasing must therefore determine not only repeat buys, but also user habits (such as brand name specifications). This is accomplished by starting with small groups of purchases by functional areas. If the areas agree, it may be possible to combine these into a larger group (based on need instead of emotion). When evaluating purchasing habits other smaller purchases may also be identified which might make sense to include with the commodity/service group. This is important because these add-ons can require disproportionate time and resources to procure and most companies strive to minimize these requirements.

Establishing Commodity/Service Teams

Having established logical groups of products and services and having identified the functions directly involved, it is time to assemble a team with responsibility for these purchases. The team should be comprised of personnel directly affected by these products or services. Typical areas most often considered are

- purchasing
- engineering
- maintenance
- stores/warehouse

It will be the team's responsibility to finalize the product/service grouping around which alliances will be formed and subsequently complete the process of discovery. Therefore, the team members must understand alliances and what must be accomplished in order to ultimately develop a good alliance.

Customer's Internal Needs Evaluation

The team must work with the users of these products and services to determine

- if the commodity/service group is actually logical
- which costs could potentially be affected
- what risks are faced by forming an alliance
- what performance factors are required from any supplier chosen.

Commodity/Service Group

The main issues in creating the commodity/service group were discussed earlier in the chapter. These issues included

- purchase volume
- level of concern
- impact on customer, environment, safety
- risk
- quality issues
- area performance
- geographical location

These issues will influence much of the final outcome of the commodity/service group. It is also advantageous to have the users identify any other products or services which might be appropriate to include in a specific grouping.

Performance Factors

While developing the commodity/service group, it is important to identify the service levels or requirements that the users might consider in choosing a supplier. These often determine the type and extent of supplier evaluations that will need to be performed.

Cost Driver Identification

The team must also work with users to identify costs associated with the supplies/services under consideration. This should include

- specialized equipment needs

- specialized product/service requirements
- inventory
- tasks performed
- paperwork requirements
- storage facilities
- operational efficiencies
- maintenance costs

Cost Driver Evaluation

After reviewing the customer's internal needs, the team must determine the cost drivers this commodity/service group could affect. Appendix A has a list of typical cost drivers based on specific categories. It is useful for the teams to review these cost drivers based on two factors—ease of improvement and dollar impact.

The teams must identify which cost drivers to pursue if an alliance is to be formed. In order to pursue those cost drivers the approximate value (cost expended) in dollars should be measured.

The results often shape the type of alliance or supplier relationship to be developed. If the potential savings are minimal, perhaps an alliance should not be formed, or at best a single source relationship could be established. If the potential savings are high, a more comprehensive alliance might be beneficial.

Internal Opportunity Identification

While the main consideration is identifying external (supplier) opportunities to reduce total cost, companies often identify internal improvement possibilities during their evaluations. If there are internal opportunities, do not ignore them.

Internal Process Improvements

As discussed earlier, alliances have evolved from the total quality movement. Therefore, many companies have established continuous improvement systems to which internal opportunities identified by the commodity/service team should be referred.

Determination To Proceed

Based on the potential total cost improvements identified and the customer's internal needs, the team must decide whether or not to proceed. The internal needs of the customer often leads to a tendency to create small commodity/service groups, resulting in few costs that can be effectively changed.

Reevaluating Commodity/Service Group

If the decision is made not to proceed, the team should reevaluate the commodity/service group to determine if an alternative grouping exists. This often leads companies to an integrated supply situation to increase the potential total cost savings.

Does A Better Commodity Service Group Exist?

If so, both the customer's internal needs and cost driver impacts may change, particularly if it is an integrated group. Usually a less thorough evaluation is necessary, but the team should reevaluate these points if it is considering any significant changes. If a better grouping does not exist, there is no point in continuing. The team disbands and Purchasing considers other possibilities.

Reviewing Potential Suppliers

Having decided to proceed the team must now begin reviewing suppliers. At this point, the review identifies those suppliers who could meet the needs defined by the team. The team should send a letter stating the direction of the company, the cost drivers to be reduced and a general list of products and services to be provided to both current and potential suppliers.

Increasingly the trend has been to include suppliers other than those historically utilized by the company. This includes suppliers that do not operate within the company's territories and those that have never before been used. In this case, competition is increased and companies have more options from which to choose. The inherent risk is that performance is more difficult to measure and increased reliance must be placed on interviewing the supplier's other customers.

Typically, a number of suppliers do not participate and subsequently drop out of the process. This usually occurs due to an inability to supply the goods and services required or a lack of resources necessary to meet the needs defined by the team. However, small local suppliers should not be dismissed. These suppliers may be part of an integrated supply group or may wish to participate on a smaller scale such as acting as a second tier supplier to the alliance supplier (small suppliers *may* provide better service locally than larger suppliers). These integrated groups allow suppliers to share resource expenditures. Currently a large number of these groups exist with fully one-half capable of participating to some extent on a regional or even national basis.

Initial Supplier Survey

From the responses received by the team, it is now time for the supplier evaluations to begin. The team must develop a list of issues and concerns to be addressed by the suppliers. The most common method used is a survey sent out to all suppliers wishing to participate.

A general example compiled from a number of companies can be found in Appendix B. Typically companies focus on systems, improvements, and other enhanced relationships that the supplier already has in place. In developing a survey instrument, the goal is to, as quickly and easily as possible, determine if the supplier has the minimum capabilities required to service the company's needs.

Evaluating Initial Supplier Surveys

Some companies have started this process with more than 100 suppliers initially involved in a single commodity service group. If a large number of suppliers is not quickly reduced to a more manageable number, nothing is likely to get accomplished. The initial supplier surveys should be used to screen the suppliers for candidates with the highest relationship potential. The specific number remaining after this evaluation can vary, but for most companies reducing the list to between five to ten suppliers is a good target figure.

Do Qualified Suppliers Exist?

After the initial review it may be found that no supplier exists who can meet even the basic needs. This is an unlikely event assuming that suppliers were initially interested and responded. Normally this first pass does not place too many limits on suppliers. The most common problems are that the parameters for the commodity/service group are not specific enough, too many cost drivers are targeted, or the expectations are too great for an immediate reduction.

Reevaluating For Different Parameters

Sometimes, a specific product or service does not lend itself easily to an alliance. This is not unusual and is one of the reasons why the majority of a customer's suppliers are not likely to become alliance partners. If this applies to a commodity/service group, simply stop the process for that group. However, reviewing the evaluations may reveal specific trends that indicate why this is occurring. By changing specific aspects such as the product mix or excessive constraints placed on the supplier in an attempt to minimize risk, a successful alliance might be formed. In such a situation, the evaluation process may need to be repeated (usually in a cursory manner).

Supplier Performance Evaluation

Having narrowed the list to qualified suppliers the evaluations become more specific and defined in nature. The first step is to determine performance abilities. A commonly used method is to determine the costs of a supplier's poor performance. Figure 2.17 demonstrates how to complete such an evaluation (The company, ABC Distributing, and all data are hypothetical in this figure).

Figure 2.17 Supplier performance evaluation model

Performance Evaluation

ABC Distributing

	(A) Ave. Time Spent	(B) Ave. Hourly Wage	(C) Personnel Costs (A * B)	(D) Other Costs	(E) Cost per Occur. (C + D)	(F) Number of Occur.	Cost per Criterion (E * F)
Billing Errors	1.5 hrs.	6.50	9.75	13.00	22.75	7	159.25
Late Delivery	1.0 hrs.	5.50	5.50	3.00	8.50	5	42.50
Early Delivery	.5 hrs.	5.50	2.75	0.00	2.75	8	22.00
Shipment Errors	2.0 hrs.	6.50	13.00	8.00	21.00	4	84.00
Poor Quality	2.5 hrs.	8.50	21.25	18.00	39.25	2	78.50

Total Non-Performance Cost for ABC Distributing	386.25

Note: Time measured in hours, instead of minutes

To use this model for evaluating the costs of poor performance, the following steps should be conducted:

1. Identify performance criteria. These are identified during the internal *customer needs* evaluation.
2. Determine the average time spent remedying the problems caused by each poor performance issue.
3. Determine the average wage of those people performing the additional work. (Some companies split this up by functional area or may include benefits in addition to wages).
4. Calculate personnel costs by multiplying results from columns A and B.
5. Document other costs such as overhead, equipment, downtime, etc.
6. Create a *cost-by-occurrence* value by adding columns C and D.
7. Track the number of occurrences for each criterion.
8. Calculate what the supplier is costing the company by multiplying columns E and F to determine the cost for each criterion and sum the last column to determine total cost due to non-performance.

In Figure 2.17 the sum of $386.25 indicates the additional cost to this customer in added work due to ABC's poor performance.

This model is somewhat simplistic but does show how to start an evaluation. Many companies simply assign values (or costs) for each criterion and then track the frequency of occurrences to determine total costs. While such a method involves less work than the hypothetical example above, the results are far more subjective. The greater the accuracy, the more useful the results.

Objective/System Evaluation

While a number of companies use the performance evaluation outlined above, the most commonly used evaluation model is the objective/system model. Appendix C provides a detailed example of how to use this model. Figure 2.18 provides a brief overview. (The data and company, ABC Distributing are hypothetical).

Figure 2.18 System/Objective supplier evaluation model

System / Objective Evaluation

ABC Distributing	(A) Criterion Weight	(B) Supplier Score	Criterion Score (A * B)
Cost Management	.25	9	2.25
Financial Strength	.20	8	1.60
Strategic Direction	.20	8	1.60
Total Quality	.25	9	2.25
Training Program	.10	7	.70
Total Score for ABC Distributing			8.40

To use this model for evaluating the supplier's systems and objective, the following steps should be conducted:

1. Determine the criteria to be used to evaluate the supplier. (see Figure 2.12 and 2.13 for commonly used criteria).

2. Develop weights for the importance of each criterion to the objectives of the company. While not required, most companies have the sum of the weights equal one. The easiest format starts with 100 points and distributes these among the criteria. The more important the criterion, the greater number of points it receives. (Note: As the example in Appendix C indicates, each criterion can be further defined by specific questions or data needs. The same methods apply for weighting each question.)

3. Score the supplier on each criterion. (Note: The example in Appendix C shows the development of a scoring system. It is important to apply such a system to reduce subjectivity.) As can be seen, as each criterion is weighted and scored, the product then creates a score for that criterion.

4. By multiplying columns A and B, an overall criterion score is calculated. When the column is summed, the overall score for the supplier is created.

The score indicates that ABC Distributing meets the overall needs of the customer by 84percent (10 was the highest supplier score possible and weights totaled 1.00).

It is usually at this point that a request for a quote is sent. Expected purchase volumes should be specified for each product as this affects the quoted prices. Also, to avoid the problem of receiving a quote for one product but being sold a slightly different product at higher prices, some form of price standardization for like products should be established. This often takes the form of an agreed upon gross margin, cost-plus, or list-less-discount scenario.

It is also at this point that the supplier is asked to formally present his company. This allows the supplier to emphasize the benefits of choosing his company and allows the team to ask any remaining questions.

Identification Of Outstanding Supplier

An outstanding supplier is selected based on the overall evaluation results, its innovations, past relationship with the company, and its ability to grow in the future with the company. The team must determine if there is one supplier who stands above the rest.

Notification To Unsuccessful Candidates

If no outstanding supplier is identified, the team should inform all suppliers and return to the pool of candidates to examine their potential under a revised set of parameters. It is helpful to the suppliers to allow a face-to-face discussion of their weaknesses and strengths so that they can maximize future opportunities.

Customer Employees And Management Endorsement

This is just a formality assuming that the team performed the customer internal needs evaluation step. However, occasionally there may be an objection or concern from internal employees or management that prevents the alliance from going forward. In such a case,the team may have to begin again. Otherwise, it moves on to the implementation stage.

CLOSING

While every stage involved in building an alliance is important, the discovery stage is a particularly important role. Discovery is the blueprint for building the alliance. A poorly prepared blue print most often results in a poorly built house or alliance. The key aspect to the alliance blueprint is a well defined commodity/service plan which spells out the risk, performance needs, and cost drivers to be addressed when choosing a supplier for a given set of commodities and services.

Time spent developing this blueprint is well worth the effort. Companies that have spent the time to work through the discovery process have dramatically reduced the time necessary to actually implement an alliance. And once it is formed they have a significantly higher probability of building an alliance that does not fail after a few years. Therefore the discovery process is more than blueprint—it is an insurance policy as well. Companies looking to form alliances would do well to consider the discovery process and spend the time and resources necessary to do it right.

CHAPTER 3

IMPLEMENTING THE ALLIANCE

Implementation begins the process of bringing companies closer in order to work together in more detail and depth than they have in the past. Yet to be able to work together in a beneficial manner companies need to decide not only on a set of common objectives, but also on the type of relationship they are trying to build and the extent to which this relationship is to be taken. In effect, the partners must determine the levels of commitment they expect from each other and the organizational structure that will allow them to work together more effectively.

This brings up one of the toughest issues in industry today: *internal organizational harmony*. A company may have many "centers of excellence"—a great purchasing department, sales staff, marketing function, manufacturing facility and accounting group. Each of these areas have their own budgets, objectives, and criteria on which they are evaluated. Often these issues differ, creating conflicting interests. As such, getting these various departments working together as a team is difficult.

Alliances compound this problem by adding another dimension. Alliances bring two or more companies together, each with its own centers of excellence and conflicting interests, with the hope of improving both companies. Now these companies must create communication systems, team work, and objectives that not only bring together the companies, but also the multiple functions of each company. While this is often difficult to accomplish, it is not an impossible task. However, in order to accomplish this, companies must plan well. It is around this planning that the Implementation stage revolves.

COMING TO AGREEMENT

When alliance companies first come together they need to create an agreement that defines the scope of the relationship and establishes their joint objectives. After the customer has evaluated a number of suppliers and chosen a single partner, there are specific objectives the customer hopes to accomplish. The supply company should also have some of its own objectives on total cost, revenues, profit, and expectations. The companies must find a way to mold these into a set of objectives and projects that will accommodate both sets of needs.

In accomplishing this task a number of successful alliances have found the following issues to be the foundation for their alliance agreements.

Common Objectives

As a team, both companies need to set the objectives that are to be accomplished. A commitment is needed from both companies, stating their willingness to work toward these goals. It is not the customer who determines the goals, but rather both companies agreeing on shared goals and the direction they will take together. These objectives need to be for the mutual benefit of all partners.

Dedication To An Ongoing Relationship

This issue is one of the defining points that distinguishes alliances from other customer/supplier relationships. For many years, contracts between customers and suppliers had an expiration date. Often the return on investment in an alliance is long term. Companies cannot expect their trading partners to always do what is in the best interest for the partner unless it is the best interest, long-term, for that company. Short term relationships foster short term thinking on profitability. Suppose, for example, a construction company knew a piece of equipment would require a three-year pay back and the contract expiration date is up in one year. The new equipment could reduce the customer's operating costs significantly but the equipment is only usable by that customer. Should the contractor purchase it? The risk to the supplier is obvious and could tip the decision away from creating the best results.

This lack of dedication to an ongoing relationship often places companies in a position where it does not make economical sense to reduce all of the possible total cost in the relationship. For this reason many alliances do not have an expiration date. Instead, these companies have an *out clause*. This will allow either company to get out of the contract or the relationship with thirty, sixty- or ninety-days written notice. This has risks too, but as concerns arise both companies work toward a satisfactory solution. This keeps most problems from becoming overwhelming. In the event a solution cannot be reached, exercise of the out clause can be used. If the out clause is used it has generally been agreed by both companies that termination is the only remedy. Interestingly enough Underhill & Associates has only found a few instances when the out clause has been used.

Commitment By Both Partners

A commitment is needed from both partners. This commitment usually comes from the management of both organizations stating why it is important to both companies to form an alliance. This statement should specify the scope of the relationship, including issues such as geographical areas covered, products/services, specialty items, and project involvement.

The supplier's commitment should be to bring all the technologies and innovations they have available to reduce the total cost of operations for the customer. It may also mean insuring that the customer has the lowest price or as competitive a price as any other customer of that supplier. This also includes developing new ideas to make the customer more competitive or to aid in reducing further costs.

Defined Requirements / Expectations

Those cost drivers that are to be impacted and the desired results must be well defined. Too often companies form an "alliance" which in reality is little more than a long-term contract and expect results to just *appear*. Total cost will not be reduced significantly unless there are specific cost drivers identified for improvement and the necessary resources to improve that cost driver are provided. This means laying out the responsibilities and schedules for the improvements.

Improved Communications

With the move toward a closer relationship, improvements in communications are critical. For many supplier/customer relationships the use of e-mail and the Internet have greatly enhanced the ability of companies to communicate. While this has helped in the office, field communications are often still weak. Attempts by some customers to improve field communications for suppliers have included getting better mobile phone rates through their greater purchasing power. Other customers are putting their own radios in suppliers' vehicles for ease of contact. Many alliance companies also use an assigned contact person. If an expedient answer, solution, or information is not available through the normal channels of communication, the assigned contact person has the responsibility to gather the information needed and relay it. However, this means of improved communication deals primarily with infrastructure and is only half the battle. Quite often the content of the information must be improved as well. Providing information on plans, activities, and standards in advance of deadlines can expedite matters. Many alliances are finding it extremely beneficial to involve the supplier on the front end, prior to the requirements being defined. By involving the supplier in the planning stage many costs can be eliminated and fewer problems occur. Understanding is greatly improved as the supplier is an integral part of the need identification.

Openness To State Needs, Problems, Concerns

In entering an alliance relationship companies may find it difficult to express the problems they are experiencing. This can be particularly true from the supplier's perspective. Bringing up areas of concern that might be politically touchy may have hurt suppliers in the past. Oftentimes suppliers try to indirectly bring up these points to minimize the risk of losing the business and in so doing may continue to live with problems and costs.

In fact, a study by the Harrigan Company consultants found that in only 45 percent of alliances were both partners satisfied. Additionally, Underhill & Associates finds that some customers are unsatisfied because the relationship is often forced upon them from above and the local needs are not being met. For the supplier, additional requirements are often added which are unrealistic or unprofitable and were not agreed to upfront. Both partners must feel free to state problems or issues, and then feel confident these issues will be satisfactorily resolved.

Shared Risks And Rewards

There is a growing trend for companies developing alliances to establish methods for sharing both the risks and the rewards generated by the alliance. As companies work on total cost, the burden is often shifted to the supplier in order to reduce the customer's cost. If a supplier's cost are driven up by the customer and price is driven down, the supplier loses. Eventually, the supplier will have to decide to end the relationship or risk making the customer unhappy by raising prices or cutting services which in turn drives up the customer's total cost. Alliances need to establish projects that aid in reducing costs or enhance profits for both the customer and the supplier. In the long run, both companies will win.

Open Books, Methods, Processes

Many companies begin an alliance by jointly mapping their processes to see where there are redundancies, waste, problems, poor methodologies, and complicated standards in order to determine how to reengineer these processes. This sharing of methodologies and processes has often resulted in some immediate gains in total cost reduction. But it is the improved understanding of each others business that provides the greatest gains. This understanding needs to be in both directions. The benefits derived from the supplier's better understanding of the customer's processes are intuitively obvious. However, in terms of driving out unnecessary costs, an understanding of the supplier's processes by the customer can be invaluable. Eventually the improved understanding leads many companies to desire an open book relationship.

Open book policies have been gaining ground in alliances as the use of *activity based costing* has taken hold. Activity based costing is simply breaking out the costs for activities the supplier provides and having the customer pay for those services in terms of how the services costs the supplier. For example, consider the payment method. Different methods incur different costs, therefore the customer is charged based on the payment method chosen. In such cases customers want some assurance that they are not paying for a supplier's inefficiencies. This open book policy can cause the supplier some discomfort when first proposed. Suppliers need to understand the validity of the request and how it can benefit them. Customers need to understand the supplier's concerns and should not expect all requests to be immediately forthcoming. Keep in mind that the supplier should have the same right to request open books from the customer. As such neither company should ask for information from the other that they would not be willing or able to provide themselves.

Trust

Neither company should pick a partner they do not trust. The occasional problems and poor performance issues can be worked through, but eventually both parties need to trust each other to do what is best for both. This means the customer should not micro-manage the supplier to ensure things are "done right," and the supplier must trust the customer not to negatively use information the supplier has provided. The reason a specific partner is chosen is because that company meets the needs of the other better than any other company. Each knows their job and what they are supposed to do in the alliance. The customer must trust that the supplier is going to work with them in such a way that the customer's total cost is reduced. It is the same for the supplier. The supplier has to trust that the customer has their best interest in mind.

BUILD THE RELATIONSHIP

A strategic alliance has to be a winning situation for both companies or it will not last. The failure rate for alliances today is fairly high, approximately 50 percent, and is likely to stay high for the next several years. This failure most often occurs because the relationship becomes a *one-way positive experience.* And it is not always the customer who ends up winning the one way tug-of-war. Almost as often, it is the supplier who wins.

Often, alliances start by focusing on reducing the cost of doing business for the customer. This is not necessarily a problem, as long as within a year's time the supplier is profiting from the alliance and some projects are now focusing on the reduction of the supplier's cost of doing business. Keep in mind that focusing on the supplier's costs for doing business is advantageous for the customer and vice versa. It is for this reason that open books of cost information become an important building block for alliances. The supplier must also understand that only through reducing the customer's costs can the customer afford to work on the supplier's cost issues.

Building a win/win relationship does not always mean the win is a reduction in cost—it can also be an increase in revenues. Many incentive programs that alliances have in place not only look at reducing the cost of doing business, but also include the enhancement of revenues in the incentive package. For the supplier, this may mean additional territories or products included in the scope of the alliance. It can also include the customer helping the supplier secure sales with other customers by offering testimonials. At the same time the suppliers can find ways to allow the customer greater output through efficiencies and minimizing downtime.

A written mission statement outlining the objectives of the alliance may not be necessary; however it is an extremely valuable tool. In a review of a number of alliances in place and doing well, it can be found that many have not only a set of objectives, but a joint mission statement. Another tie-in is a *Letter of Intent* explaining the scope of the contract, resources being dedicated, main product/service groups included and how the alliance is governed.

This brings up an additional concern for implementation; how the alliance is going to be evaluated. There are numerous activities customers require that drive costs into the supplier's operations. Somehow the customer will ultimately pay for the increased costs if the supplier is going to be a profitable organization. So being able to score each other for the common good and determining the current total cost for the relationship should be one of the primary concerns of the alliance team. These total cost issues should also be remeasured on an ongoing basis to ensure that both parties are experiencing mutual benefits.

In achieving these savings in total costs there will be projects that one partner or the other wants to work on which may benefit that party and cost the other. This is one of the unique traits of alliances. Very few projects will be equally advantageous to both companies—in fact, the improvement generally increases the costs for one of the companies involved. However, the cost increases to the partner should still be less than the value received, thereby resulting in a lower total cost. If not, the cost should not be transferred. This also incorporates the need to ensure that the partner incurring the higher cost is compensated through other improvements. Additionally, partners must agree upfront on what they will actually be able to do and are willing to work toward when setting the initial agreements. For example, one partner may wish to use e-mail or EDI. If the other partner cannot immediately afford to do this, it must be accepted by the one desiring the tool. This inability to make things happen immediately occurs quite frequently and must be worked around to ensure the relationship stays mutually beneficial.

To accomplish their goals companies must set up an operating structure to determine which projects to focus on. And yet it is surprising to find how little time companies spend setting up an operating structure between alliance partners. Without some form of improved operating means, other than simply the improvements derived from one-to-one business transactions, the alliance is likely to fail. This is particularly true as the form of the alliance intensifies and harder-to-achieve cost savings are attached.

The alliance companies need to determine a structure for tackling the process. For example, partnering generally requires less structural support than outsourcing. Figure 3.1 depicts a structure that is both effective and typical of successful alliances. The oval shapes at the top of the figure represent both the customer's organization and the supplier's organization. Normally, when an alliance is formed, there is some sort of joint steering committee or management team that interacts with the improvement teams as well as the two companies to guide the alliance. It is the creation and support of these structural entities that is essential.

Figure 3.1 Alliance structure and interaction

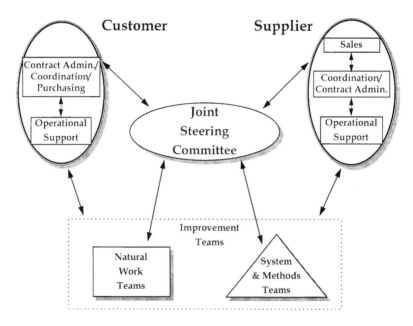

The Importance Of Structure

An important point to keep in mind when building an alliance structure is that the strength of the structure must increase as alliances move up in scope. The structure portrayed in Figure 3.1 need not always be accomplished to the degree it is shown here. In a single source alliance, for example, where the main cost driver under consideration is price, there is little need for anything other than better communication between the customer and supplier organizations. A steering committee, a natural work team, or systems and methods teams are not needed. However, as the type of alliance relationship intensifies and more difficult cost drivers are focused upon the two companies will need to work together more closely for greater impact. This increased intensity can be achieved with a structure of responsibilities for *the customer, the supplier, the joint steering committee, natural work teams*, and *system and methods teams*.

Customer

For the customer there are four essential activities:

- purchasing
- contract administration
- alliance coordination
- operational support

Purchasing. At first glance there seems little difference between current practice and this supposedly new structure, but there are some important distinctions. The purchasing agent's role changes substantially. As discussed in Chapter 2, the purchasing department must work closely with all areas of the company that might be impacted by a purchase or the selection of a supplier. As goods and services not currently in a commodity/service group are purchased, it should be decided whether or not to add them to an existing group, with the decision based on the lowest possible total cost. Additionally, purchasing often takes the lead role for improvement efforts and is therefore responsible for assessing risks, performance needs, and potential value of making any improvements.

Contract administration. This involves the evaluation of objectives, improvement projects, and performance by both companies to ensure that the total cost of acquisition, possession, and disposal is being reduced. When applicable it also includes the amendment of the commodity/service offerings and scope of the alliance. To accomplish this the purchasing department (or area responsible) must work with all functions and the supplier to contract the agreements.

Alliance coordination. Working more closely together requires improved communications and response to immediate needs. Many organizations create a single contact point to answer questions pertaining to the alliance. The contact is usually the purchasing agent or the buyer who is heading up that commodity/service group. This party will act as coordinator, juggling the day-to-day business needs between parties, handling any performance concerns by either company, and ensuring improvement projects are progressing.

Operational support. This involves the personnel responsible for working on the teams that actually make improvements between partners. This can be time consuming, particularly as the costs targeted for improvement go beyond the more easily identified and improved issues of ordering, invoicing, inventory, and performance Operational personnel will also need to be part of the joint steering committee to ensure the alliance is affecting systems and methods positively. This often requires a closer working relationship than in the past.

Supplier

The supplier's organization requires similar functions to those needed in the customer's organization, including

* sales
* contract administration
* alliance coordination
* operational support

There are, however, some differences.

Sales. In many cases, as an account moves from a traditional buyer/supplier relationship toward an alliance, the role of the salesperson changes. Many suppliers have teams dedicated to selling alliances who understand which cost drivers can be affected and how to sell the concept. These teams often support the individual salesperson in making the alliance calls. Once the alliance is in place the customer is less in need of a salesperson and more in need of a customer service representative who knows processes and how to make improvements. For some salespersons this is already part of their job description. For others it is a new expectation—and one the salesperson or the supplier may not be willing to meet. In such cases the salesperson focuses on other accounts and the supplier appoints an alliance representative for the alliance account.

Alliance coordination. At the same time, the supplier's alliance coordinator provides support to the improvement teams and examines problems, finds answers, and gathers data to help the alliance sales team sell new accounts (See Chapter 5 for more details). The alliance coordinator is often an operational person who does not travel much and is easy to contact. The need for an alliance coordinator increases as the size of the alliance increases. If multiple regions are affected a coordinator is essential as improvement data is collected and compiled from a number of locations.

Contract administration and **operational support** are basically the same as for the customer. The administration is most often performed by the corporate staff responsible for the coordination of the alliance.

Joint Steering Committee

Typically, as the alliance moves from a single source to a partnering alliance the focus shifts to inventory, the ordering process, scheduling of work crews, and the invoicing process. In such cases the alliance may need a joint steering committee to take on the limited responsibilities of both the improvement teams and the committee activities. The overriding theme under which the steering committee functions is to determine *how* total cost can be driven down for both companies. Often in partnering relationships, the joint steering committee can do all the work involved in the natural work teams and the systems and methods teams. The committee members not only oversee the direction of the alliance but also work to resolve problems and reduce total cost. As the relationship moves up to an integrated supply, supply chain management, or an outsourcing relationship, the need to form the structure in Figure 3.1 becomes greater. Simply put, the more cost drivers an alliance is attempting to reduce, the more steering committee needs to share the responsibilities for improving with improvement teams.

Contract administration. The joint steering committee also holds responsibility for contract administration, cooperatively looking at how the agreement between the two companies operates and if any changes are needed.

The most common points to address in contract administration are pricing issues, objective evaluation, scope changes, and performance problems. The steering committee holds responsibility for determining how these issues are to be handled and what changes are needed. The steering committee is also responsible for ensuring that both parties understand and agree to the changes and are held accountable for making the changes.

Objectives. The agreed objectives should be spelled out by the steering committee. Keep in mind that the steering committee must live up to it's name. It is responsible for guiding the companies through the relationship being formed.

Managing the change. Entering into an alliance relationship can be hard to accept by personnel at many levels in either organization. It is the steering committee's responsibility to smooth the transition among the personnel in both companies. This can include an explanation of the intent, cost drivers, expected outcomes and benefits of the alliance.

Projects. It is the steering committee's responsibility to prioritize the processes and projects for improvement in the alliance. After making a determination of priorities, the committee selects the improvement to be made based on the available resources. Improvement teams are then formed, based upon the nature of the project undertaken.

Total cost evaluations. The steering committee is also responsible for total cost evaluations. The steering committee must ensure that improvement projects are measured and documented to determine their impact on revenues and total costs. Chapter 4 explains how the committee, working with the improvement teams, can measure the value of the improvements made.

Problem solving. The steering committee is also responsible for the identification and resolution of any problems that develop in the newly-formed alliance. This requires the committee to work with all areas within both organizations. Identifying and documenting problems for smoother resolution is crucial for the long-term health of the relationship. Left unaddressed, small problems can fester into major ones so it is best to solve the issues as quickly as possible. For example, in the initial stages of any alliance, personnel for the purchasing company will often find better pricing in the marketplace. Part of this can be attributed to suppliers outside of the alliance who will cut prices in an attempt to get back lost business. Other times there may be legitimate pricing problems, which the steer committee must handle, or the price comparison may not take all factors into consideration.

> *WEPCO personnel complained of a situation involving a hand tool supplier. In comparing the price paid after the alliance was formed to the former price they found that on the average WEPCO was paying approximately 5 percent less over all than before. However, on some items (less than 5 percent) WEPCO was paying a higher price. They also found that the supplier had also brought these price issues to WEPCO's attention. However, WEPCO chose to pay the high price for these items because when other value-added*

aspects were included, the total cost of acquisition and possession was lower. For instance, all hand tools had a no charge exchange if items broke for any reason. (Other suppliers did not have this policy). Overall it was determined that, although the supplier was not price competitive on everything, total cost was still lower due to reduced lead times, free delivery, reduced transaction costs and lower inventory costs. Once WEPCO personnel were informed of the facts complaints stopped.

To overcome such problems, both companies must work with the steering committee to identify and correct any kinks in the process. The committee must respond to these issues to assure concerned personnel that the steering committee is making competent decisions.

Natural Work Teams

Natural work teams are groups of people from both companies who work together in the natural course of their jobs. For example, a contractor who lays pipe might have a natural work team with the customer's employees responsible for inspecting the work. The team is responsible for working together on a given project and for determining how to work together better. Amoco and Mobil, for example, will often include the supplier in their plant or field operational discussions either daily, weekly or monthly. Both companies invited contractors and suppliers into these meetings to offer input into projects, share each company's limitations and concerns, and to offer solutions for more effective teamwork. These natural work teams can also identify additional projects and improvement opportunities. They are expected to document and measure any cost saving ideas that are implemented and provide this information to the steering committee for review.

System & Methods Team

The systems and methods teams are groups that work on issues that are greater in scope than the processes managed by natural work teams. For example, they would address communications problems, computer system needs, or any processes that have an impact on several areas or functions. A system and methods team may also be formed when an opportunity exists relating to a number of natural work teams. In such a case, a standardized method may make more sense than having all the natural work teams make individual improvements. Systems and methods teams should always be formed by the steering committee and include personnel from each functional area affected by the process under study.

Interaction Of All Groups

Obviously the groups depicted in Figure 3.1 cannot operate independently of each other. There must be some form of communications, accountability and direction. The arrows connecting the entities indicate the flow of interactions.

Joint steering committee and improvement teams. The steering committee is responsible for developing communications methods and determining the accountability of each team. These responsibilities include: designated projects, cost measurements, and the limitations under which the teams must work. The teams are also accountable for ensuring that improvements are made, barriers are overcome, performance is tracked, and information is provided to the steering committee. The steering committee is responsible for making the teams understand why the changes are needed, and providing direction, resources, and support in developing and implementing solutions. Additionally, most solutions should be passed to the committee for approval prior to their implementation.

Joint steering committee and companies. The steering committee cannot achieve the objectives of either company without guidance from both the customer's and the supplier's management. Again, the steering committee is responsible for directing the relationship, but much of that direction comes from the needs of both companies. Usually the committee members can make most of the decisions however, a number of companies use *sponsors* to address any major issues.

The sponsor is a high level manager from each company who receives regular updates on the relationships within the alliance, total cost improvements, and improvement projects. The sponsor provides resources, support, and direction as needed. The sponsor can help provide needed credibility to teams and support in maneuvering through political issues. The sponsor also keeps other top managers informed so there are fewer surprises. The sponsor is only periodically involved with the actual working of the steering committee but is kept informed on a regular basis.

Improvement teams and companies. The improvement teams need to coordinate changes and receive input from those people and functions affected within both operations. Without this coordination, problems will multiply and improvements will be slow in implementation.

MANAGING THE CHANGE

Almost every company needs a way to manage the transition from the traditional roles of purchaser/supplier to the new roles found in alliances. As problems arise (and they always do), issues must be resolved quickly and information communicated to the affected parties.

New Customer Attitudes

For the customer, managing change will require new ways of thinking on issues such as:

Price: In most alliances the supplier of choice has one of the lowest total price packages on items. However while the supplier will likely be low or competitive on the majority of the items, it will be possible to find a lower price on individual items everyday. The product or service users are not likely to be concerned with the low or competitive prices, but any amount paid over market price may create a stir. The joint steering committee must be well versed on total cost and able to communicate the advantage in not bidding out the higher priced items. Otherwise these items may need to be removed from the commodity/service group if it does not currently offset the lowest total cost.

Service relationship: The "we call, you haul" mentality or other traditional roles between customer and supplier will need to be replaced with one of cooperation. The customer's employees should understand that the supplier is now a partner working with the customer to reduce costs and that the customer is paying (in some form) for all these services.

New Supplier Attitudes

The supplier must develop a new mindset to handle:

Ability to discuss total cost: Within the confines of an alliance relationship service companies must convincingly define the difference between price and cost. In other words, what value, in dollars, does the service company bring to the customer?

Changing service needs: Alliances often require *teams* to make improvements and manage the alliance in addition to many new operational requirements. Suppliers must understand the importance of these new requirements and how to participate in meeting them effectively.

There are four primary issues in managing the change. Companies must

- create a *vision* or mission for the people involved in the relationship
- develop implementation plans that spell out how the vision will be accomplished
- identify and remove barriers to the implementation
- establish an environment where the companies can work together for the greatest mutual benefit

Creating The Vision

Figure 3.2 demonstrates the importance of creating the vision or alliance mission. Imagine for a moment that you are a field, plant, or warehouse employee and do not understand the nature of alliances, your role in them, or the alliance's impact on your field of expertise. If you are unaware of your role, you can be an unintentional barrier to the newly formed alliance.

Figure 3.2 The clearer the understanding of the alliance vision, the higher the probability of success.

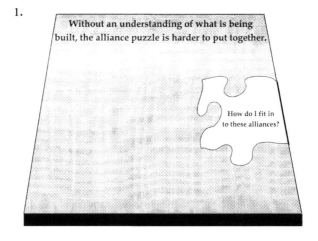

1.

> Without an understanding of what is being built, the alliance puzzle is harder to put together.

> How do I fit in to these alliances?

2.

3.

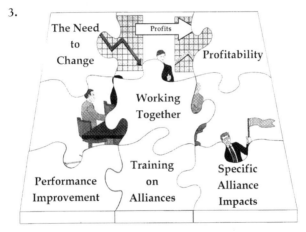

4.

The steering committee's first job is to create the vision for both the supplier's and customer's employees, showing what the companies wish to accomplish. The second picture in Figure 3.2 shows the typical pieces to the *successful alliance* puzzle.

Some employees may ask why changes are needed when both companies are already successful. The past relationship has been profitable for both. Why change? What is "out there" driving this move to an alliance?

For the utility industry it could be the competitive concerns due to deregulation. For the oil and gas industry it could be increasing global competition, resulting in reduced prices in the face of increasing domestic costs. For manufacturing firms it may be the need to respond more quickly to changing technology and market conditions.

Many steering committees also convey the mission and objectives, so that everyone knows what is being undertaken. They answer questions such as:
- What is an alliance?
- How was the supplier selection accomplished?
- How do the companies intend to work together?
- What is the profitability picture if things do not change?
- What structures exists?
- What performance standards will exist and what improvement measures are expected?
- What are the roles and responsibilities for the employees affected?
- What is total cost and why is it different from price?
- What specific impact is the alliance expected to have on various areas inside both companies?

As people start to understand the answers to these questions a picture starts to emerge from the puzzle. The more those involved understand the nature of alliances and their benefits, the more likely they are to help accomplish the goal. Without knowing what the puzzle is suppose to look like, it is difficult for everyone to help fit the pieces together.

Developing The Implementation Plan

The steering committee also must develop a plan that ties into the vision. Companies need to show not only where they are going but how they plan to get there. An implementation plan will spell out the objectives, projects, and time frames the companies are operating under, and who is accountable for these projects. Figure 3.3 illustrates the primary tasks that the steering committee and improvement teams must accomplish during implementation.

Several points deserve further discussion. First, during the initial implementation phase, the assigned improvement projects should be small and easy to accomplish. Nothing promotes success like building on success, and nothing hinders enthusiasm faster than initial failures. Second, continuing to create the vision should be incorporated into the plan, both to sharpen the focus for current participants as well as to bring others into the alliance framework. Third, ensure that the main cost drivers are identified and incentive schemes are developed that benefit both companies. This usually includes projects important to both companies. Most alliances start improvements by going after quick hits in order to build the momentum needed for larger projects.

Figure 3.3 General alliance implementation plan

General Implementation Plan

Months

Steering Committee Action Items	1	2	3	4	5	6	Key Points
Set Agreement (Starts Plan)							Terms, conditions, scope
Set Joint Mission							Commitment, direction
Set Joint Objectives							Where at, where going
Management Commitment							Involvement, support, understanding
Train: Alliance Concepts							Basic understanding - everyone
Specifics of Relationship							For those people impacted
Identify Cost Drivers							Systems, Equipment, Inventory
Develop Incentive Schemes							How will both companies benefit
Set Improvement Projects (Initial)							Based on cost drivers & objectives
Improvement Team Action Items							
Define Project Mission							Objectives & limitations
Define Project Goals							Specific outcomes desired
Map Processes							Critical to alliance
Brainstorm Opportunities							Waste, redundancies, improvements
Rate/Evaluate Opportunities							Easy first then impact
Develop Improvement Methodology							How to move forward
Determine Measurement Method(s)							Baseline & Total Cost improvements
Assign Resources							Time, people, money
Implement Improvements							Inform everyone involved
Track Performance							Total Cost improved?
Reengineer Processes							Re-map, evaluate, continue

The implementation plan is critical for success. Consider the last vacation you took. Did you know your destination? Did you know whether you were going to fly or drive to get to your destination? Were accommodations ready upon your arrival? Did you know a little bit of what you wanted to do during your vacation?

People tend to plan their vacations better than they plan their strategic alliances. There is often a mentality in which partners "kick back and relax" once alliances are set up. In an alliance this can cause failure. Partners need an implementation plan that defines the alliance goals, how they are to be achieved, the methods to be used, and the initial projects to be undertaken.

The implementation plan depicted is not meant to be the only method for accomplishing an alliance. Instead, it is a general plan based on actual company implementations and the approximate time frames used to put them in place. It should also be remembered that these companies are often able to accomplish this stage in a six-month period because the discovery was properly done, easing the path for implementation. If discovery is not handled properly, the general implementation plan may often be stretched to 18 or even 24 months before companies settle into a good working relationship, *if they ever do.*

Identify And Remove Barriers

While numerous barriers exist there are typically four barriers that occur frequently:

Communication: In the rush to start alliances, companies often fail to explain the basics to their employees. This ties back to creating the vision, and if done poorly can create barriers. For example; employees often hear about alliances in terms of outsourcing. Even when the point is made that jobs are not at stake, it is still what they "hear." With jobs at stake and the high alliance failure rate, miscommunications about alliances are likely since people relate what they hear to their past experiences.

Lack of direction: Often after the alliance is put together, no one knows how to proceed. How are the teams supposed to operate? How are they to measure total cost? Which cost drivers do they work on first? When do they get started? It really is important to set the direction not only for the whole alliance, but also for the individuals within the alliance.

Change: People are often uncomfortable with change, usually out of fears and lack of understanding the plans. While it is difficult to always work one-on-one with everyone, there are usually key people within each area who need to fully understand the plans. These are people with whom alliance leaders should work closely and coach. In turn, these people help those they work with in working through change.

Internal barriers: Internal barriers will exist inside almost every organization. These barriers are most often departmental conflicts. Budgets and evaluations differ among departments and are often not in agreement with the alliance goals, and improvements for one area may be detrimental to another. As such, the alliance and any subsequent changes should be evaluated by all affected areas based on risk, performance requirements, and the value added by the change. Then internal budgets and evaluations mayl need to be adjusted.

Figure 3.4 Opposing forces in implementation of alliances

Alliance Forces

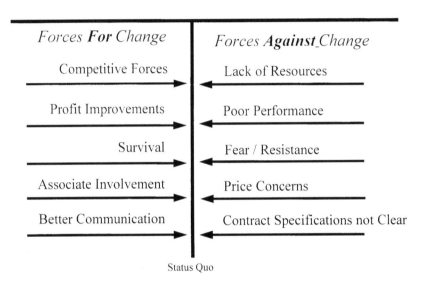

Forces *For* Change	Forces *Against* Change
Competitive Forces	Lack of Resources
Profit Improvements	Poor Performance
Survival	Fear / Resistance
Associate Involvement	Price Concerns
Better Communication	Contract Specifications not Clear

Status Quo

A helpful tool for companies to use in implementing alliances is illustrated in Figure 3.4. Steering committees need to identify those forces which both promote and constrain the implementation of an alliance. These issues are then listed and addressed in the implementation plan. The left side of the figure shows the forces creating the desire to have an alliance. The right side represents those forces against change which ensure the customer/supplier relationship will remain at status quo. Alliances can build forces for change by encouraging participants to share their ideas. Then, as the companies develop an implementation plan, the members include ways to strengthen those forces for and minimize those forces against the alliance.

For example: Amoco used a newsletter and production graphs to strengthen the forces for alliance by showing employees why alliances were necessary (Figure 3.5). As production declined due to depleting reserves and rising costs, survival and profitability were at stake. Then, to help minimize the forces against alliances (such as concerns over the price paid for goods), Amoco and Red Man Pipe & Supply created a joint newsletter to show some of the cost savings occurring (see Appendix E), in addition to performing a comparison of current prices to prices actually paid prior to the alliances. The result, with hundreds of thousands of dollars in documented savings, concerns over price dropped dramatically. The impact was so great, Red Man has now started newsletters with some of its other alliance partners including Mobil and Chevron.

Figure 3.5 Graph of production decline and rising costs helps Amoco show the need for alliances.

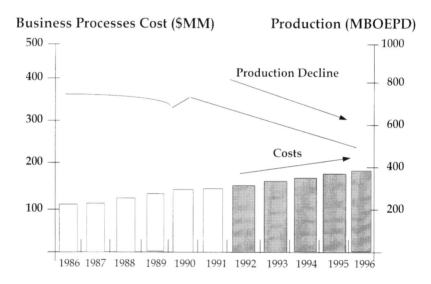

Create The Environment
The last component for managing change is to create an environment where both companies feel comfortable and can be open with each other. Simply putting people together in natural work teams breaks down many walls between the companies and encourages working together toward common goals. It is helpful to make sure these meetings are "hats off," meaning the supplier's say has equal weight with that of the customer. Each company needs to feel free to discuss problems caused by the other company, how those problems have increased the cost of doing business, and how to fix the situation.

THE "HOW TO" OF IMPLEMENTATION

Up to this point the focus has been on the *what* and *why* of implementation. Now the focus shifts to the *how*. The two flowcharts in Figures 3.6 and 3.7 explain the step-by-step process used in developing successful alliances. It is important to keep in mind that, while the process diagram in Chapter 2 involved only internal personnel, the vast majority of this process is performed as a team between alliance partners.

Figure 3.6 Implementation process, chart 1 of 2 (See also Figures 2.15 and 2.16 for Discovery process)

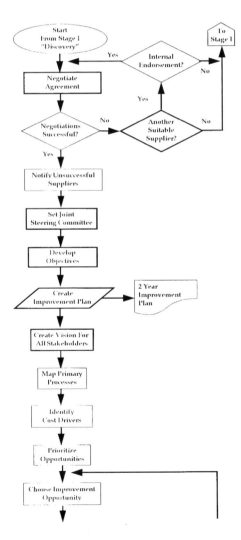

Figure 3.7 Implementation process, chart 2 of 2 (See also Figures 2.15 and 2.16 for Discovery process)

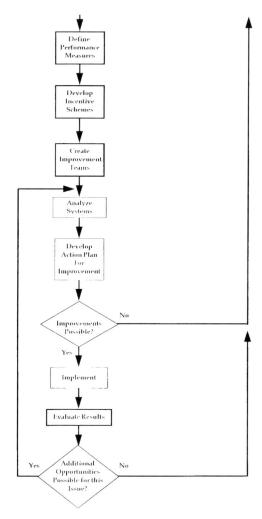

Negotiate Agreement

Implementation begins with negotiating an agreement. The term *agreement* is used because a number of alliances do not use a contract in the traditional sense of the word. An interesting point is that there does not seem to be a correlation between successful alliances and those that fail, based on the use of a contract. But with the failure rate running at 50 percent the cost of ending an alliance is often higher if a contract does not define each company's responsibilities.

While the use of a contract does not guarantee success, there is a correlation between success and the use of measurable objectives with some form of statement indicating commitment. Negotiations therefore must go beyond the typical debate of rewarding a contract based primarily on price. An agreement should be negotiated that includes

- *a scope statement* on the geographical area involved and the products and services to be included
- *an outline of the basic objectives*, usually very broad at this stage and expanded further immediately after the alliance is set
- *improvement specifications* such as the use of improvement teams, expected savings, incentives for improvement, measurement of improvements, and the roles and responsibilities of each party

Many alliances start with some combination of a joint letter of intent or mission statement and a contract. The letter of intent and mission statement often spell out the spirit of the agreement, while the contract is used due to corporate tradition or management requirements. The result, unfortunately, is often a contract that is not utilized and as the relationship changes and grows these changes are often not incorporated into the contract. This can lead to trouble down the road, particularly if the letter of intent or mission statement was updated and is now in conflict with the contract, as these documents can be considered part of the contract To help avoid this conflict, the contract should be a document that is easy to read and use and should be considered an integral part of the alliance framework. This is one reason that contract administration is a vital part of the alliance structure.

If a contract is used there are often a number of points to be added or that should be expanded upon, including:

Definition of legal relationship. One form of strategic alliance is known as *partnering* or a *partnership*. This has caused some legal concerns as "partner" is also the legal term for a form of ownership. Additionally, many people refer to the other company in the alliance as their partner. Many contracts spell out the relationship to avoid confusion.

Confidentiality. As relationships move closer more information is shared and the improvements made can provide a competitive advantage. This causes both suppliers and customers enough concern that they want to limit the spread of this information. The jointly-developed ideas (other than product technologies) can often help the supplier with other customers and the customer with other suppliers. Many alliances that start with a confidentiality clause decide to drop it on the day-to-day operational concerns. Some have even agreed to show competitors and other companies the improvements made in order to help the supplier sell that new account or help the customer work with another supplier. This also allows the supplier to feel more comfortable in sharing any improvement ideas coming from other customers. Specifics concerning what can or cannot be shared need a to be documented.

Contract duration. Long term contracts have been used in purchasing for some time. These contracts have term limits or expiration dates. However, alliance contracts are, with increasing frequency, eliminating any ending dates. Instead, the relationship is in place until one party or the other provides a written statement of intent to end the relationship. Some contracts spell out acceptable reasons for termination, such as performance criteria; others have a no-fault clause, so that no reason has to be given. Most contracts that exclude expiration dates have a stated number of days from written notice until expiration. This number should not be set arbitrarily. It should be based on the time needed to find and set up suppliers to meet the customers needs and allow for depletion of inventories by the supplier. Commonly used time frames are between 30 and 90 days.

Inventory. A number of contracts have included an inventory classification that ties into the amount of inventory a supplier will carry. An inventory maintenance level is set based on historical usage to insure availability and minimize the risk of delivery delays. When just-in-time or other inventory reduction programs are used by the customer, this clause becomes more prevalent.

Specialty items. If the supplier is expected to provide special equipment, supplies or personnel, the customer's purchase obligations concerning these items should be documented. And, in the event the alliance is terminated, the supplier's compensation for these items should be outlined.

Relational governance. In an alliance situation, contract maintenance is usually performed by the joint steering committee on an ongoing basis. However, any large changes may require corporate approvals.

Conflict resolution. The steering committee is usually responsible for resolving conflict. If a resolution cannot be achieved, either party can invoke the termination clause and the alliance dissolves. It is for this reason that contracts should be considered. Keep in mind that fully half of all alliances fail. Without a contract to fall back on, any letter of agreement, established objectives, or verbal and non-verbal language can be held against either party.

While it is unusual, negotiations sometimes do not result in the development of a mutually beneficial situation. If the commodity/service team was unsuccessful in its negotiation with one supplier it should review any other suppliers interested in the alliance that had good overall evaluations. If another suitable supplier does exist, the team must restart the process of getting an internal endorsement from all parties as outlined in Chapter 2.

When There Are No Other Suitable Suppliers

While another supplier with good alliance potential may exist, it is not always the case. The team should not simply jump to the next supplier in line—rather it should look at the supplier's qualifications to determine how to proceed. If no other supplier looks suitable, all suppliers should be notified that an alliance is not possible at this time. This courtesy often includes an explanation of why they were unsuccessful. The commodity/service team should then consider modifying the parameters. For example, maybe a commodity/service group of telecommunications and computer services was the wrong mix. Perhaps a group of only telecommunications services would better serve the company's needs. If the commodity/service group parameters are redefined, the supplier search begins again with reevaluations for using the new parameters.

The Successful Negotiation

Once the alliance partner is chosen and an agreement is successfully negotiated, the remaining suppliers should be notified that the search has ended

Form Joint Steering Committee

Once the agreement is set a joint steering committee should be formed to spell out the objectives, measure current costs, and create the initial implementation plan. In the beginning, the committee will meet fairly often—for some alliances as often as once a week, for others it may be once a month. Over time most alliances find that the need for frequent meetings decreases as the implementation projects are completed and everything is running smoothly. As a result the steering committee meetings may taper off to quarterly or semiannually, based on the size and number of projects, their importance, established time frames, and complexity of the alliance.

The steering committee should include decision makers from both companies, and represent all areas directly impacted. These people should have the authority to change the contract or make recommendations to change most of the day-to-day operations under the contract. While the team has the responsibility to pick projects and resolve problems, their focus should be on developing objectives, setting the plan, and getting everyone on board.

Develop Objectives

One of the easiest methods for developing objectives is to have both the customer and the supplier create wish lists of what each wants to accomplish. Most companies consider
- profitability
- improved communications
- relational factors
- performance measures or what type of performance each wants from the other company
- improving the competitive situation
- better planning

After the companies develop their wish lists, the steering committee reviews and modifies the lists to reflect where the desires of both companies are in agreement. For example, the supplier may wish for better forecasting from the customer in order to better meet the customer's needs. The customer may want shorter lead times on work crews. Put together, the alliance objective might be to improve joint planning. Once the objectives are named, the committee needs to sharpen their focus. One of the most effective means to do this is to take each objective and break it down into three parts. Each part should be defined with a short paragraph.
- *Current state*. Explain where the relationship is today in relation to the objective.
- *Impact of current state*. Explain what is wrong with the current state, and what problems or costs are created because of this state.
- *Desired state:* Where does the steering committee hope to take the alliance?

Example (abbreviated):
- *Objective:* Improve joint planning.
- *Current state.* Companies A and B perform operational planning independently of each other.
- *Impact of current state.* Because planning is performed by each company individually, delays occur, schedules are often changed, resources are redirected, and jobs are often rushed to be completed. The result is increased costs for both companies, wasted resources, missed completion dates, and poorly completed jobs.
- *Desired state.* Through better planning and joint efforts scheduling can be achieved more easily and accurately.

Why go to all this trouble? There may no need at first—however, as the alliance grows, both in work and geographically, the need increases. The steering committee members understand the objectives and may not need to have them spelled out so completely. However, the further removed people are from the committee, the greater the need to show current status and reasons for change, so these people can more easily accept the new relationship. Remember that the real power of an alliance is to involve and motivate those people performing the tasks in the primary processes to support and move the relationship forward.

Create Improvement Plan

The steering committee must create an improvement plan based on the developed objectives, the tasks necessary to manage the change, and the general implementation projects. Figure 3.8 provides an example of how companies can get started. Wisconsin Gas and Arby Construction identified 94 opportunities, then chose these 17 to begin with, based on impact and ease of implementation.

It is important to start with some easy wins. Most alliances desire to start quickly and so identify projects with a high degree of impact on total cost that can be accomplished quickly. This allows some improvements to happen quickly so people can see the benefits upfront which can help companies overcome some of the potential barriers. While it is good to start by "picking the low hanging fruit," eventually companies need to focus on the high impact projects as well.

Figure 3.8 Categorizing opportunities (Wisconsin Gas and Arby Construction)

Ease of Implementing

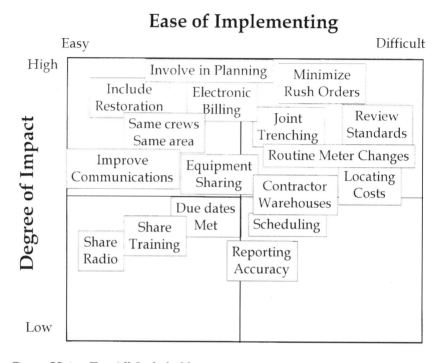

Create Vision For All Stakeholders

It is important that the steering committee identify all the areas that the alliance will affect. This could include engineering, accounting, purchasing, the warehouse, field personnel, plant personnel, maintenance operations, administration, and information systems, just to name a few. Having identified the primary people involved, the steering committee must then determine which personnel will feel the most effect, based particularly on those projects and cost drivers chosen for initial focus. These people will need training on the concept and goals of the alliance, quickly and in greater detail than those people less affected. This training should include information on

- their role in this alliance
- how their specific jobs will be altered
- what new expectations will be placed on them
- how they are to solve any problems they might encounter
- what resources will be made available to the (particularly time)

Even if these people are not resisting the alliance, they will not know what to do nor how to do it without clear definition of these issues. Through sheer lack of understanding they may create problems, simply because they are blind to the goals of the alliance. For those who are less involved, it is usually sufficient to give a general introduction on the alliance concept and a short discussion on how it will affect them. When companies attempt to create the vision, it is often valuable to show and discuss the commitment from top management and from the management in their areas. For example, if the alliance has an impact on operations, it would be helpful to have the operations manager or supervisor involved in presenting this information. This way the employees knows that management understands that area's specific needs and concerns about the upcoming changes. Providing a copy of the general implementation plan can be helpful as well.

Mapping Primary Processes

More and more companies are finding that by mapping out the processes they share, each company's understanding of how the other operates is improved. While this understanding alone is valuable, the mapping process can also point out where efforts are duplicated, how the processes come together, and what data is generated for tracking and measurement purposes.

Mapping is most commonly achieved with flowcharts. However, any method which creates a picture of the process is valuable (such as diagrams and arrow graphs). They must be kept up-to-date and be readily understandable by their users.

Identify Cost Drivers

Cost drivers are occurrences that create an expenditure of resources or loss of revenues. Each process will have a set of cost drivers ranging from people and equipment to downtime and lost production. A list of commonly identified cost drivers can be found in Appendix A. It is not comprehensive but does provide some insight and can be used as a starting point, since each company will have its own unique cost drivers.

Prioritize Opportunities

Figure 3.9 Evaluating cost drivers to prioritize opportunities

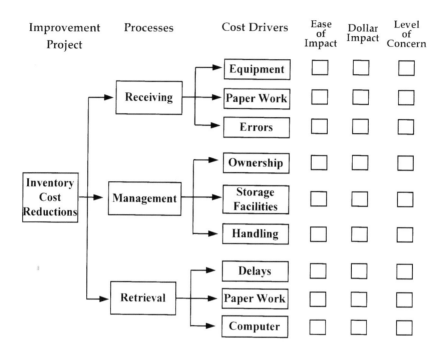

To prioritize opportunities for improvement, consider Figure 3.9. It breaks down an improvement project into the systems and cost drivers that would be affected. Once the cost drivers are listed they should be prioritized according to which ones can be worked on immediately and to the dollar impact each cost driver would have on total cost. However, any change to a cost driver should also take into consideration any concerns that may exist if a change is implemented. The two most common concerns revolve around the risks and performance issues. Obviously, not all projects can have an affect on all cost drivers, so the team must pick and choose which cost drivers to focus on based on these issues.

Choose Improvement Opportunities

Given that a single project may target a number of cost drivers and various options for improving them, the team working on the project must decide in what order to proceed. For example, using Figure 3.9, how should a team proceed? The most common opportunities pursued include:

- consignment by distributor/contractor
- consignment by manufacturer through the distributor
- vendor-managed inventory
- just-in-time delivery
- shelf management
- warehouse outsourcing
- inventory buy-backs
- promotion of the sale of dead/excess inventory to other companies

Each of these opportunities is based on targeting different cost drivers involved in inventory management. The starting point is based on the priorities set by the team. The priorities are usually based on ease of implementation, risk factors, performance issues, and the dollar impact on both companies as shown in Figures 3.8 and 3.9.

Define Performance Measures

Performance measures need to be defined from the start. When building a car you would not want to wait until it is completed to determine its performance features. The same is true for these improvements. What level of service is required on which items? Chrysler, for example, working with some of its suppliers, has classified items based on usage rates to determine consignment levels, delivery lead times, and other service factors. But these are not the only criteria to consider.

The supplier also has performance issues with the customer which can affect the system's ability to function. These often include a lack of scheduling or standardization, changing requirements at the last minute, or general lack of planning on the customer's part. Often a customer does not realize how much expense is added by these issues, therefore it is important that the supplier spell out the costs. Usually, the performance criteria focused on upfront are price and a few supplier performance measures. While this is not unusual it is somewhat short-sighted—companies need to work together in setting performance measures for each other.

It is valuable to develop baselines around the objectives and the cost drivers under study. What is today's total systems cost? This requires the team to walk through the processes of both companies, and is one reason that flow charts are so valuable. Two variables drive the cost of a process. The first is the cost of each step in a process—this includes personnel time, equipment, and overhead expenses such as the computer and office space. The second cost driver variable is how often that system or process is used. These variables provide two ways to cut cost: 1) reducing the number of times the process is used and 2) reducing the cost of the steps themselves.

Returning to the inventory example above, if the team chooses to pursue a just-in-time delivery system which performance issues are important? For the customer it might include
- providing accurate usage history
- setting scheduling plans
- adequate lead times

Standardized product requirements for the supplier might include
- little variation in lead times
- accurate deliveries
- defect free products

Only by advance knowledge of the performance standards can a system be built to meet those needs.

Develop Incentive Schemes

Once the baseline costs are determined, some form of incentive plan must be developed so that any derived benefits can be shared. Figure 3.10 outlines the basic incentives to the customer and supplier to work together. However, for the long term viability the incentive schemes should go beyond these basic issues. For instance, if the burden is shifted from the customer to the supplier, there is only so much additional cost the supplier can absorb without becoming unprofitable.

Figure 3.10 Understanding why the customer or supplier should help its partner.

Why should....

...the customer work to reduce the supplier's cost of doing business?	...the supplier expend resources to reduce the customer's cost of doing business?

- Helps to reduce total channel costs which can result in;
  - improved processes
  - reduced prices
  - improved supplier performance
  - minimized inventories
  - transfer of effort
 	
- Promotes the ability to plan better
 	
- Creates increased understanding
 	
- Identifies efficiency opportunities
 	
* **Insurance policy** for continuous help with increasing revenue and reducing costs
	- Increased revenues
	
	- Helps reduce the costs of doing business;
	  - improved processes
	  - increased leverage with manufacturers
	  - increased understanding
	  - improved planning ability
	
	- Improved cash flow
	
	- Creates increased understanding
	
	- Improves ability to sell on total cost to other customers
	
	* **Investment Strategy** to reduce the risk of Sales, inventory & people

One way that suppliers can cover this increased cost is to allow prices to go up. However, some suppliers have found that they do not look competitive in the marketplace if the price of goods or services go up. This often results in increased resistance, therefore many suppliers do not like to use price as the incentive. Fortunately, there are a number of alternative methods for creating incentives valuable to both partners.

- *Help create more business for the supplier.* Increase the scope of the agreement geographically, thereby enlarging the sales territories involved. Add to the *market basket* (additional products and services the supplier wants to provide), or help them secure additional business with other customers.
- *Actively work on reducing the supplier's cost of doing business.* The manner in which a customer does business with its supplier drives up cost in the supplier's business. The price can actually drop while a supplier increases its profitability on that account if companies work together to drive the waste or costs out of the supplier's system.
- *Allow the supplier a surcharge.* This method is gaining in use, due in part to a concept called *activity-based costing* (ABC). In its

simplest form ABC means the customer pays the supplier for each service provided, such as deliver or consignment based on the cost incurred by the supplier. A management or service charge is then developed and applied to all such activities.

The next question is *how much do the partners share?* While some alliances have a 50/50 incentive plan where all savings are shared equally, the majority do not. A number of companies use a method whereby the relationship must save the customer a certain amount each year for a specified number of years (three years is a common duration). For example, a supplier may be required to work with the customer to save $500,000 a year. Any savings derived are measured as having only a one year lifespan. Therefore savings from a new process can only be applied to the $500,000 once even if it reduces costs in all three years as shown in Figure 3.11. Normally any savings beyond the specified amount in a given year and after the third year are shared equally between the partners.

Figure 3.11 Front-loaded step incentive plan

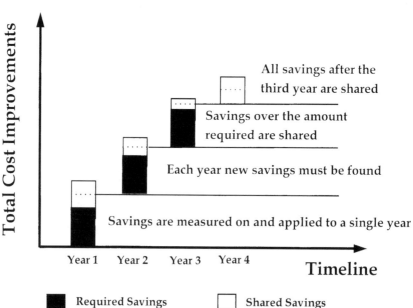

Other alliances do not set goals; rather, they look for continuous improvements which are shared on 1:1 to 1:2 ratio. An additional twist is to create a bonus incentive for the supplier of a shared percentage based on how much a given project came in under budget. This method is gaining in use, particularly with outsourcing alliances. The added risk to the supplier is that if the budget is exceeded the supplier pays part of the additional costs.

Remember that any incentive plan must allow the supplier to have some control over events, such as in the previously mentioned outsourcing method. Otherwise the advantage of using that supplier is lost because their expertise is negated by the very methods the customer is trying to change. Additionally, the measurement and control of total costs should include any possible increases as well as any reductions in costs. Savings derived from an improvement that increases other costs may not be an improvement unless the total cost is actually lowered.

Create Improvement Teams

Improvement teams are created around the specific projects and systems selected as the best opportunities for total cost reduction projects. In addition to developing improvement ideas, the team is normally responsible for measuring cost improvements, finding additional improvement opportunities, and implementing the solutions developed. These teams will be comprised of the personnel directly responsible for performing the affected tasks in the systems of both companies.

Analyze Systems

The improvement team should become the alliance experts on the system under study. Before jumping in to make improvements, the team needs to study the processes to understand
- what the input and output requirements are
- why these requirements exist
- which activities are redundant
- where problems surface and why
- what cost drivers exist

Having analyzed the system the team must now develop its plan of action for the process of improvement.

Determining Improvement Viability

The team may not develop any viable solutions. If this is the case the team usually disbands and the steering committee chooses another opportunity on which to work. The decision on viability is usually made by the steering committee after the team's presentation. If the solution is viable, it is now time to implement it.

Implement

Normally the team that developed the solution is responsible for its implementation. If the solution impacts a number of areas or people it may be best to run a pilot study to work out the bugs and ease the implementation. The team is responsible for providing any required training.

Evaluate Results

Sometimes a change can be easy to accomplish. But a change in and of itself does not necessarily mean it is the best thing for the company, nor does the change always take into consideration the actual results. The team must now document the improvement and its cost and value to both companies. If this information is not documented, no proof will exist as to the total cost reductions. Additionally, a number of processes and areas may be impacted so the team needs to look at and evaluate the impact through out the system. This includes documenting the increase in total cost in addition to the improvements.

REMINDERS

- Implementation can be accomplished quickly and easily if all the partners can work together to develop a set of common objectives and a comprehensive plan for building the alliance. Most companies find the use of a joint management team or steering committee to be extremely valuable.
- It is this steering committee which develops the objectives, sets the direction of the alliance, and begins the implementation plan for accomplishing the objectives. Objectives need to be clear, concise, and communicated to all personnel directly affected by this new relationship. These objectives are most helpful in creating the vision for all parties which is the first step in managing the change.
- Managing the change is one of the key points of the implementation plan. To manage the change effectively companies must create an understanding of what is to be accomplished and why, as well as how this change will be accomplished. Any barriers to accomplishment need to be identified and removed and any personal concerns about the new relationship minimized.
- In addition to managing the change, the implementation plan needs to include several projects for improvements that can be readily achieved to show that reducing costs is possible. Each project should be assigned to a responsible party for its completion. Once the change is accomplished and proceeding smoothly, the alliance can move into an ongoing maintenance stage where continued success and reduction of total cost is pursued by everyone.

CHAPTER 4

MAINTAINING
THE ALLIANCE

INTRODUCTION

The Discovery stage focused on determining the customer's commodity/service needs and identifying the company that could best meet those needs. Implementation dealt with developing the relationship to accomplish the fulfillment of both companies' needs. The maintenance stage of alliance deals with the efforts required to keep alliance relationships performing and returning positive results. Companies reaching this stage are usually doing fairly well, because the majority of unsuccessful alliances usually fail before reaching this point. This stage is not so much about having reached a length of time in the relationship as it is about having progressed to a specific relationship level.

The objectives and cost drivers developed during the implementation stage now guide the alliance in the direction set by both companies. However, many aspects of the alliance will change as new industry trends emerge, company directions and objectives are redefined to meet new needs, and the alliance grows. These two issues—trends and growth—make alliance management an important issue. Alliances are dynamic in nature and are surrounded by continuous change; if the alliance does not remain dynamic, it can stagnate and eventually may fall apart.

Alliance Management

Alliance maintenance involves managing both the contract and the relationship itself. Unlike the typical long-term contract, which is often static except for a few price changes, alliance contracts are dynamic. Changes will often occur to the scope of business, resulting in expanded products or services (or the removal of specific items), additional geographical areas, enhanced objectives, and new cost drivers. The contract tends to be amended more often than a normal contract, resulting in a steady need to ensure that the contract's objectives and scope are still accepted and committed to by all parties.

In addition to the administrative aspects of managing the alliance, this stage is critical in moving the alliance forward. During the implementation stage the idea of working more closely together was tested, usually with small projects, to see if both companies could work better together. Having determined that this is possible and advantageous, it is now time for growth of the alliance. To achieve this growth, two major items are needed: 1) *advancement of the objectives*, and 2) *removal of any barriers*. These two items have an interesting interrelationship. It is easier to advance the objectives when barriers are removed, but it is also easier to remove barriers if objectives are being achieved. It is for this reason, and the long-term health of the alliance, that another objective of this maintenance stage is to measure the improvements made in total cost.

Alliance Measurement

Alliances are formed for one reason—to improve the profit picture of those companies involved. If costs go up or revenues fall for either company as a result of the alliance, it is likely the alliance will end. However, many variables impact a company's profit. Simply looking at the bottom line or a profit and loss statement will reveal little of the actual impact an alliance has on the companies involved.

Alliance measurement assesses the impact of the projects undertaken as part of accomplishing the objectives. It would be impossible to capture this value or reduction in total cost on every improvement because many cost improvements will be unknown. For example, improvements in communications or planning may result in savings due to improved use of resources, reduced errors, and less work. Much of this can be measured, but how do companies measure the improvement in morale, reduction in frustration, or time spent complaining? Even if companies could somehow measure these intangibles, the cost to do so could eliminate the benefit that was obtained.

Instead companies should select which cost drivers to measure and simply keep the other savings in mind. Some of the key aspects of total cost improvements that companies measure include

- price improvements
- revenue enhancements
- increases in efficiency
- elimination of non value added activities
- process improvements
- transfer of effort
- technological advancements

By measuring the reduction in total cost based on the improvements in these variables, the partners can better manage the alliance. These results show that advancement on the objectives is being achieved, or that other plans or projects should be initiated to accomplish the objectives. In effect, these measurements are guideposts that help to keep the alliance on course.

Additionally, by measuring the improvements, the alliance is developing resources to overcome the barriers that surface. Different barriers surface at different times—some will have surfaced during implementation. These barriers should be addressed as soon as possible, as discussed in the previous chapter. Therefore, it would be advisable to start measuring improvements during the implementation of the alliance. The methods are described at this point simply because far more total cost savings will be instituted during maintenance than at any other stage.

MANAGEMENT

Alliance maintenance continues the work begun in implementation. A solid, well-designed agreement or contract can help build the alliance further. The partners must create a plan which becomes the blueprint for building the alliance. But it is the agreement which sets the dimensions and specifications of what goes into the plan.

Those companies accomplishing the most in total cost savings almost invariably have well-defined expectations, incentives, and evaluation methods. Often these were not developed until the maintenance stage was reached and the companies realized the need. The plan should be based on the objectives and around the organizational structure that supports the alliance (discussed in Chapter 3). It should focus primarily on improvement projects but should also include any contract maintenance that might be required.

The primary source for total cost improvements projects will be the issues identified during the commodity/service planning and from the objectives set fourth in the Implementation stage. However, both improvement projects and contract maintenance needs may be determined from the barriers encountered within and between both companies. These could include performance issues, lack of available resources, and pricing issues. However, many other barriers will surface in addition to the contractual and total cost improvements that the team needs to address such as changes in personnel, fear of job loss, and resistance to the change. The steering committee is responsible for managing these aspects of the alliance.

Advancement Of Objectives

The most effective method for achieving objectives is to develop a plan and a system for logically working through the process of improvement. The diagram in Figure 4.1 shows this process. It also includes several other equally important aspects—the initiatives that enable the process to actually succeed.

Too often, projects are begun without communication to those affected because there is no method for identifying critical processes or people. As a result, neither positive nor negative effects on key cost drivers are identified, making any incentives ineffective and meaningless. In the rush to change processes, opportunities can be missed that could result in better improvements than are actually achieved. Because of the problems that arise, training is delayed or becomes a session on justification instead of instruction or direction. Any evaluation actually conducted is discounted because the results are suspect due to having missed many of the cost drivers. Hence, the measurement of cost improvements, or *score carding*, is ignored.

Figure 4.1 Primary components of alliance maintenance

Score Carding   **Communication**

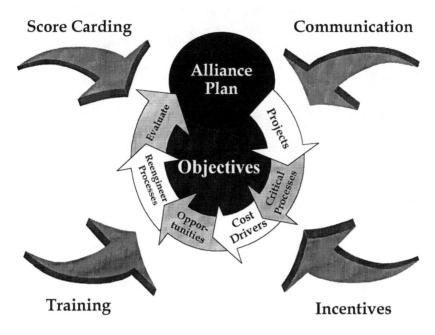

Training   **Incentives**

Obviously, this is an exaggeration of what could occur. However, alliance partners would do well to consider how a number of successful alliances achieve their results. The intent is not to show the only method possible, but to show how those results are achieved by the companies most successful at reducing costs beyond the simple transactional aspects.

Objectives

In managing the alliance, it is the objectives set forth in the implementation stage that provide the guideposts for the steering committee. Mobil Oil and Red Man Pipe & Supply established the objective of improving the inventory management system between both companies. To meet this objective, projects and teams in various areas were created. The result has been extremely beneficial for both companies in a number of locations. The savings at a single location has amounted to $758,760 per year for Mobil Oil. These results were only possible because the steering committee could use this objective and others as guideposts to direct the actions of the project teams. All of the members were working together toward a mutual set of goals that allowed the alliance to reach its destination. Figure 4.1 illustrates how each task or aspect is either centered around or directed towards these objectives.

Chapter 3 discussed how to set these objectives and develop them into tools which could help in managing change. These objectives will change as the alliance grows. Objectives can be both a vehicle for moving forward and a guard against going too far. Both aspects are necessary parts of the objectives. Projects can take on a life of their own, often becoming bigger and providing "opportunities" beyond those that a partner can actually accept. This occurs most often when people get caught up in the idea of improving matters beyond the scope of the project. It is more important for companies to focus on continuous improvement than on building the perfect system the first time. Building the perfect system usually requires too much time and resources, and by the time it is built, the system may be obsolete. Tremendous gains can be made by working on smaller "bite size" opportunities. Therefore, as progress is made the steering committee must ensure that the project remains within the scope of the objectives.

For this reason, objectives should be linked to form the limits desired by both companies. Failing to link the objectives can create gaps in the overall scope of the alliance, resulting in wasted time and effort as it becomes necessary to restructure projects.

Alliance Plan

The main purpose in creating an alliance improvement plan is to ensure the projects that are chosen help to meet the objectives of the alliance. AMOCO Production Company developed such a plan with one of its suppliers to combine and standardize the processing requirements of a half dozen plants. Teams were set up to determine how to minimize inventories, standardize products, and reduce processing costs. In addition to these improvement projects alliance plans should include time to

- review changes in price
- consider any additional products/services (or to delete any products/services)
- discuss how to handle any problems or barriers that may have developed
- review and modify the agreement or objectives if needed

These issues and the projects for improvement should be examined periodically to ensure the ongoing health of the alliance.

The plan itself should be presented in a format that is easy to use and understand. Many alliances use the diagram format as shown in Chapter 3. However, any format the alliance chooses to use, so long as it is used, will suffice. To be user friendly the plan should include:

- *Projects underway:* Opportunities currently being pursued.
- *Primary responsibilities:* Identify one person to be accountable for each project. Some companies prefer to appoint a person from each company. If this method is utilized, one of them should be designated as the leader.
- *Time frames:* The progression from the start to completion of each project and any milestones if the project is performed in stages.
- *Team members:* The leader and other members working on the project.
- *Project scope:* The project mission as it relates to the objectives and the limitations under which the project must operate.

Projects

From the alliance improvement plan will come the projects that the companies are going to work on to improve. For Wisconsin Gas and Arby Construction more than 90 opportunities were identified. The steering committee chose five projects to start with, including several "quick win" projects involving communication improvements and longer term projects such as improved scheduling. Most alliances, even large alliances, have found that limits should be placed on the number of projects to be undertaken at any one time. These limits are based on available resources—of these resources, man-hours tend to be the most scarce. Based on the type of alliance in place there may not be a need for many ongoing improvement projects. However, if total costs are not being reduced, competitive nature often reasserts itself, resulting in a shift in focus back to price as other suppliers use price in trying to break apart the alliance. As one AMOCO employee put it, "A low-maintenance alliance has a tendency to become a no-alliance situation."

Projects stem from ideas or opportunities coming from other project teams, studying other companies or industries, mapping processes, evaluation results, and plant or field personnel. The steering committee selects a team based upon such factors as risk, performance concerns, dollar impact, personnel capabilities, and how the opportunities affect the potential achievement of the alliance objectives.

Critical Processes

As each project begins, the first action the team takes is to identify all processes or systems likely to be affected. WEPCO, in working with several construction companies, identified inspection, scheduling, and planning as the primary processes involved with project construction. They then focused on these processes in the pursuit of lowering total costs. The projects were first examined for their affect on all processes in both companies prior to proceeding. The reason for this is simple: changes create a ripple effect. A small change in one process could create serious problems in another.

By identifying all the processes likely to be affected by the project, the team is in a stronger position to control the ripples. The critical processes are those mostly likely to result in the largest reductions in cost and that will be most affected by any planned changes. At this point the team should evaluate whether it has the required expertise and resources or if additional resources are required.

If these critical processes for both companies are not already mapped out, it is advantageous to do so at this point. By studying the processes, the team can often find easy improvements, waste, and duplicate efforts or costs in addition to the key cost drivers. Using this information, the team can determine how to proceed.

Cost Drivers

Every process and task within a process has cost drivers. Border States and WEPCO identified a dozen potential cost drivers within their systems. These cost drivers included over-engineered requirements, changes to standards, process improvements, and inventory efficiencies as well as pricing issues. The result in the first nine months has been a reduction in total costs of more than 3 million dollars on 10 million dollars of purchases. Appendix A lists some of the more commonly identified cost drivers to help other companies get started. Each cost driver can actually be viewed as an opportunity. The important task for the team is to identify the degree of impact or savings (value), risk or concerns, and performance needs imposed by working on a specific cost driver. Figure 4.3 was introduced in Chapter 3 and has been slightly modified for use in this stage.

Figure 4.2 Cost driver breakdown and evaluation

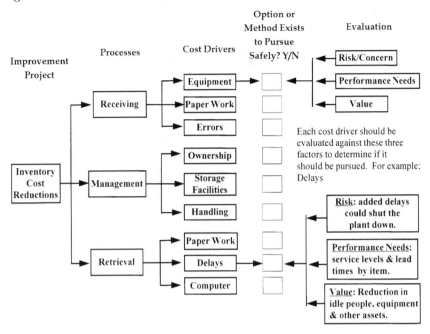

Risks and Concerns. Assets, tasks and other cost drivers that are already in place exist because at some point in time there was a need for them. That need may remain, and changing or eliminating the cost driver could result in greater costs than any potential savings to be achieved. The team needs to weigh the risks and concerns of the user in selecting options to reduce costs.

Performance needs. If a change is to occur, such as a transfer of effort or the elimination of duplicate efforts, the requirements of the user must still be met. For example, while it is true that there is often a certain amount of duplicated effort, the task may be duplicated because of different output requirements for that user. Considerations for change must include the needs of the users, determination of the requirements, and how to best meet these requirements.

Value. The value of a cost driver is based on several criteria including:

Today's value: The yearly expenditure or loss of revenues that occurs due to this cost driver. For example, a piece of equipment can have an asset value, maintenance costs to keep it running, operating costs, personnel costs to run it, storage, and insurance. All of these aspects are cost drivers that result in expenditures.

Transfer value. The cost to change the system or cost driver and the new cost for the modified system. This new cost could be the cost involved for the partner to perform the work. If a warehouse is being outsourced, what does it cost the supplier to take over the warehouse? What does the customer pay for this transfer of effort? And what is the cost to develop and implement the change?

The actual savings or value to a company for changing a specific cost driver would be today's value less the transfer value. This value need not be calculated exactly—a close approximation is usually adequate. This information is used simply to help determine what the savings could be if that cost driver is pursued.

Opportunities

Opportunities are developed from those cost drivers that were identified and evaluated as being worth the risk of changing. In working with a number of different alliance partners Red Man Pipe & Supply has come to realize that not all companies have the ability to change the same cost driver in the same way as another customer. As a result they have built numerous methods for attacking a specific cost driver. Teams take the evaluation factors and determine whether an opportunity exists based on current methods. If not, new methods may be developed to meet the customer's needs.

Reengineering Processes

The term reengineering is used for a purpose. Some of the most successful teams use the reengineering concept to make the improvements to the systems under study. Both Haynes International and Navistar are developing new processes and systems with their suppliers to minimize the costs for the companies involved. Simply put, the team starts with the scenario of how a perfect system would operate. Based on the concerns or risks and performance issues already identified, safeguards are added to the system.

The new system is then mapped and the team presents it to the end users to identify potential weaknesses or opportunities for improvement. In some cases, once the new system is finalized, it is implemented. However, this has caused problems for some companies, particularly when the systems were outsourced. A test pilot or slow transition into the new system may be a better option. The downside of these methods is that savings are slower to materialize and transfer costs become greater. However, this may be worthwhile since mistakes are minimized and the process can be fine tuned prior to full utilization. In any event the new system must be implemented and it is the team's responsibility to facilitate a smooth transition.

Evaluate

Once the new system is implemented, it is important to assess whether it is operating smoothly and at the predicted lower cost. Coastal Management Corporation evaluated the delivery, inventory, and service levels prior to improving the systems involved with its suppliers. The results of the system changes have totally eliminated inventories (no consignment) while at the same time cutting deliveries to approximately ten percent of their previous number. The impact on operations has been dramatic—crews no longer wait on materials, output has increased significantly, and operation costs have dropped. How? The companies now all work together as one. The information gathered during the cost driver evaluation served as the baseline for subsequent evaluations and for providing the reasoning and direction for the changes made.

The improvement team looks at the risks or concerns identified and determines if these have been minimized and if the system is in at least as strong a position as it was prior to the change. Performance measurement is based on the new input and output to ensure that the user's needs are being met.

If any problems exist, the team should implement minor corrective action until the system can be totally corrected. It is also important for the team to assess the cost drivers in the new system and determine the new cost of operations. The total cost measurement concept and methods will be explained later in this chapter.

Enablers

An enabler is an action taken by the team that helps ensure success. There are four primary enablers to consider in managing alliances. These can help overcome barriers and promote action for the alliance if used appropriately.

- *Communication.* Almost every company talks about the need for better communication. This need is even greater as companies are working together in an alliance. Every project undertaken requires communication to the appropriate users in order to manage the change and gain the users' assistance in developing the new systems. By not informing the affected employees of the pending changes and allowing them to voice their concerns, they can become barriers. To facilitate communication,

Redman sets up joint newsletters with its alliance partners to show the changes taking place. AMOCO also increases communication by bringing its suppliers into plant and field operational meetings.

- *Incentives.* Once the value of the change is determined it is important to consider how each party is to be compensated for the planned improvements. This is the key to determining how many hours and resources each partner is willing to expend. This concern can also be relayed to the departmental and personnel levels for each of the companies as well. With limited budgets and resources, the various areas affected need to determine whether they have the time or the ability to work on specific projects. WEPCO uses this enabler by going on sales calls with its primary alliance partners to help the supplier generate added revenues. With other partners WEPCO shares part of the savings derived. Consumers Power is looking at opening additional territories for the alliance partners that provide the greatest improvements.

- *Training.* Training is required for any new processes, technologies, techniques, and products initiated by the team. Without training, it will take longer to achieve the expected results. Additionally, resistance to these changes will be greater because people will not have been introduced to them and therefore will remain uncomfortable. Red Man starts all of its primary alliances with two days of alliance training in various areas to bring everyone together. Red Man then works through processes and cost drivers to improve understanding of the impact each company has for the other.

- *Score carding.* Score carding is the task of tracking the dollar impact on the bottom line of the improvement for both partners. This information allows the partners to see the impact each is having on the other, both positive and negative. In turn, it can provide incentives to do more and help to eliminate some barriers. AMOCO held a three day symposium on the results achieved worldwide from alliances. The results help to foster support by showing that alliances work. One example showed how the cost to drill a well of equal depth has been reduced from $1.1 million in 1991 to $550 thousand in 1995.

The methods that companies use will differ based on the cost drivers chosen for improvement. Most alliances develop a set of methods that can generally be applied to a number of similar improvement situations. Examples of these methods can be found later in this chapter.

Removing Barriers

In managing the alliance it is important to consider not just the enablers but also the disablers—the barriers to moving forward. Alliances have a number of inherent barriers that can prevent the relationship from becoming a success. Some of these were touched on in Chapter 3 but deserve greater attention given the impact these issues have had in industry.

Typically, the barriers fall under four classifications as shown in Figure 4.3. Failure to address them can halt the alliance before it gets off the ground. The steering committee must monitor these barriers on an ongoing basis and remove them.

Figure 4.3 Typical barriers found in building alliances

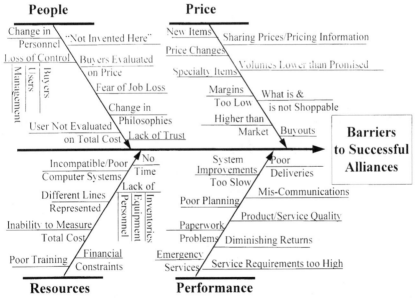

People. With all the changes affecting companies today, employees feel increasingly vulnerable. Sometimes these changes directly influence jobs in terms of both security and the method of evaluation. Alliances are often viewed as having a negative impact on jobs, which is sometimes the case. Often jobs are lost in reengineering and alliances are used to help manage procurement when staffs are reduced or outsourcing eliminates positions. At other times, alliances can have an overall positive effect on people throughout the company, but in specific areas the results might be negative.

Given that these concerns are often real, if not addressed they can impede any progress. How these barriers are handled goes back to the earlier discussion of enablers. Communication and training can eliminate many of these concerns. For example, Amoco, Mobil, Chevron, WEPCO and others have used joint training sessions with their alliance partners. The results have been extremely beneficial. Both parties have an opportunity to voice concerns, receive feedback, and start to develop opportunities to move forward together. Naturally this forum cannot cover all issues, such as fear of job loss when the loss of jobs is imminent, but it can clarify many of the other issues. Subsequent smaller sessions can handle new personnel or areas as the alliance grows.

The steering committee must also address the incompatibility between total cost and current internal evaluation methods for various departments with corporate management. For example, some car manufacturers did not traditionally include inventories as part of the plant's total asset base. Therefore, the plant manager had no reason to lower inventories, particularly since lower inventories could affect output, which was a criterion on which the plant managers were evaluated. When the inventory was targeted as an option to lower costs, resistance was encountered due to the conflict in interest. The solution was that inventory became part of the plant manager's evaluation and resistance all but disappeared. In effect, there was now incentive for the managers to reduce this aspect of total cost.

Price. While the main force that drives alliances is total cost reduction, price is still an important factor and one that can put the brakes on hard. For some companies price has been the only factor on which a supplier's total cost was evaluated. Yet in alliances it should be only one of many pieces of total cost. And when a supplier is forced to lower prices in order to receive the alliance business, it can cause problems. If a supplier's margins are too low, services may suffer.

However, the greatest resistance comes when a lower price is found. Not if it is found, but when it is found. In any alliance, almost any day of the week, lower prices can always be found on given products. Usually the number of products is small, but the mere fact that a lower price was found, implies that too many of the remaining prices might be high. Even though a few prices are likely to be higher than can be found in the market, usually the total price paid on all goods is lower and the total cost to acquire and possess the goods or services is much lower.

The committee must address this issue immediately. If it can be shown that the total price paid for goods and services is shown to be competitive overall, and that the higher priced goods have little impact on the total amount paid when compared to expected savings, many of the concerns can be eliminated.

The price paid can also affect an area's evaluation. If total cost is decreased but the evaluation for an area is negatively affected by price, the evaluation method must change. Otherwise, resistance to the alliance initiative will increase.

Another price issue is the handling of items not on the contract, or specialty items. This concern has increased due to integrated supply. Many distributors have as many buyout sales as stock sales due to the purchase of these specialty items, and buyouts usually have very low margins. This causes problems for both parties because the customer has to explain when prices are slightly higher (although total cost is less since the supplier must now source the material and the supplier performs more tasks for a lower return.) Large projects may also cause problems—the supplier may feel these projects should be part of the contract, while the customer may believe the volume of project purchases would result in price concessions worth the extra costs involved in sourcing and managing the purchases themselves.

Many of these issues should be addressed up front and agreed upon in the contract. For example, the dollar volume to be reached before the project can go out for bid can be specified. Or the creation of *tiered pricing*, which allows for lower prices based on various volumes, can prevent projects from becoming an issue later. Another commonly used method is to score card the savings generated and then use projects over a specified dollar amount as the incentive to the supplier for having reduced total costs.

Resources. Many alliances are started with the best of intentions, but when the reality hits in terms of resources required, they just never happen. Limited resources can only be spread so far. Many customers entering alliances have just downsized and finding the time to work on improvements with the supplier is often difficult. For the supplier, the additional services required and the lower margins experienced place limits on what the supplier can do.

In this circumstance proceeding slowly makes the most sense. Most companies must select the projects and cost drivers on which to carefully spend the available resources during this time period. The models discussed later in this chapter under *Alliance Measurement*, offer a way to evaluate these opportunities. A little time invested upfront in planning which issues to work on goes a long way.

Performance. Performance has always been a source of concern to customers and suppliers. It is not just an issue of the *supplier* doing things right. The customer's performance needs to be considered as well. In either case poor performance raises costs and barriers.

Performance can be a project in and of itself. Realistic expectations should be set for both companies. This requires understanding of each other's costs and needs. Joint systems can then be developed which allow for better performance at a lower total cost. Coastal Management, in evaluating the cost of delivery from Red Man Pipe & Supply found that the supplier had five trucks on location at the same time. Each was delivering five separate small orders. After creating a new system for deliveries, the trips were cut to two scheduled runs per day and have now been reduced to one run a day. The initial reaction was less than favorable, but through training and working with the various personnel it actually became easier for the customer's crews to do it that way. This is a common finding by many companies. Change is initially resisted, but through training and communication, people come to understand the need to change and how to change without creating additional costs.

Diminishing Returns

There is one barrier that deserves special attention. A number of companies experience diminishing returns after the alliance has been successful for both parties. The law of diminishing returns applies when a certain level of savings is achieved, then the amount of cost reductions levels out.

Figure 4.4 Diminishing returns can lead to trouble

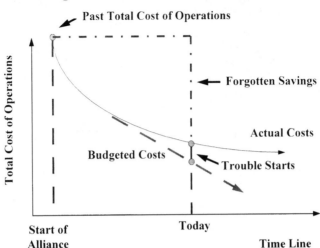

Figure 4.4 shows the effect of diminishing returns. This barrier particularly applies to companies that have been involved in an alliance for some time. The graph shows that the total cost of operation has come down tremendously over time. Unfortunately, neither company documented many of the total cost reductions; therefore the savings have been forgotten. It is quite common for undocumented savings to be forgotten or considered not to exist, particularly when changes in personnel take place and alliances do not involve multiple levels or multiple areas in the management of the alliance.

The trouble starts when either a new manager attempts to improve things or management's need to drive down costs creates a budget based on savings that have little chance of occurring. In reality there are often still some large savings possible but the change in focus shifts resources away from making these improvements. When the new expectations are not met, the emphasis often reverts back to price.

*Figure 4.5 Diminishing returns encourage companies to refocus on price,
leading to increases in other costs.*

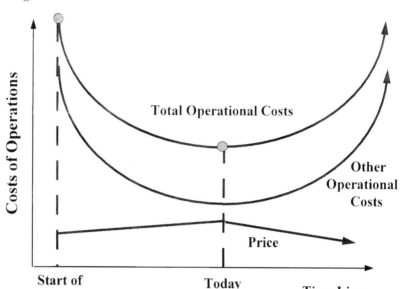

This shift back to price can be seen in Figure 4.5. Over time, price
has been allowed to creep up because of the previously illustrated forgotten savings. The increased price was the incentive for reduction of
other costs and for the supplier taking on more of the burden. At first
the reduction in price seems to have little effect on total cost except to
decrease it further.

Unfortunately, the effect is only temporary. For example, inventories do not simply reappear overnight. But as the supplier attempts to
reduce its costs, much of the burden is shifted back to the customer
and systems that were eliminated earlier now evolve again. Over time
total costs go up and the customer finds itself in a position of higher
operating costs. The end result—the initial gains are lost, therefore
everyone loses.

It is for this reason perhaps more than any other that score carding, tied to an incentive plan, is needed. Many added-value activities
performed by each company for the other are taken for granted. No
two companies perform alike; each company drives costs in and out of
their trading partners differently. Without measuring the added value,
the true cost is difficult to monitor.

ALLIANCE MEASUREMENT

Throughout this book the concept of total cost has been used as the primary reason to institute alliances. The concept of total cost is nothing new. Suppliers have often used the concept in an attempt to distinguish themselves from other suppliers. The problem has always been in trying to quantify the worth of the value added by a supplier.

In an alliance this value must be measured, and in a manner accepted by both companies. This includes both the methods for measuring total cost and the level of accuracy. Keep in mind that as the methods become more detailed, the information is generally more accurate and, therefore, acceptance is higher—but the cost to gather it is higher as well. Many companies use approximations based on a study of the cost driver, which is then applied to that cost driver in similar processes.

The following examples are simple in nature and meant to illustrate that added value can be measured. In actual practice gathering the information will require much more effort. Only six general score card models will be illustrated. These score cards document improvements and the added value to customers. Forms following this methodology can be found in Appendix D. Many more exist and others can be developed based on the needs of the users. Underhill & Associates has developed more than 40 different ones and is developing a number of new ones for use with its clients.

Inventory Reductions

Inventory is one of the most frequently targeted cost drivers in alliances. This is due both to its visibility and of the dollar amount involved. However, the savings derived from inventory reductions is not the actual dollar amount freed from being tied up in inventory; instead it is the reduced cost associated with the possession of an item that results in savings. The possession costs for inventory include two aspects:

Hard costs. Cost improvements or savings that will have an immediate and direct impact on profits. Inventory hard costs include:

- *Interest expense:* Tieing up dollars in inventory limits the ability to invest that money elsewhere and receive a return and may create a need to borrow funds.
- *Taxes:* Most states apply an annual inventory tax based on the amount invested in the inventory.
- *Shrinkage and spoilage:* The loss of inventory due to pilferage and damage, which are not covered by insurance.

- *Insurance:* some companies are self-insured; others carry insurance on the value of inventory. If insurance is paid, it is a hard cost; if the inventory is self-insured, the cost is soft.

Soft costs. These are cost improvements or savings that only impact a company's profit if assets are redeployed. This means the asset still exists and is held by the company for use but is now idle. For example, if just-in-time inventory management is instituted, the warehouse becomes idle (assuming no inventory). The potential exists to save resources if the warehouse can be sold or put to another use. With soft costs there is a potential savings, but until the potential is changed to reality through some action, it never actually lowers the cost of doing business. Inventory soft costs include:

- *Warehouse:* Storage space is soft because, unless the area is put to another useful purpose or is sold, there is no actual savings from reduced expenditures. The sale of a warehouse would turn this into a hard cost improvement as would redeployment. Redeployment creates a hard cost improvement because it eliminates the need for an expenditure (a new building for another purpose).
- *Equipment:* Shelving, handling equipment, and inventory control equipment may be freed for sale or other uses.
- *People:* As inventories are reduced, personnel can be shifted to other more "added value" positions, limiting the hiring of new personnel.
- *Processes:* In some cases the need to perform specific tasks is reduced or eliminated. This is covered in more detail later in this section.

Figure 4.6 Calculating inventory carrying cost savings

Inventory Items	(A) Past Average Quantities	(B) Average Quantities now in Inventory	(C) Average Value of the Item	(D) Dollars Freed (A-B)*C	Savings = D*K Cost
2" Ball Valves (consign)	30	0	45	1,350	270
3" Ball Valves (consign)	30	0	55	1,650	330
Check Valves (all sizes)	65	0	95	6,175	1,235
Fasteners (J.I.T.)	10,000	1,000	21	189,000	37,800
General Supplies	5,500	200	12	63,600	12,720
Pipe Nipples	200	0	15	3,000	600
				264,775	52,955
				Total Dollars Freed	Total Carrying Cost Savings

Note: "K Cost" is used to denote Carrying Costs;
Interest, taxes, insurance and shrinkage/spoilage.
A K Cost of 20% was used in these examples.

There are numerous ways to reduce inventories, many of which have been mentioned in earlier chapters. A number of these methods reduce some of the soft costs mentioned above. These savings should be reflected in other score cards such as process savings or an asset improvement model (not shown here). The score card in Figure 4.6 shows how to capture the hard savings from inventory reductions.

Step 1: Inventory items. The team responsible for inventory reductions must first determine which items should be reduced. This can be done on an item-by-item basis (such as 2 inch ball valves), by family group (motors), or total inventory. Keep in mind that the more specific the information provided is, the more accurate the score card will be.

Step 2: Past average quantities. Prior to eliminating the inventories, the alliance partner must determine how much inventory exists (in dollars) for each inventory item.

Step 3: Average quantities now in inventory. Once the new system is in place, determination must be made of the quantity of goods now in inventory and still owned by the customer. For example; if consignment is the new method used, inventories may remain at the same level but are no longer owned by the customer. In such a situation the quantity would be zero since all ownership was transferred; therefore, the customer does not incur the carrying costs.

Step 4: Average value of the item. Individual item prices may vary so an average price per item must be determined. If exact prices are not available, use current market prices to show the replenishment cost.

Step 5: Dollars freed. Subtract current quantities from the past quantities in order to determine the reduction in units. Then multiply this amount by the unit price. This determines the total dollars freed or now available for other uses.

Step 6: Savings. The amount freed is not the amount saved. What is saved is the cost for carrying inventories (or K cost). K cost is a derived percentage that includes all of the hard saving parameters. For many companies this works out to between 18 and 21 percent (Figure 4.6 used 20percent). This will show the hard savings for each item. By totaling the last two columns the total dollars freed and total savings can be calculated.

By using this method Border States was able to document a $742,000 in hard savings for WEPCO in the first year of their alliance.

Process Savings

Unlike the inventory score card, process savings are soft in nature. However, these savings are still real and should be measured. As stated earlier the term "soft" means the savings will not normally have a direct impact on the bottom line unless assets are re-deployed. While any process can be improved and consequently generate savings, the most commonly focused on processes are the transactional ones between partners. Examples include:

- ordering process
- bar coding of shipments, products, invoices
- use of EDI (electronic data interchange) for ordering and invoicing
- use of EFT or ACH (electronic funds transfers and automated clearinghouse)
- procurement cards
- summary billing (billing statements bi-weekly or monthly rather than per order)

Many other examples exist of methods and means to reduce the transaction costs associated with ordering, invoicing and payments. All of these and any improvements to maintenance and operational processes and systems occur when at least one of two variables change:

Task cost. A process is a series of steps or tasks and each task creates an expenditure. This expenditure could be supplies, personnel time, equipment usage, overhead usage and many other costs. Savings can be derived by reducing the cost of a single step or many steps in the process.

Figure 4.7 Process cost comparison between traditional and EDI invoicing

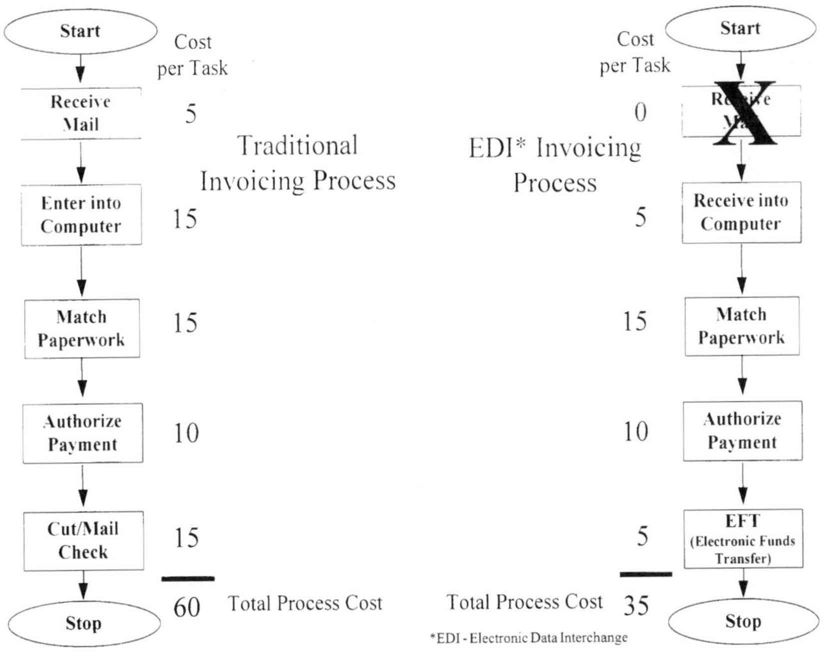

Figure 4.7 shows the potential savings using the example of implementing EDI for invoicing. Some tasks are eliminated and other modifications made that result in some savings. Changes in processes, however, do not always result in improvements at each step. In some cases, the cost for a given task may go up. This can still be advantageous if the total process cost is less. If the cost of the process increases, it can still be advantageous if the second variable drives the savings.

Process usage. The other variable that drives process costs is usage. A process used 10 times, with a cost of $10 for each use, will cost the company the same amount as a $100 process which is used once. Many companies emphasize the reduction in the number of times a system is used in addition to reduction of the cost of the system. For example, line changeovers at a manufacturing facility drives costs into the system if performed frequently. To minimize the cost, manufacturers often attempt to plan needs better and reduce the number of line changes. This same idea holds true for other systems.

Figure 4.8 Changing the utilization rate of a process can reduce the total cost

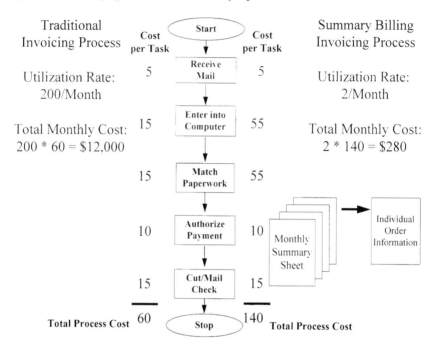

The flow chart in Figure 4.8 shows the increased total process costs incurred due to summary billing increasing from $60 to $140. However, because the process utilization rate is reduced from 200 times per month to twice a month, there is an overall savings in total monthly cost. These variables are not an either/or option and can be combined to reduce costs. Although the savings are soft, with a little extra effort the savings can start to generate actual results.

Figure 4.9 Calculating process savings

Processes Improved	(A) Past Process Cost	(B) Past Frequency of Use	(C) Current Process Cost	(D) Current Frequency of Use	Savings = (A*B) - (C*D)
EDI Invoicing	60	1,000	35	1000	25,000
Order Processing	55	1,000	250	30	47,500
Manufacturing Process	150	10,000	148	10,000	20,000
Inventory Management	6	30	0	0	180

Note: Process savings should be annualized to reflect the savings for one year. Total Process Savings **92,680**

The score card shown in Figure 4.9 is used to capture process improvements. It should be noted that some process improvements result in revenue enhancements instead of savings; in that case, use the revenues score card shown in this chapter in Figure 4.10.

Step 1: *Processes improved.* The alliance studies the critical processes and determines which processes to improve or which were improved.

Step 2: *Past process cost.* As was explained in Chapter 3, baseline cost information on all critical processes should be developed. If it has not been done, the team must determine the cost prior to changing the process. The easiest method to do this is to "paper chase" the process. For each step apply a percentage of the overhead charged to the department as well as any direct costs. (Overhead is prorated based on the number of transactions and percentage of time dedicated to that process).

Step 3: *Past frequency of use.* Determine the approximate number of times the process is used on a yearly basis. (If a weekly or monthly usage rate is determined, annualize the usage rate).

Step 4: *Current process costs.* After the process change is made, determine the new cost using the same method in Step 2.

Step 5: *Current frequency of use.* Determine how often the new system is used (annualize the usage rate again).

Step 6: *Savings.* The savings resulting from the improvement of any one process can be determined by 1) multiplying the past process costs by the past frequency of use and 2) multiplying the current process cost by the current frequency of use. Finally, subtract the current value from the past value. [(A * B) - (C * D)].

Step 7: *Total process savings.* Sometimes more than a single process is affected. If so, sum the savings column to determine total savings from all process improvements. AMOCO and Red Man documented more than $125,000 in potential process improvements in the first six months of their alliance. This resulted in the expansion of the alliance scope to include additional areas of coverage for Red Man.

Revenue Enhancements

Not all improvements deal with savings. The value a supplier adds can be a result of increased output or revenues. Revenue enhancements usually occur because of direct material suppliers or service companies. However, MRO (maintenance, repairs, operations) suppliers can be involved as well. Revenue enhancements other than direct materials are usually a result of operating efficiencies and reduced downtimes. Often use of increases in costs also occur when revenue is enhanced due to either equipment, people, or products and these increases should be determined as well.

Figure 4.10 Calculating the profit improvement from revenue enhancements

Date	Event	(A)Annual Unit Improvement	(B) Unit Value	(C) Increased Cost	Profit Improvement = (A*B) - C
3/96	Back on-line 3 days early	300	100	11,000	19,000
4/96	System Improvement	250	75	1,000	17,750
4/96	New Product Used	50	100	1,500	3,500

Note: Process savings should be annualized to reflect the savings for one year.	Total Profit Improvement	40,250

The score card in Figure 4.10 is used for capturing revenue enhancements. There are two types of improvement in revenues:

- *Situational:* A one-time increase such as when the supplier helps the customer get back on line more quickly.
- *Continuous:* The increase in revenues will occur many items from this point forward.

Step 1: Date. Document the occurrence by date, particularly when it was a one-time event.

Step 2: Event. Describe the event as it occurred.

Step 3: Annual unit improvement. Determine the number of additional units produced. If the improvement is continuous, determine an annualized amount. For situational improvements, the one-time amount is the annualized increase.

Step 4: Unit value. Determine selling price for these additional units.

Step 5: Increased costs. Identify any increased costs. Do not apply costs such as overhead since these costs already exist. Consider only those increases in expenditures directly due to these units (direct material, new supplies, etc).

Step 6: Profit improvement. To determine the improvement to profits, multiply the annualized increase in output by the unit value for each event, then subtract any additional expenditures.

Step 7: Total profit improvements. Sum the profit improvement column to determine the total profit.

WEPCO worked with two of its suppliers and their union, Local 317, to minimize the effects of a forced plant shutdown. Repairs were estimated at requiring 11 days to complete. However, by working together the plant was back on line in four days. An unplanned cost of $250,000 was incurred, but the seven additional days of generation prevented the loss of several million in revenues.

Price Savings

Price is, and perhaps may always be, the most emphasized cost driver. There is no question that its visibility and comparative ease to evaluate makes it a prime target. However, it is not always scored correctly. Savings from price issues come in many forms including:

Alliance Pricing. Alliances often start with guaranteed pricing that is lower than the customer's previous price. An item-by-item analysis can be performed—however the most common method is to develop a market basket (a list of some commonly used items on the contract) and determine the average price paid during the year prior to the alliance. The average difference by item or market basket can then be used to estimate the approximate savings (if any exist).

Plateau Pricing. Rebates or further reductions in price for specific periods of time due to total purchases should also be measured.

Tier Pricing. This is a discount on certain levels of quantity purchases.

Price Protection. Many contracts hold the supplier to a given price that cannot be raised for a specific period of time. Any increased costs that would commonly be passed to the customer must be absorbed by the supplier. For example, a bearing distributor agrees on prices with its customer, then the manufacturer increases prices to this distributor. The price time period in which the increased price was not passed on is a savings to the customer. The distributor is helping the customer to avoid an expense.

Figure 4.11 Calculating price savings

Items	(A) Annual Purchase Quantities	(B) Price Differences	Annual Savings (A*B)
Alliance (Market Basket)	1	100,000	100,000
Price Protection (Widgets)	1,000	2	2,000
Project Tier	1	8,545	8,545
Year End Rebate	1	6,500	6,500
Integrated Products	500	3	1,500

	Total Price Savings	118,545

The score card in Figure 4.11 is used to track price savings to the customer. Of all score cards this could be the most critical. Price is always an issue. By documenting and communicating the overall savings on price, the day-to-day issues that often surface can be minimized.

Step 1: Items. Determine the items or situations for which a savings in price occurred. This could be a project where tiered pricing is the issue, a market basket for initial savings, or individual items as savings occur.

Step 2: Annual Purchasing Quantities. How many items will be purchased in a year's time that will incur these savings? The annual quantity for a tier is one and is documented each time a tier occurs; the initial alliance pricing has a usage of one if done as a whole with volumes included. For protection, only the estimated purchases during the protection period are counted.

Step 3: Price Differences. Once usage volumes are determined, calculate the actual savings in dollars for each unit.

Step 4: Annual Savings. Multiply estimated annual usage by the dollar savings to determine the price savings for each item.

Step 5: Total Price Savings. Sum the annual savings column to determine the total savings incurred. Mobil Oil saved tens of thousands of dollars over a one year period by using tiered pricing with one of its suppliers. Additional price improvements with the same supplier have amounted to more than $500,000.

Service Provided

Many suppliers provide services for which there is no direct charge. This could include training, deliveries, field/technical support, project coordination, and a host of other services. Sometimes the service is an industry standard—every supplier provides it. In this case, determining the value added by this service may not provide any acceptable data to use in showing total cost reductions.

However, where the service provided goes beyond the norm, the added value should be calculated. All suppliers might make trips to deliver supplies, but does the alliance partner provide 24 hour service or make multiple runs a day or week?

Keep in mind that this score card is perhaps the simplest in nature of any of the score cards shown and is being applied to complicated issues. Alliances, where the services provided are critical and require more depth, must develop score cards specific to their needs based on the costs affected. While this is true for all these simplified score cards, it is particularly true for services.

Figure 4.12 Calculating the added value for services provided

Service Provided	(A) Fair Market Value of the Service (or Training)	(B) Time Spent on Service (or People Trained)	Value Added = (A*B)
Product Safety Training	50 / person	30 people	1,500
Technical Support	60 / hour	11 hours	660
Project Planning	450 / day	6 days	2,700
Technical Training	250 / person	10 people	2,500
		Total Value Added	7,360

Step 1: Service Provided. The alliance partners must identify those services provided that go beyond the industry norms for which the additional value must be measured.

Step 2: Fair Market Valve of the Services. This can be a difficult value to determine. Most partners try to determine how much it would cost on a hourly or daily rate to hire another company to provide that service.

Step 3: Time Spent on Service. The alliance partners should track the time spent performing these services. Most often this is done on an on-going basis. Some alliances do, however, annualize the service provided to avoid the continuous need for documentation. The method should be determined by how important it is to show the added value per occasion for this service.

Step 4: Value Added. The value added by the service provided is calculated by multiplying the market value by the time provided.

Step 5: Total Value Added. Total added value is determined by adding together the individual values for each service provided.

Like Material Exchange

There are many cost drivers that do not fall into one of the generalized score cards shown above. When such a cost driver is encountered, it may be still important to determine the savings generated. The score card on like equipment is used as an example to show how companies can develop their own. Keep in mind that the simpler it is to use the more likely a score card is to be used.

Figure 4.13 Calculating savings from like material exchange

Material to be Exchanged	(A) Market Value	(B) Book Value	(C) Investment Tax Impact (A-B)*Tax Rate	(D) Value After Tax (A-C)	(E) Exchange Value	Savings = (E-D)
Motors	10,000	0	2,800	7,200	9,000	1,800
Cross Over Equipment	8,000	500	2,100	5,900	8,000	2,100
Lift Generators	12,000	6,000	1,680	10,320	12,000	1,680

tment Tax can vary year to year based on the tax code.
ose of this example an investment rate of 28% was used.

Total Material Exchange Savings | 5,580

Step 1: Name the Savings. In this case the savings is "material to be exchanged." But what does this mean? Many companies have used equipment that is put up for sale because it still has value for another company. When the equipment is sold there may be taxes due. These taxes are due if the market value is greater than the book value of the asset sold. Because the equipment was capitalized or depreciated, any amount in excess of the book value for which the equipment is sold is therefore subject to an investment tax.

To avoid this tax a number of companies are using a concept called like material exchange. The exchange normally involves three companies. The customer gives the assets to the company desiring these assets. The company receiving the assets pays the supplier (alliance partner) who in turn delivers like kind materials to the original owner. (Note: There are some legal issues involved and the tax is only avoided unless the new material has no market value after it is used. Companies considering the use of like equipment exchange would be well advised to seek council from tax experts prior to initiating any action, as there are a number of legal and tax issues not described in this book.).

Step 2: Determine the Cost Drivers. In describing the concept of like material exchange there are four factors that drive the potential savings. Teams assigned to improvement opportunities must determine what drives the cost on their projects.

- *Market value.* What the assets being sold can bring in the market.
- *Book value.* The asset value carried on the company's books.
- *Investment tax rate.* The tax rate on the excess value of the asset sold (the example above used 28 percent, but this varies based on the tax code).
- *Exchange value.* Usually this is the same as market value; however, it can be less. It is the value of the goods provided to the customer.

Step 3: Create Calculations. Once the cost drivers are determined, their interactions must be determined. In this example there are three calculations including:

- *Investment tax impact.* The market value less the book value determines the amount of the sale subject to the investment tax. Multiple this amount by the investment tax rate to calculate taxes.
- *Value after tax.* This determines how much purchasing power is left after the sale of the asset is made and taxes are paid.

- *Savings.* Based on the value of the equipment after tax less the value of supplies that will be provided if the exchange takes place.

Step 4: Format. Create a format that is easy to complete and understand. Make the formulas short and simple.

Score cards are beneficial to use in alliances for several reasons. They enable the alliance to see the value added and focus on issues other than price to reduce costs. They provide a means for determining what has been saved and to what degree incentives should be applied. But most of all, they provide the proof that the alliance is valuable and advantageous to both companies.

THE TOTAL COST PICTURE

Score cards most often measure the added value or the positive outcomes in an alliance—however score cards can measure the added cost as well. Yet the added value is only a piece of the total cost. Total cost is comprised of the following four elements:

- *Price.* Total annual purchases made from the alliance partner.
- *Performance.* Increased costs due to poor performance.
- *System/objectives.* Intangible costs associated with incompatible systems or conflicting objectives.
- *Added value.* Both hard and soft savings or profit enhancements captured through score carding.

It is the combination of these elements that measures total cost. It is also important to understand that the supplier needs to score the customer on these issues as well. The customer's actions will drive a part of the price paid for goods and services. Companies must manage all the costs in the supply chain if the alliance is to be truly beneficial in the long run. To calculate this total cost companies can combine two models with the score cards just presented.

Performance

Calculating the cost of poor performance was explained in Chapter 2 and that model is presented again in Figure 4.14. The important point is that the cost of poor performance can be easily captured. The $386.25 shown as the total non-performance cost is the amount to include in the calculation of total cost.

Figure 4.14 Capturing non-performance costs as part of total costs

Performance Evaluation

ABC Distributing

	(A) Ave. Time Spent	(B) Ave. Hourly Wage	(C) Personnel Costs (A * B)	(D) Other Costs	(E) Cost per Occur. (C + D)	(F) Number of Occur.	Cost per Criterion (E * F)
Billing Errors	1.5 hrs.	6.50	9.75	13.00	22.75	7	159.25
Late Delivery	1.0 hrs.	5.50	5.50	3.00	8.50	5	42.50
Early Delivery	.5 hrs.	5.50	2.75	0.00	2.75	8	22.00
Shipment Errors	2.0 hrs.	6.50	13.00	8.00	21.00	4	84.00
Poor Quality	2.5 hrs.	8.50	21.25	18.00	39.25	2	78.50

Total Non-Performance Cost for ABC Distributing	386.25

Note: Time measured in hours, instead of minutes

Added Value

The graph in Figure 4.15 was created from the score cards shown earlier in this chapter to show the total added value. The table at the bottom depicts the numbers in the graph. The use of tables and charts is an excellent method for presenting and disseminating the information on the added value to employees and management of both companies. It should be noted that the $317,370 in added value includes both soft and hard costs. Alliance partners need to make the decisions concerning soft cost measurements and how much should actually be documented as savings.

Additionally, the chart show some savings spread out over the entire year while others are calculated by the month. The distribution of any given savings must be documented by its nature—one time or continuous—and shown accordingly. For example: alliance price savings were spread out over the entire year; but price protection only applied to three months, which is why the savings in price for April through June is higher.

System/Objectives

The system and objective to aspects of alliance measurement are the hardest costs to assign value because the are often intangible. When values are assigned they are usually very subjective. In practice most companies do not try to create an actual value to assign to this cost; however, some have attempted this by taking the alliance market basket price and dividing it by a cost factor. The cost factor is derived by taking the supplier's score (8.40 from Figure 4.16) and dividing it by the total possible points (in this case 10). While this is sometimes practiced it is not often accepted. Instead the partners use the score as a reference point against which improvements are measured. This measurement is important to ensure that both companies continue to move in the same direction and stay viable to the needs of both companies.

Figure 4.15 Compiling total cost initiatives

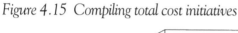

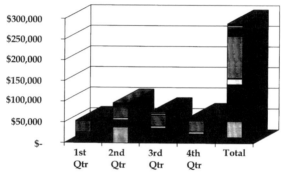

	1st Qtr	2nd Qtr	3rd Qtr	4th Qtr	Total
Consignment	270				270
Consignment	330				330
Invent. Reduct.	1,235		12,720		13,955
J.I.T.		37,800	600		38,400
* EDI Process	6,250	6,250	6,250	6,250	25,000
* Order Process		11,875	11,875	11,875	35,625
* Manufacturing			5,000	5,000	10,000
* Invent. Mgmt.				45	45
Back On-Line	19,000				19,000
* Sys. Improve.		4,438	4,438	4,438	13,314
* New Product		875	875	875	2,625
* Alliance (MB)	25,000	25,000	25,000	25,000	100,000
* Price Protect.		1,000	1,000		2,000
Project Tier		8,545			8,545
Year End				6,500	6,500
* Integrated Prod.		375	375	375	1,125
Training	1,500			2,500	4,000
Tech. Support		660			660
Project Plan.			2,700		2,700
Motors			1,800		1,800
Cross Over Equ.			2,100		2,100
Left Generators			1,680		1,680
Total	**53,585**	**96,818**	**76,413**	**62,858**	**289,674**

* Indicates savings are shown over a one year period from point of initial improvement. Therefore, not all of the $317,370 in savings will be applied to the current year (from examples shown previously).

Figure 4.16 Combining the value added by the supplier

System / Objective Evaluation

ABC Distributing	(A) Criterion Weight	(B) Supplier Score	Criterion Score (A * B)
Cost Management	.25	9	2.25
Financial Strength	.20	8	1.60
Strategic Direction	.20	8	1.60
Total Quality	.25	9	2.25
Training Program	.10	7	.70
	Total Score for ABC Distributing		8.40

Alliance Management And Total Cost

The model introduced at the beginning of this chapter emphasized the importance of ensuring all procedures and efforts revolve around the objectives set by the alliance partners. These objectives set the direction for which projects and processes will be targeted. From this cost drivers will be identified which provide opportunities to reduce total cost.

When managing the alliance initiatives the companies need to keep both the risks and performances needs in mind in addition to the value of the opportunities. Total cost should be calculated by the costs reduced but should also include the additional costs incurred. Without the ability to calculate both costs the alliances long term prospects will be less favorable.

The ability to measure these cost is the first step in being able to manage them. Alliances that cannot document the improvements made will find it difficult to keep the alliance in place and moving forward. The steering committee must develop the means necessary to allow everyone affected to measure the costs impacted.

Score carding is the simplest means for measuring this aspect of total cost. But it is only one method. As new opportunities present themselves new methods may be necessary. With total cost evaluations and managing the alliance going hand in hand the steering committee must develop these new methods to ensure the continued existence of the alliance.

CHAPTER 5

THE SUPPLIER SIDE OF ALLIANCES

As industries and customers have embraced alliances, suppliers have started jumping onboard, sometimes without first looking at what they are getting into. The prospect of losing a major account or the possibility of securing all of an account's business can make a supplier act before carefully considering the consequences. Considering the haste with which some customers move into alliances, often without truly knowing what they are starting, it is no wonder that suppliers also react quickly.

As was pointed out in earlier chapters, these alliances do provide many benefits to suppliers. Often it is those suppliers who react quickly that walk away with the prize—the customer. Some of these suppliers, however, have learned the hard way when to jump onboard and when to walk away.

Alliances bring both sales, with the potential for greater profits, and costs, with a greater risk of being less profitable. Suppliers pursuing alliances need to identify what the costs might be and how best to target those accounts that offer the greatest returns. The supplier then must understand how to work with the customer to secure the alliance.

REALITIES AND ANALYSIS

The realities of alliances are somewhat harsh. Studies continue to show that one-half of all alliances fail. Both customers and suppliers fail to meet the promises made when setting up the alliance, often because neither party understood the necessary procedures to make the alliance successful.

Suppliers first should determine which costs or burdens are likely to be shifted onto them and then reach a mutual agreement with the customer on the associated value for shifting this burden. This step can set the Stage for a win/win relationship which has a much greater chance of succeeding. It also can ensure that the supplier's profits remain healthy as attention is refocused to reducing his costs as well as the customer's.

Prior to participation in the alliance, the supplier should evaluate both the potential sales and profitability of the customer's account to ensure its own profitability in the alliance. In effect the supplier should perform its own discovery on the customer just as the customer performs discovery on the supplier. This provides the supplier with a better understanding of which actions can be afforded as well as what type of alliance would be most beneficial for that account.

Shifting Burden

The impact that an alliance has on suppliers can be beneficial or harmful. Usually it is not one or the other, but somewhere in-between; therefore, it is the supplier's responsibility to maintain some distance from the harmful side. As industries and companies downsize due to competition and profitability, the customer is often left in the position of performing as many tasks as previously but with fewer people.

One way companies accomplish this feat is shown in Figure 5.1. Some of the burden is shifted to the supplier, meaning the supplier must perform some of these tasks or develop systems to minimize the tasks. Unfortunately, the customer's personnel often have little or no time available to change the system in-house because of fewer resources. Also, due to these increased profitability pressures, the buyers are under pressure to get the lowest prices possible.

Figure 5.1 Alliances can have a negative impact on a supplier's profit

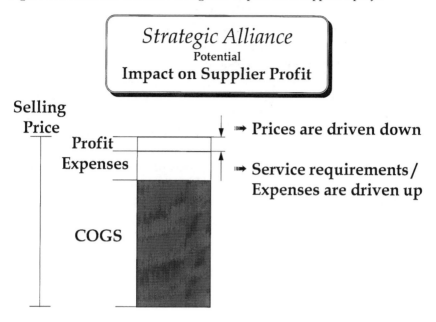

The result is a squeeze on profits; the same scenario applies whether it involves the hard goods distributor, the manufacturer, or a service company. Market pressures are forcing prices down while at the same time driving service requirements and expenses up. Now imagine the effect for this distributor if the cost of goods sold (COGS) were to be raised. If any long-term price protection agreements are in place with the customer, the results could be devastating.

Price

The pressure put on price reduction is not completely unjustified. The supplier often receives enough benefit from being the only source (true in almost every type of alliance) that price concessions appropriately may be expected by the customer. Even if the concession simply is to hold prices at current levels, the concept of risk compared to reward surfaces. In the past, the supplier's risk was high because inventories were stocked to meet potential demand. This resulted in higher inventory carrying costs when the product was not sold or the supplier had personnel (crews, salespeople, technicians, engineers) and equipment on hand in hope of obtaining the sales to justify these assets.

The risk of increased costs and poor returns on these assets was higher than that associated with the alliance relationship. Now, sales are "guaranteed" before the purchase is made. The competitive risks are, therefore, reduced and a lower return *may* be justified. The reverse is true as well: lower prices may not be justified if higher costs of doing business also come with the lower competitive risks.

Another justification for a lower price is *synergy*. Synergy occurs when volume increases as all of the business comes to one supplier. Then certain advantages can evolve that allow for lower costs of doing business which consequently can support lower prices. For example, a hard goods supplier delivers $500 of goods per run instead of $50 per run. The operational cost to deliver $500 in goods is only slightly higher than the cost to deliver $50 in goods. The lower expense per dollar of sale could potentially increase profits and create an opportunity to share with the customer some of the savings through lower prices. This idea also applies to the service company. A crew is hired to do a number of jobs instead of only one. This practice results in reduced travel time and expenses, better utilization of crews and equipment, and easier scheduling.

This concept actually works in some alliances; unfortunately, it fails to materialize in many other alliances. Failure usually occurs because the customer's systems and planning processes were not developed with this scenario in mind. Instead, orders and deliveries are made as needs arise. The $500 in purchases does occur, but in five orders and deliveries instead of one. Some improvement exists, but often not enough to justify any real price concessions.

Service Requirements/Expenses

The expectations placed on the alliance supplier can be high. Customers may look to the suppliers to provide better service levels or new services. One of the most common requirements is to have the supplier manage the inventory at the customer's location. This management can include every task from taking over the customer's warehouse to simple shelf management. Shelf management requires suppliers to ensure that inventory levels stay within specified minimum or maximum parameters. Also included in the supplier's duties may be the actual stocking and receiving of that inventory.

For some suppliers, shelf management causes no additional burden; for others, it does. But when service requirements include employing people in the customer's warehouse, crib, or store room or having dedicated support personnel, this burden can lower profits. When this situation occurs, price concessions by the supplier become more difficult to justify. Sometimes the added volume can justify the added service, but not in all cases. A supplier's costs may increase to a greater extent than the increased sales will justify when requirements include procuring and delivering non-stock items (which can account for over 50% of a supplier's sales), specialty items not often sold, or participating in improvement teams and restructuring processes.

Suppliers often have some "excess" personnel, inventories, or equipment that can cover some of the increased service requirements. However, usually these assets do not include great excesses. They exist because the supplier feels that he cannot sell what is not available. Often the thinking is that any additional needs will be covered by these excess assets, but the reality is different. Prior to the formation of an alliance, four or five suppliers may have taken care of a given customer's business. When only one supplier remains, that supplier's previously excess assets may become dedicated. If these assets are used consistently by one customer, additional just-in-case assets will be needed for other accounts.

The customer also may wish to eliminate inventories and may expect the supplier to buy those existing inventories. Even when buybacks or consignment is not required, the suppliers may be obligated to increase inventory to cover the customer's needs when his inventories are depleted. This practice drives costs up. Additionally, new systems created to satisfy the customer result in increased costs in both development and maintenance.

The supplier must learn how to work with the customer to balance the increased service requirements and expenses against the price expected by the customer. If this balance is not addressed and the supplier's profits decrease, the alliance will fail. An alliance must be profitable for both companies.

Targeting Opportunities

Suppliers sometimes focus on getting the sale and not on examining the profitability of that sale; the ultimate result may be unprofitable accounts. In fact, because of this tendency, a number of suppliers have started analyzing their profitability by individual customer accounts. The results have shown that as much as 10–20% of a supplier's customers may be subsidized by other customers. This conclusion means some customers are unprofitable to the supplier. Research by the faculty and staff at the Industrial Distribution Program at Texas A&M have produced similar findings.

Unfortunately, such customer analysis is performed too infrequently, particularly in the evaluation of potential alliance relationships. One method gaining popularity is activity-based costing (ABC). ABC is a form of cost accounting. In its simplest form, ABC determines the cost for each activity performed by the supplier. The supplier creates a menu of products (the goods and services normally purchased) plus the add-on services. (Add-on services are the secondary processes usually not directly contracted for by the customer such as payment method, warehousing, and equipment changeovers.)

The customer now buys the add-on services along with the products. The product is sold at cost plus a small percentage of profit. For example, in the past a distributor might buy a machine for $1000 and sell it for $1250. The $250 markup covered the supplier's costs of warehousing, accounting systems, salespeople and other expenses in addition to the supplier's profit. Under ABC, the same machine might sell for $1050 plus the cost for any other activities performed (the $50 represents the supplier's profit). If the customer wanted the machine immediately (from stock), planned on paying in 30 days, and wanted this machine delivered, an additional $200 charge would be added. However, if the customer paid cash and picked up the machine when it arrived from the manufacturer, perhaps only a $50 charge for the add-on services might be applied.

The advantage of ABC is that it allows customers to pay for only those services used and forces companies responsible for high service costs to pay those costs. The disadvantage lies in the difficulty of determining actual costs and keeping those costs current as overhead can change as customer requirements change.

Cost Of Business

Although the use of ABC may not be possible for all companies, it is a potentially useful tool and companies should consider its use. However, the work required to ensure accuracy may be too time consuming for some companies to justify its use. Another method is of the "quick and dirty" type, meaning that while it is faster and easier to implement, it is not nearly as accurate. Yet for companies evaluating alliance opportunities it can provide valuable information in terms of what factors to target and how to present the alliance in a profitable manner.

Figure 5.2 illustrates how this method works. The strategy behind this method is to categorize customers into levels of current profitability. This concept is similar to the old ABC method for classifying inventory. For classification of customers, suppliers must determine the basic cost of business for each customer. This cost is based on two factors: service requirements and performance.

Service requirements. Service requirements deal with any procedure the supplier is expected to perform for the customer. This can include inventory of items specific to a given customer, use of special equipment, the number of runs made to the customer, training requirements, and technical support. Each service requirement is a cost-driver for the supply company.

Low service requirements can reduce operating costs greatly and potentially improve profits just as high service requirements can increase costs and reduce profits. The supplier needs to identify the expectations and requirements of all customers and then determine the costs for the services provided to each customer. Exact values are, of course, the most helpful, but classification between low and high can provide useful guidelines. For example, if the average customer places orders valued at $100, and customer A places $200 orders and customer B places $50 orders, one factor of profitability already has been determined. In this case, customer A has a low service requirement cost and customer B has a high service requirement cost. (Sales volume will be taken into consideration later).

Performance factors. Service requirements consider the work the supplier performs as part of doing business with a customer. Another facet of cost is the work associated with poor performance by the customer. That is correct, the customer's performance is evaluated; or as one supplier put it, "the hassle factor." This aspect of the cost of doing business deals with re-work, wasted efforts, and costs driven into the supplier's operations due to the customer's actions. Included are:

- late payments
- changing orders
- inventory, people, equipment and other assets required by the customer but not well-utilized (or not utilized enough to justify the expense)
- rush orders
- inadequate information
- poor paperwork (note: excessive or special paperwork is a service requirement)

Each of these examples raises costs in the supplier's operation and affects profitability. The model introduced in Chapter 2, which shows how customers can measure the cost of poor supplier performance can be used here as well. The supplier tracks the costs incurred and the number of occurrences as documentation of the increased cost of doing business. If this is not possible, the supplier can simply rate the customer on a high/low basis.

Utilizing the concepts of service requirements and performance, a supplier can categorize customers based on the cost of doing business with them. Again, remember that the more accurate and objective the data is, the more useful it will be in evaluating the customer.

Figure 5.2 Development of a quick measure of a customer's profitability

Cost of Business

Service Requirements

	Low	High
Low	Low	Medium
High	Medium	High

(Performance Factors on vertical axis: Low to High)

Profitability

Gross Margin

	High		Low
Low	High	Good	Average
Med.	Good	Average	Weak
High	Average	Weak	Low

(Cost of Business on vertical axis: Low to High)

Profitability

The second chart, entitled profitability, uses the information from the determination of the cost of business and connects it with the gross margins involved. Individual account profitability is primarily driven by these two elements. This model shows the profitability of each account, identifying which ones need improvement and which ones might be risky alliance partners, but it does not provide the complete picture. Sales volume is the final consideration. For now, however, consider only the information provided so far. Weak or poor profitability is most often multiplied in an alliance. The result is increased sales with the same low profit. Increasing profitability is not likely unless a major change occurs in the customer's philosophy and operational methods.

For years, most customers have pushed on three fronts: price, delivery, and price. With price as two of the fronts, an improvement in margins is unlikely. In such cases improvements in performance or reduced service requirements need to be demonstrated before any price reductions make sense. While these customers may be valuable, they may be of more value to the supplier by *giving* them to the competition; therefore, the competition's limited resources are depleted by these accounts while the original supplier's assets can be used more profitably.

On the other hand, those customers which allow the supplier good to high profits need to be given more attention so that they are not lost to the competition.

Targeting Alliance Opportunities

The final step in evaluation of customers is determination of existing opportunities. By comparing account profitability to sales (volume of business), the supplier better understands the type of relationship and cost-drivers involved with that customer and the potential consequences of an alliance.

Obviously the best targets are those customers which offer higher profitability and high sales. For customers falling into these categories any type of alliance most likely would be beneficial to the supplier but to maintain the alliance long-term, the supplier should work on every total cost reduction which will help bind the customer to the supplier. In this way the business can be "locked up," eliminating competition. This agreement in turn can minimize sales efforts required and allow the service and support resources additional time to work with the customer. In actuality however, very few customers will fall in this category.

Figure 5.3 Account profitability and sales volume identify which customers

Alliance Targeting

Sales Opportunity

	High		Low
High			
Good	Prime Opportunity		Value Added
Average			
Weak	Partnering & Single Source		Little Opportunity for a Profitable Alliance
Low			

Profitability (vertical axis label)

the supplier should target

The lower left hand side of Figure 5.3 shows the two most common types of alliances formed when sales volume is high but profitability is average to low. If structured properly, a single source alliance can be advantageous to both companies. There can be a reduction in a supplier's costs if the purchasing is centralized or coordinated in a planned schedule. Usually in a single source situation the result is a slight overall increase in profitability. The reason is a lower price is often required and the improvement in operating costs only occurs if the customer's performance and service, as a percentage of sales, changes.

Partnering, on the other hand, does offer a higher prospect of improved profitability. In Chapter 2 partnering was defined as *emphasis on transactional costs* such as ordering, invoicing and inventories. If customers view partnering as a means of reducing total costs, the supplier's costs also may be reduced, because these are often tied to service requirements and performance. By showing the customers how their costs may be lowered and what the supplier's role is in reducing these costs, systems can be built which benefit both companies. Unfortunately, the solutions are sometimes already determined and the supplier may be required to add additional service costs to his own system.

When joint efforts are expected to reduce costs, the supplier should spend time educating the customer about the supplier's cost of business and how this affects the price and services to be provided to the customer. In these cases, the customer can see the payoff in lower total costs. But to have any real benefits for either company, there must be adequate volume to justify the added cost of making the improvements.

This concept brings up another point to keep in mind. Without adequate sales volume to justify the added workload and costs which are often associated with an alliance, there may be no justification to form one. The entire right side of Figure 5.3 is devoted to non-alliance relationships. When profits for a given account are high, yet sales volume is low, it may be more advantageous to show the value added without trying to form an alliance. This insight helps the customer as well since purchase volume often drives the alliance opportunities from the customer's perspective. The primary exception to this occurs when the customer is willing to pay for the supplier's added costs.

For those customers categorized in the bottom right-hand side of Figure 5.3 there will be little opportunity for a profitable alliance, but integrated supply is another possibility. For those customers interested in integrated supply and who fall under the "Little Opportunity for a Profitable Alliance" category it usually means becoming a second-tier supplier. The auto industry has almost perfected this supplier classification and other industries are following suit. For the second-tier supplier it usually means losing direct contact with the end-user, instead, selling to or through other suppliers.

The risk in being a second-tier supplier is the loss of control. The supplier who owns the account often has the ability to find and use other suppliers. Suppliers often become wary of involvement as a second-tier but this fear may not be justified. Second-tier suppliers simply need to treat the integrator as a real customer. With low sales on given goods or services, the integrator usually will not spend much time and effort looking for new sources, if the service and performance from the supplier has been good, because the cost is often too high. On the other hand, the opportunity to reduce costs is available for the second-tier supplier. By setting up agreements with the integrator that result in reduction of the second-tier supplier's service requirements and performance costs, profitability can be improved for those sales actually serviced by the integrator. The integrator also may increase the second-tier's sales by adding new accounts.

Long-Term Outlook

It is surprising how similar the customer's supplier base and the supplier's customer base are likely to look in a few year's time. When Underhill & Associates reviewed a number of suppliers' customer bases and discussed trends concerning future expectations, they found several trends. These are depicted in Figure 5.4 and are not meant to be an examples of best practice, but examples of how the sales and customer base may look for the typical tier-one supplier of tomorrow. Second- and third-tier suppliers are likely to have far fewer sales tied to alliances and many more in traditional bid-buy transactions.

Figure 5.4 Customer relationship to sales comparison

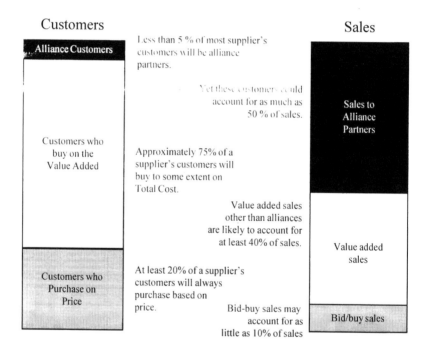

Figure 5.4 shows that very few customers are likely to be alliance partners. Even suppliers in industries dominated by alliances feel that the vast majority of their customers will not form alliances in given commodity/service groups. The reasoning is fairly simple: not all customers considering alliances have sufficient volume needs in a given commodity or service to justify an alliance; also specific value-added

requirements limit many commodities and services from being includ-ed in an integrated relationship. Additionally the majority of most suppliers' customers are small- to medium-sized companies where sig-nificant cost savings are harder to achieve; therefore, alliances become harder to justify.

Obviously markets and industries may change as conditions change and the concept of alliances mature. At that point the demo-graphics shown here may no longer be valid; for now, however, fewer than 5% of a supplier's customer base will likely be alliance partners. There were several exceptions where some suppliers forecast as many as 8% of their customers would be alliances, but most predicted less than 5% of their customers would be alliance partners in the final out-come. An interesting point is several suppliers found that over one-half of their sales are tied to alliances now with less than 2% of their customers actually being alliances, and these suppliers fully expect a number of additional customers to form alliances. If this holds true, the sales portion for some suppliers potentially would show far more than the 50% of sales tied to alliances as depicted in Figure 5.4.

Another trend suppliers are seeing is the increase in value-added buying. Where alliances have not started or may not be form for a given commodity or service, a more thorough understanding among purchasing personnel about value-added buying is signaling a positive trend. As alliances focus on total cost and the results begin to material-ize, the *value* part of what suppliers offer is receiving greater attention. However, the forecast that 75% of customers may buy to some extent on the value added could be overly optimistic, because it also includes any sale where price and delivery were not the only deciding factors. It does, however, indicate that the customer is starting to understand the importance of factors other than price.

Focus On Win/Win

With the trend towards alliances strong enough potentially to impact 50% of a supplier's sales, and with many alliances being unprof-itable, suppliers seem to be in a difficult position. It need not be that way because suppliers who take a proactive approach and sell the alliance concept to customers often can set the tone so both the cus-tomer and the supplier can win.

This focus on win/win is a key element to successful alliances. Webster defines an alliance as "an association to further the common interest of the members." When alliances stop being of *common inter-*

est, they disband. Some customers do approach alliances in this fashion; others jump onboard without understanding their supplier's costs and needs. In such cases the drive is to cut costs quickly and the result can be expensive for the supplier and the customer.

Yet when suppliers take the concept and the know how to their customers, it is more likely to be a winning relationship for the supplier than if the customer initiates it. This occurs because when the supplier initiates an alliance he knows that the customer will not accept the alliance unless there is some value in it. He also knows that he needs to receive something back which pays for the value added.

Therefore it is to the suppliers advantage to use a strategy to target alliance opportunities similar to that discussed earlier in this chapter. Once the likely accounts are targeted, the supplier helps the customer discover total cost improvements and the need to form alliances. Selling the fact that costs are driven into all links of the supply chain should take place in day-to-day contact. The customer needs to be shown that the greatest returns will come from reducing these costs throughout the supply chain and not just within his own operations. Why? Because the customer pays for any cost driven into the supply chain, as shown in the Amoco example in Chapter 1.

Reduce The Cost Of Doing Business

The supplier needs to reduce the cost of doing business. This includes internal improvements the supplier must perform alone and external improvements performed in concert with its trading partners both upstream and downstream. The customer has a direct effect on service requirements and performance. While these are significant cost-drivers to the supplier as shown in Figure 5.5, there are other areas that the customer can affect.

One such area the customer can influence is the supplier's supplier or the manufacturer. The manufacturer often will be more willing to work with the supplier to reduce channel costs when the customer is directly involved. The supplier needs to convince the customer that the customer's participation can improve profitability by reducing these supply chain costs and problems.

Figure 5.5 The supplier's costs must be reduced to ensure the long term viability of the alliance.

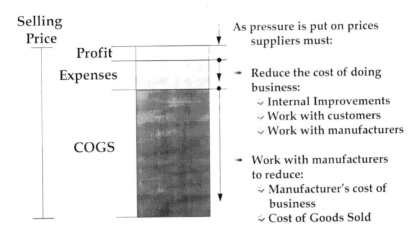

Strategic Alliance

Selling Price

Profit

Expenses

COGS

As pressure is put on prices suppliers must:

➥ Reduce the cost of doing business:
  ∿ Internal Improvements
  ∿ Work with customers
  ∿ Work with manufacturers

➥ Work with manufacturers to reduce:
  ∿ Manufacturer's cost of business
  ∿ Cost of Goods Sold

Work With Manufacturers To Reduce Costs

While the customer can provide some support to the supplier, particularly on their joint processes, much of the work with manufacturers is the responsibility of the supplier.

The effort required to work with manufacturers will be great. Customers see an immediate and direct positive effect while many manufacturers only see a disruption of the distribution channel with potentially little to gain and much to lose (discussed further in Chapter 6). But it is necessary to pull these companies into alliances, because many of tomorrow's costs likely will be reduced through supply chain management. The reasoning for this is fairly simple: in today's alliances, most of the emphasis is placed on reducing the costs between a customer and its immediate suppliers; over time as these costs are minimized fewer improvements will be possible without moving toward the upstream side of the supply chain.

SELLING ALLIANCES

The best advice for suppliers interested in alliances is not to wait for the customer to become ready to create an alliance. Suppliers need to become proactive, guiding the customer in setting the stage to create an alliance. Unfortunately, the task of selling alliances is often left in the hands of a national sales team or alliance group. While these teams are usually effective, they cannot be everywhere at once and tuned in to the nuances of a specific customer's needs, as the sales person could if he understood how to uncover all of these needs.

With the trend growing more prominently each year toward regional and national alliances, the need for the salesperson's active involvement in alliance selling is growing. Suppliers should have all their salespeople involved in understanding and selling the concept of alliances in an informal manner that ties into the day-to-day aspects of being problem solvers. This approach can enlighten the customer about the many attributes of alliances, in effect, allowing the supplier to help set the pace. This approach often requires the salesperson to sell at multiple levels and multiple functions while identifying needs, concerns, problems, and performance issues in an efficient manner.

This multi-level, multi-functional approach can also be connected to the customer's discovery process and offers the supplier a tremendous advantage when a;;lied. When this approach is taken, the discovery process for that commodity or service group can become the pilot study for other alliances within the customer's company. Because the supplier becomes part of the commodity/service planning team, vendor evaluations for that commodity/service group are bypassed. The supplier is selected based on its contributions to the team.

The risk to the supplier is that the customer may choose someone else after all the groundwork is performed. The risk to the customer is the possibility of missing a better partner. However, with some care and study by both parties these risks can be minimized.

If the supplier fails to sell the alliance at this entry level, a competent showing of the supplier's abilities to reduce costs during the evaluation stage and through the sales presentations which are often a part of the final selection, may convince the customer of the supplier's competency.

Day-to-Day Selling

Alliances need to be based on an ongoing relationship which extends beyond a few people in either company. Alliances which are set and operate just between the salesperson and purchasing, for instance, have a high probability of failure. Why? Practically speaking, how long will the same salesperson remain in that position? Both salespeople and buyers know how difficult it is to break-in new counterparts and often any improvements previously made are forgotten or are unfamiliar to the new person. Additionally, many of the costs affected are outside of purchasing's control and evaluation. Saving a million dollars in inventory costs is noteworthy; however, little might actually be accomplished if the buyer or decision-maker is not held accountable for this cost. Consider the position the buyer is in if price, a performance measure on which the buyer is evaluated, were to increase a hundred thousand dollars annually as a result of saving one million dollars in inventory costs, a performance measure on which the buyer is not measured. At that point the buyer actually may be penalized for his performance, and therefore may not make the decision which is best for the company.

For this reason it is important for the supplier to do some homework about the company, discovering information about employees in many different positions. Granted, many salespeople regularly interface with numerous individuals, but this assignment includes developing a profile on these people.

The first step is to identify the areas which directly would be affected by an alliance, including, purchasing, operations, maintenance, engineering, and accounting. Once the primary players have been established the supplier needs to create a profile for each department and each major player in that department, gathering information on the operational responsibilities, the evaluation criterion on which personal performance is judged, and the supplier performance factors important to each player.

This acusorary example of the information needed is illustrated in Figure 5.6 and can make selling the alliance more productive. Obviously, this information cannot be gathered in one meeting and it is not always easy to obtain. The idea is to target primary accounts and begin to gather the information so that when it is time to sell the alliance, the specific concerns and needs of each player can be better targeted.

Figure 5.6 Simplified example of a customer profile

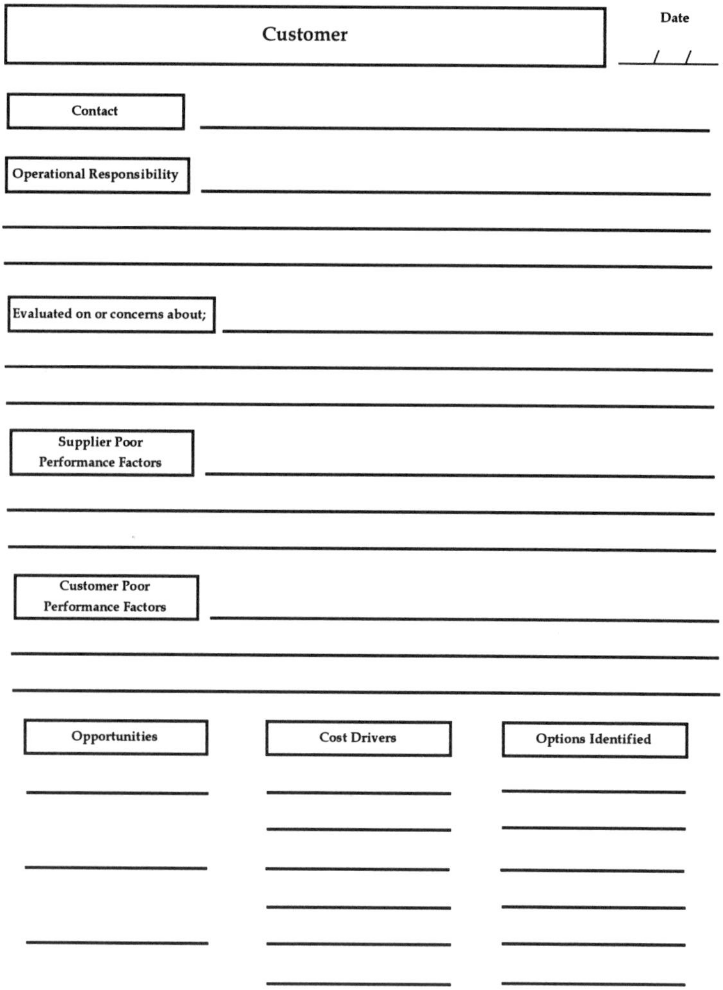

Customer	Date __/__/__

Contact _____

Operational Responsibility _____

_____

_____

Evaluated on or concerns about; _____

_____

_____

Supplier Poor
Performance Factors _____

_____

_____

Customer Poor
Performance Factors _____

_____

_____

Opportunities	Cost Drivers	Options Identified
_____	_____	_____
	_____	_____
_____	_____	_____
	_____	_____
_____	_____	_____

Most good salespeople have bits and pieces of this information in their heads, so the intent of this exercise is to develop this information into a working plan. Also, for multi-locational accounts, sending this information to the alliance sales team can be most effective in curtailing any ill-prepared presentations. Tie-ins to specific concerns and issues can highlight the team's preparedness and the suppliers understanding of the customers needs.

Positioning The Customer

The idea is not to go to customers and tell them how alliances will solve all their problems or even reduce their costs; this should come later. Initially the information gathered on the profile will be used to understand how to change the customer's position. Figure 5.7 on the left-hand side illustrates the position of the typical customer on alliances.

At this point the customer usually does not have a strong opinion in favor *of* or *against* forming an alliance, but here comes the salesperson trying to sell the idea of alliances. This is almost always the wrong approach because customers will form alliances only if they see their problems being solved, cost-drivers reduced, or revenues improved. Also they will resist forming alliances if they perceive their concerns, risks, price, and performance issues will be negatively affected. This dilemma requires the salesperson to attack on two fronts to minimize the negatives and to maximize the benefits.

Figure 5.7 Customers may or may not wish to form an alliance. The wrong sales approach can position the customer into rejecting the idea.

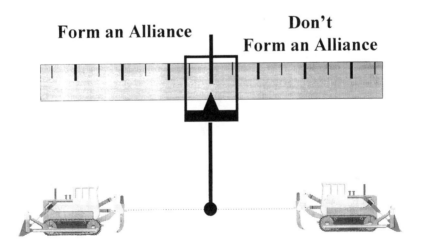

Form an Alliance

Don't Form an Alliance

Problems Solved
Cost Drivers Reduced
Increased Revenues

Risk / Concerns
Price
Performance Issues

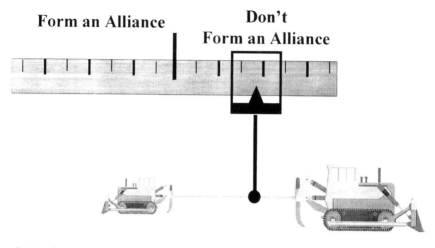

Form an Alliance

**Don't
Form an Alliance**

**Solutions and cost
reductions viewed
as minimal.**

**Objections reduce
probability that an
alliance will be formed.**

Here is an exercise to practice the attack on these two fronts. Imagine for a moment you are talking to one of the players identified and business is going as smoothly as usual. Management is not pushing for the alliance and you (the salesperson) begin the topic of alliances and inventory reductions with all the possible opportunities.

What will be the likely response? Concerns about plant shut-downs, prices rising due to lack of competition, poor services, and so on.

In effect, the exact opposite of what the salesperson had hoped for occurred. As objections are raised, the perceived benefits are seen as minimal, and the risks and concerns are magnified. This position is depicted in the second half of Figure 5.7. Sales personnel must keep this scenario in mind when raising new ideas and suggestions (and alliances), and thinking first about the decision process many people work through.

The easiest way to get customer acceptance is if it is *their* idea. This approach is often far more effective in selling alliances, but how does the salesperson get the customer to come up with the idea of an alliance?

The best proven method is to sell each idea or cost improvement separately. Then connect the ideas and improvements through the formation of an alliance. This concept is not new, but in alliance selling there are some added twists.

For each of the main players at the customer's locations the salespeople can use the information gathered on the profile sheets to identify potential problems or opportunities on which an alliance can focus. In each case multiple cost-drivers that the supplier is willing to help reduce should be determined. Then potential solutions are developed. Based on these, the supplier now works backward to identify the cost-drivers affected. From these cost-drivers a list of questions can be created which guides the customer toward an understanding of the need to change and then the potential solution. Figure 5.8 and the explanation which follows shows the use of this method. The intent is to ask questions which gets the customer to state a problem and determing its significants.

Figure 5.8 A methodology for selling alliances

Opportunity - Inventory

Stage 1 - get the customer to see inventory as a problem.
a. How much inventory is being carried?
   What is the turn rate?
   How much stock is dead/obsolete?

b. How often is there a stock out?

c. How much time is spent finding material?

d. Could the inventory space be put to better uses?

Stage 2 - get the customer to identify the cost drivers and the value of these cost drivers.
a. What does carrying the inventory cost your company? (interest expense, shrinkage/spoilage, taxes, insurance, equipment, people, space)

b. What do stock outs cost? (lost output, shut downs, idle people and equipment, lost sales and missed customer deadlines, order expediting)

c. What are the costs involved in retrieving inventory? (time spent finding, idle people and equipment)

d. What does this lost space cost? (loss of production space, new building needs, maintenance costs, insurance, investment cost)

Stage 3 - solution development.
a. Consignment
   VMI
   Shelf Management
   Outsourcing of the warehouse

b. VMI
   Outsourcing of the warehouse

c. Outsourcing of the warehouse

d. Just-in-time delivery

Stage 1 gets the customer to state that a problem exists or that there is a need to improve. A number of Stage 1 questions should be prepared. If one avenue of questioning is closed by the customer, be prepared with other avenues to address the same issues. By asking questions the salesperson can see what problems seem most important to the customer. Keep in mind that while it is easier to state the problem and solution, this procedure often results in objections being raised which are hard to overcome. By asking questions and leading the customer to the desired conclusion, fewer objections are raised. Once the customer agrees that a problem does exist, it is time to move to Stage 2 and identify the cost of this problem.

Stage 2 questions will uncover the costs by asking about cost-drivers. As a reminder, there is partial list of cost-drivers in Appendix A. It is important to get the customer to state a close, approximate cost for each cost-driver. Then by recapping the costs disclosed by the customer the magnitude of the total cost can be brought out. If the salesperson chose the right opportunities and asked the right questions, there should be a number of items which together amount to a high monetary value. If so, the customer should be ready to talk solutions to those items.

Until the customer perceives the existence of a high cost, there will likely be little action toward making improvements. By asking questions, and not offering solutions, the customer has developed the need for a solution himself, as opposed to the solution being thrust upon him for something he sees no need. The customer also supplied the information and therefore is less likely to dispute the conclusions drawn.

When developing the questions, the salesperson should refer to the profile which he developed. Only solutions to issues which are of direct concern to the person present should be discussed. Otherwise the customer will have little reason to act on the need to change. For example, if the plant manager is not responsible for inventory, do not pursue that issue; focus on something else.

Now, it is time for Stage 3, the development of solutions if the perceived value is there. Again the supplier should not offer to "save the world," but work with the customer to develop options and ask more questions about concerns in solution development. The supplier should offer examples of various methods used to solve other problems with other customers and then help build parameters that cover that customer's needs. Potential solutions should be developed prior to going into the meeting. If a given solution is not feasible, or acceptable to that supplier, he should stay away from that option. This action may require certain cost-drivers be avoided. If, as in Figure 5.8, the supplier cannot invest in a warehouse and the closest facilities are too far away to operate a J.I.T. system, the supplier should refrain from discussing the cost-drivers involved in owning the warehouse.

This approach should be followed with each of the main players at the customer's locations. Naturally, each will have some similar and some unique concerns, so different problems will be attacked. In this way, the supplier can determine the needs of an alliance at multiple levels and through multiple functions—creating a higher need for the alliance throughout the company. When managed appropriately, the positive results are similar to those depicted in Figure 5.9. These results may take several calls to achieve. Therefore developing a complete profile will lay the groundwork for successfully selling an alliance.

Figure 5.9 Shifting the customer's perception toward the need to form an alliance.

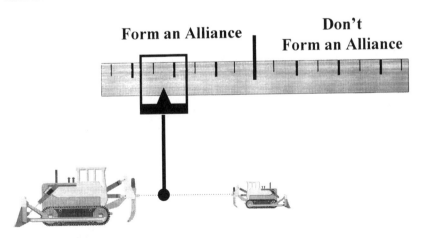

Form an Alliance

Don't Form an Alliance

Involve the customer in developing ideas & solutions
- Decreases objections
- Increases understanding of the cost drivers
involved and the value of changing them

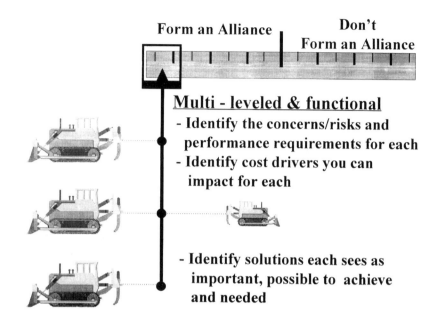

Form an Alliance **Don't Form an Alliance**

Multi - leveled & functional
- Identify the concerns/risks and performance requirements for each
- Identify cost drivers you can impact for each

- Identify solutions each sees as important, possible to achieve and needed

As the salesperson develops the needs and potential solutions with each key person, logical "next step" possibilities also must be determined. Once the customer sees the need to change, the salesperson should be ready to suggest where to go from there. Otherwise there may be no movement toward action. The next step could be taking the alliance plan to management, starting a pilot project, making a formal presentation to an improvement committee, or gathering specific information. Just keep the momentum going and work the process together.

Working Discovery Together
Chapter 2 focused on the customer performing a strong discovery or needs determination and then choosing a supplier based on those needs. Without a strong discovery there is a higher level of risk of failure. This has not changed—discovery needs to be performed—the difference is who does it and how it is done.

If the salesperson works with each key player, identifies his needs, concerns, and performance factors, and builds solutions with the customer, much of discovery process has been performed. It is simply performed with a supplier as part of the team.

The biggest advantage is less resistance. Each area now wants the alliance because of what it can do for them. The risk is missing opportunities the supplier steered away from which might have been advantageous to the customer but costly to that supplier. Obviously, the salesperson may not wish to bring up these points, but usually someone does. This necessarily does not mean the supplier who helped develop the plan for an alliance is replaced.

On the contrary, usually that supplier has an inside track. It was the supplier who helped each of the key customer players develop his goals and objectives. It was the supplier who helped create the basis for the commodity or service team and helped develop the criterion for success. This groundwork provides the supplier with a distinct advantage in selling his company as the supplier of choice.

Handling Evaluations

It would be nice if evaluations came to the supplier ahead of time to allow the supplier to find the driving force behind the customer's questions. Sadly, many evaluations are not even reviewed by the customer upon being returned; they are simply filed. Sometimes the evaluation is simply a "quick fix" to an ISO 9000 requirement or another quality program. Other times it is in response to the requirements the customer must meet for its customers; and sometimes it is used to help form alliances.

Some customers are straight forward and do state the intent of the evaluations, but many do not. So, with all the evaluations coming in how does the supplier handle them? Unfortunately, the best answer is to treat everyone seriously. Contact the salespeople, find out if any word has gotten out about the reason for the evaluations, then respond accordingly.

With the number of evaluations on the rise, having some preset data can be helpful. The evaluation in Appendix B is a composite of issues and questions compiled from several companies' evaluation tools. While some standard information can be helpful, each response should be tailored to the specific customer.

Perhaps not surprisingly, many evaluations are filled out by personnel who are not in direct contact with the account, because many questions call for information outside the salespersons' expertise.

Yet, it is important for suppliers to appear knowledgeable about the customer's needs on these surveys and evaluations. A number of suppliers have been eliminated from consideration because they were harder on themselves than the customer would have been. A useful strategy to use in completing surveys is to attempt to determine the cost-drivers behind each question and show the supplier's abilities in reducing total costs. This method is not always easy but studying the examples in Appendix A and B might make it easier to understand the customer's intent and respond accordingly.

Sales Presentation

The need to present the supplier's capabilities is usually required at some point for most customers. The most effective presentations are those geared specifically to that customer and based on the information coming from the profile.

The management group and the commodity/service team are the two groups who most likely will review the supplier's capabilities at some time. A management group is used most often when the alliance initiative is focused on national or company-wide alliances. The main objective of this group tends to be price concessions due to sales volume and transaction cost reductions, due to a reduced vendor base. The commodity/service team is generally more interested in ensuring specific aspects of risk, performance, and reduced costs.

Understanding the subtle difference needed to present to each of these groups is important. The management group is usually less interested in the mechanics and wants to be told the estimated savings. They are less likely to be concerned with the specifics of performance issues and service requirements. They deal with "the big picture" and want assurance of a high dollar difference.

The commodity/service team has representatives from various areas with totally different and often conflicting concerns. For this group the profiles become a valuable asset. Even if a profile were built for an individual who is not a team member, his counterpart likely is a part of the team. Performance issues, service requirements, and cost effects and methods must be presented. The more successfully the supplier can show an understanding of each area's concerns and needs, the more likely that supplier will be chosen for the alliance.

The presentation outlined below is focused on the commodity or service team and should be modified if presented to management to meet their focus. When developing an alliance presentation, the supplier should determine what objectives it hopes to accomplish and build around them. Common objectives revolve around the following:
- understanding total costs and the ability to reduce them
- knowledge of and ability to form alliances. The potential solutions developed can be used as the foundation to start building the alliance

- service requirements and performance, tied to functional evaluations and concerns
- presenting the supplier's company

There are two points to remember during this process. First, while many of the team members know *of* the supplier's company, misperceptions may exist. The supplier should spend some time promoting his company. Second, every supplier has its strengths and weaknesses. Be direct. Hoping the weaknesses will not be mentioned is simply courting disaster. Once the issue is brought up by the customer, the supplier is put in a defensive mode, making it harder to sell the strengths of the company. The best method is to present the strengths a company has to offer in such a way as to negate the weaknesses. To help in understanding this concept, complete the evaluation exercise in Figure 5.10.

Strengths & Weaknesses

Identify 10 activities which you do that adds value or reduces your customers Total Cost. Then identify 10 weaknesses you need to overcome.

#	Activity	Magnitude
S1		
S2		
S3		
S4		
S5		
S6		
S7		
S8		
S9		
S10		
W1		
W2		
W3		
W4		
W5		
W6		
W7		
W8		
W9		
W10		

Review both the strengths and weaknesses and determine which relate to each other. For example, one supplier who used this concept was a comparatively small supplier competing against companies many times its size. The supplier knew its size would be a weakness. To prevent this situation from becoming a real issue the supplier concentrated on its industry focus, importance of the customer to total sales (high service expectations), and a national network set up of similar size companies through an industry association allowing it to meet any and all product needs. Concern was thereby turned away from the size issue.

Another supplier had a computer system which performed well but was missing the bells and whistles of its competitor's computers. This supplier's presentation presented the computer as a strength because of the reports and systems the computer did allow and connected these to the documented savings that other alliance customers were enjoying.

Presentation Layout

The presentation should have three sections. The first is a brief profile of the supplier's company. This section should focus on reducing any concerns the commodity/service team members might have about why the supplier has "the right" to be there. The second section is the focal point, the supplier's ability to reduce costs and minimize concerns for the customer. Also it is important to show a strong understanding of alliances and proof of abilities in making an alliance successful. The last section is the detailed assets and strengths about the supplier.

Company Profile

A short company profile will show the supplier's strengths. Some members of the commodity/service team might not know the supplier well. Others may have some doubts about its abilities. If these questions and doubts are not minimized at the beginning, some customers likely will be too preoccupied with these issues to really hear what the supplier can do for the customer. On the other hand, the supplier should not spend too much time on itself, rather it should quickly move on to ways it can provide for the customer's needs. As such, the profile should last no more than 10 to 15 minutes during any two- four hour presentations.

The primary topics to cover in this profile of the supplier are:

- *Primary assets to service the customer:* People, inventory, locations, equipment.
- *Strengths:* The supplier's strengths or its competitive advantage. This is also a good time to minimize the company's weaknesses through the strengths the supplier has to offer.
- *Growth:* Nothing shows a company's abilities as much as growth—this reflects success. Growth can be in locations, sales,

employees, and product or service offerings.

- *Awards:* customer, industry, business, manufacturer, anything which shows outside agencies consider the supplier to be outstanding.
- *Historical Highlights:* significant events which further emphasize and introduce the supplier's company.

Keep this section short and to the point. If too much time is spent here, the supplier may never get the chance to present how it actually can help the customer.

Ability To Help The Customer And Reduce Costs

The most important part of the alliance presentation is for the supplier to show how it will lower the customer's costs. The supplier must show its understanding of the forces driving the customer's needs, such as; competition, deregulation, re-engineering or other issues. Understanding the customer's point of view builds the supplier's credibility.

Now it is time to address the various concerns, issues, and cost-drivers identified in the day-to-day selling documented in the customer profile. As the issues are addressed, the supplier should name the specific operational areas where these issues were identified and the potential solutions developed with the customer personnel. Another technique which works well is to provide a list of cost-drivers similar to that found in Appendix A and introduce the idea that many costs can be eliminated. Then focus on those costs outlined in the customer profiles.

Since alliances are long-term, it is important for the supplier to show its understanding of the various aspects of the alliance including: the structure, management changes, implementation plans, and methods to avoid pitfalls. The idea is to first show that the supplier understands the needs and concerns of each area and then demonstrate that he has the skills and knowledge to help build the alliance in an intelligent fashion. Here is the moment when the customer is looking for proof.

A common method is to have case histories explaining the alliance relationship and results. More and more suppliers are starting to record this on video or CD-ROM in order to build credibility by having other customers testify to the value added by the supplier. If a written case study is used, try to get the customer to endorse it; this adds greater credibility.

Graphic results such as those shown in Figure 5.11 and/or joint newsletters, such as those in Appendix E, also should be considered. If multiple case histories exist, space them, relating each to specific topics and concerns being discussed with the customer during the presentation.

Figure 5.11 Savings for Amoco from one area of their alliance with Red Man Pipe and Supply

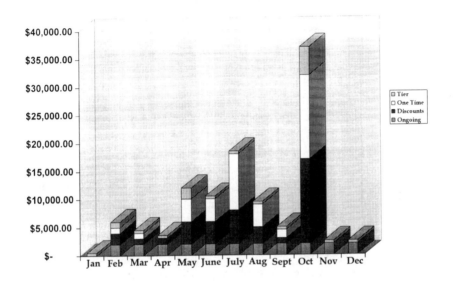

Amoco / Red Man Alliance

Company Overview

While the ability to reduce a customer's costs should represent the majority of the presentation, some time should be spent presenting the supplier's company. Although a cursory company profile was used as an introduction, it is time to show what the supplier has the ability to back up its promises. At this point the objective is to have the customer feel good about the supplier. This means the customer understands who the supplier is and how the supplier operates. Briefly, the supplier should present the following:

Company Philosophy: The history, mission or vision, objectives, and operating philosophy of the supplier. Gear this toward meeting the performance concerns listed on the customer profile. An organization chart also can be advantageous.

Asset Detail: People, services, equipment, location matchup, financial strengths, and manufacturing strengths (if applicable). Basically it is time to show the muscle the supplier has to offer in backing up its stated ability to make things happen.

Computer Capabilities: Reports available to help reduce and track costs, inventory management, e-mail, EDI, bar coding, automated processes, and tracking capabilities. Computers are emphasized in alliances; therefore, it makes sense to emphasize this asset separately.

Total Quality: Points tracked, charts, S.P.C., supplier evaluations, and ISO 9000 are all important aspects to present. Basically, anything which shows the customer what is being done internally at the supplier's locations to reduce the costs of doing business.

The points of this presentation are to ensure all the primary customer concerns are addressed and the flow of the presentation is smooth and logical. If the customer walks away feeling good about the supplier, but has little knowledge of how that supplier actually can reduce company costs, the prognosis for being chosen is not good.

However, the best presentations are based on knowing the customer's needs and how willing the supplier is to accommodate those needs based on the expected profits. To accomplish this suppliers should evaluate their customers in much the same way that customers evaluate suppliers.

To evaluate customers the supplier must create its own team of experts throughout the company. Alliances cannot operate with just the salesperson; alliances require the entire company to understand, support, and work through this improved relationship.

The salesperson can and should provide the lead role in its development. Much of this development revolves around creating a base from which to launch the alliance. This means identifying the risks, performance requirements, and critical cost-drivers important to each customer, then working with the customer to develop solutions and move the relationship forward.

CHAPTER 6

PERIPHERAL CONCERNS AND PROSPECTS

Alliances are usually complex relationships that can result in changes to the market place as well as the supply chain and operating practices of the companies involved. Until this point the chapters have focused on the primary aspects of developing alliances, and in so doing have raised a number of questions to be addressed. This chapter looks at the most common concerns raised by companies that are entering, or considering entry, into an alliance relationship.

LOSS OF COMPETITIVE MARKET FORCES

Potentially allotting all the business to a single entity often generates fear of a negative outcome among members of the customer's company. The concern usually revolves around one of these three issues:

- that the supplier will start to dominate the marketplace
- that once the business is secured, service will drop off
- that once the business is secured, there will be no checks and balances for protection against price gouging

Unfortunately, there may occasionally be some validity to these issues and they must be addressed in order to build confidence in the alliance and make a smooth transition into the new relationship.

To make matters worse, suppliers who are not chosen as the alliance partners often echo these issues to get the business back. In some cases the supplier who was not chosen may even offer "loss leaders" to break the alliance, selling below cost in some cases. This serves to heighten the concerns of some of the customer's personnel who do not realize these special prices cannot be maintained.

Although these issues are real and need to be addressed, in the majority of alliances these problems can be avoided if the alliance partners deal with them both in the contracts and joint steering committees to prevent them from becoming major obstacles.

Supplier Domination of the Market

The issue most often raised that if one supplier is given all of the business the other suppliers will go out of business or the alliance partner will dominate the market and become too large to be effectively controlled. Both concerns reflect the fear of reduced competition among suppliers. These concerns are depicted in Figure 6.1, which shows the shift from the traditional markets to the perceived future markets that alliances will create. The most often cited example is the impact that some Wal-Mart stores and warehouse-type stores have on smaller more traditional stores.

Figure 6.1 As alliance suppliers grow some people perceive the supplier dominating the market.

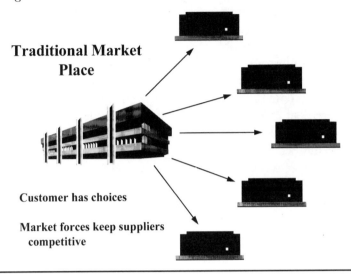

Traditional Market Place

Customer has choices

Market forces keep suppliers competitive

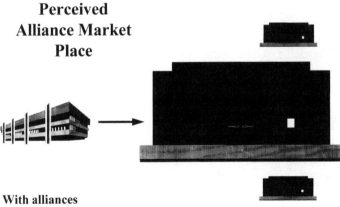

Perceived Alliance Market Place

With alliances
- **choices disappear (go out of business / become too small)**
- **competitive forces do not exist**
- **customer is at the supplier's mercy**

While it is true that alliances will take some business away from other suppliers, this normally does not result in the supplier's demise. Most suppliers have many customers and though the loss of a major account can be detrimental, it will usually not result in the supplier going out of business unless other factors are involved. The oil industry provides an example of one of these "other factors." Many oil fields within the United States are declining because reserves are being depleted. As a result, some suppliers find it difficult to maintain enough sales to stay profitable. Consequently, when a large customer gives an alliance to a particular supplier, the other suppliers who were not selected may not be able to survive.

In most industries, however, this is not likely to be the case. The loss of one customer out of hundreds (or even thousands) is not devastating even if a major account is involved. Resources are shifted to the development of other accounts; the supplier may even start alliances of its own with some of its other accounts. Only rarely is a single customer so important to a supplier that the loss of that customer will drive him out of business. Referring again to the Wal-Mart example, it is not the loss of a single customer or even ten customers that hurts the traditional small store, it is the loss of many customers.

The loss of many customers also signals a shift in customer needs. In a competitive market, it is those companies that are able to identify the needs of the customer and then adapt and provide those needs, who will survive. This type of change will be ongoing. It is not a debate of good or bad; it is an issue of reality not fantasy and suppliers must adjust accordingly. These changes can be seen in almost every aspect of society today. The economy has shifted from agricultural to industrial and is now moving towards service. The economy has also moved from local to state to regional to national and is now moving towards a global perspective. For some people and companies, these changes have been beneficial; for others, the changes have been detrimental. The reason Wal-Mart has been successful is that it was able to better meet customer's demands. This is what alliances are accomplishing—better means for meeting customer needs.

Another reason that alliances are not likely to create suppliers that dominate a market is due to the number of customers in multiple industries that will not form alliances. Smaller companies as well as some medium-size companies will not perceive enough benefit in forming such relationships—the cost is often greater than the return. Suppliers will therefore always have customers for their products if they are meeting their customer's needs.

Additionally, suppliers face few barriers to forming alliances, and large numbers are starting to take advantage of the opportunities that alliances allow. Suppliers are not necessarily limited by size in alliances in the way that customers often are. Small suppliers can form alliances with large companies by proving that they bring greater value or through involvement in an integrated selling group.

However, while the likelyhood is small that a single supplier will dominate the market as a result of alliances, the alliances will heighten the speed at which changes already impacting the market occur. Customers need to evaluate these changes and determine the affect an alliance will have on their abilities to achieve their objectives.

Supplier Loses the Customer Focus

The other two most common concerns address the loss of services or competitive prices. These issues are dealt with together because often they are not mutually exclusive. In many cases the supplier will "buy" the business with a lower price. This price may not allow the supplier to be profitable unless he pulls back on services or adds hidden charges. Some construction companies use high margins on products to recapture the loss of profits from low hourly rates. In other cases, the supplier is asked to perform more services and, in return, is given a higher price to pay for these services.

This situation goes back to the total cost consideration that companies must assimilate when creating alliances. But there are other, less legitimate reasons for this issue to come to the forefront. Sometimes a supplier is unable or unwilling to provide the service at a level agreed to or expected. The reason may be that the supplier lacks the resources or that the customer's requirements are excessive. The customer does not always consider the supplier's cost-drivers and the result can be higher costs for the supplier instead of the promised lower costs due to the synergy from the commitment of all the customer's business.

To overcome these concerns and prevent interruption of the alliance relationship, the steering committee must develop systems for responding to employee concerns by using defined and measurable performance and service criteria for both companies. One goal of the steering committee is to measure total cost and show the demonstrated improvement to those personnel directly involved. Another is to help them understand the need to change operational practices that add in costs for both companies.

From the service standpoint, the performance model discussed in Chapter 2 can be used to evaluate both the supplier and customer and to determine how poor service and performance can affect total cost. The partners must then work together to satisfy the needs of both companies.

From a price standpoint, a set price structure must be in place. Most customers also require a cost-plus or margin to be set to insure against the risk of abuse. Some companies also perform random audits as a means of ongoing assessment. However, perhaps the best method is to compare prices at the start of the alliance to identify the changes from previous costs. Then any and all price changes must be worked out according to the contract by the steering committee. If, at any time, large variations from market prices are found, these should be brought to the attention of the steering committee for evaluation. In some cases, the lower total cost of using the alliance supplier justifies a higher price. In others, it may be better to have a different supplier provide the commodity or service.

LEGALITIES

The question of legalities of alliances often is raised. A commonly cited concern involves antitrust legalities. From the customer's perspective, the worry is market domination over suppliers or artificial prices. The supplier's concerns are integrated supply and the discussion of price with potential competitors. It may be necessary to seek legal advice to assess potential risk. This discussion is not intended to provide such legal counsel because without specific knowledge of a circumstance, the points made here may differ.

The Customer Issues

Most of the legal concerns revolve around the price. Is it legal to give all of a customer's business to one supplier and force a better price? Or in a regulated industry, such as utilities, can products and services be purchased at a price higher than market? As is the case with many legal questions, the answer should be phrased as *yes and no*. This means that the answer depends on the circumstances and may not always be straightforward.

Customers forcing a better price is normal day-to-day business. Leveraging purchases with volume is not in itself illegal; this practice is one of the benefits that a customer derives from an alliance. The exception to this, from a legal perspective, is when a customer dominates an industry. In such cases, there may be a perception of coercion that makes such leveraging illegal. The general rule of thumb defines dominance as a situation when the customer controls 60% or more of the market.

Regulated industries operate from a different perspective. If the alliance partner is paid a price greater than market prices, regulatory agencies take a dim view. The key here is to demonstrate the total value received for the price paid. If the alliance supplier has taken on some of the burden of business normally performed by the customer, this information needs to be documented, otherwise the price may indeed be considered inappropriate.

The last issue is joint ventures. Typically one of the owners runs the company and is held accountable to the other owners. The contract between joint partners often specifies any purchasing limitations or restrictions; many times only certain types of purchases are restricted. Customers in joint ventures would be well-advised to work with all the owners when setting up alliances, particularly on restricted purchases. These owners must be shown the value received if higher prices are paid and the potential affect of the alliance on the company. The contract between the owners sometimes may need to be rewritten to include changes to the purchasing restrictions.

The Supplier Issues

For suppliers the major consideration is integrated supply. In many integrated supply relationships either one supplier sells to another supplier or suppliers may work together to sell to a customer. In either case, prices must be discussed. This often involves disclosure of price on competing products and services. So, is it legal for these companies to discuss prices? So far the courts have said "yes," if the price is set for a specific customer and not for the market (assuming of course that the suppliers discussing price do not dominate the market with their combined companies).

However, this is one of the reasons that suppliers who wish to sell together often need to form a separate company; to set a market strategy legally. Most often the suppliers interested in integrated supply will form a limited liability company that is little more than a shell company operated in one of the supplier's offices. This company can now buy from the partners and prices can in most cases be set and discussed legally.

Contract

While on the topic of legalities, the issue of contracts between the customer and supplier should also be mentioned. Contracts also were discussed in Chapter 3. Contracts should be used to minimize the risks and manage the issues associated with establishing and maintaining the alliance, but also with ending the alliance. The contract should be used as a joint management tool and should allow a certain amount of flexibility. Overly complicated contracts often impose so much legal jargon that they are neither understood nor followed by either company. This practice results in higher risks and costs if the alliance does fail.

LABOR UNIONS

Alliances often are viewed as a threat by labor unions. This is particularly true when the alliance involves service companies or when outsourcing is the type of alliance being considered. But even alliances centered around products can be viewed as "job killers" when efficiencies or shifted burdens result in lower staffing needs.

The truth is that while alliances do sometimes eliminate jobs, they also protect many others by securing the company's competitive position. Customers and suppliers are faced with changing technologies and global markets and competitors, resulting in changing needs. How customers and suppliers adjust to these changing needs can decide a company's fate. Unions face the same issue: change or perish. True, unions can flex their muscles and limit some changes, yet this can hurt the union in the long-term, if the company is put at a competitive disadvantage.

Unions need to learn how to manage this change the same as the customer and supplier have learned how to manage it. The relationship and conflicts are really quite similar. The supplier wants its products to be used and purchased at the best price for the services provided. The customer wants these at the lowest total cost. While somewhat simplified, the union issue is much the same.

Some unions have attempted win/win agreements with their customer partners. Many failed, like many alliances failed, but a number have succeeded as well. So there is room for hope. Yet as alliances grow, they will increasingly come head-to-head with union issues and concerns. So what is in it for unions and how can they interact with the alliance initiatives?

The first issue is understanding the changing dynamics that are taking place. If companies cannot improve their efficiencies, they may be forced to move or even go out of business. Neither option holds good job security. But the union also must show the value it truly brings to the company. For example, suppliers often get "beat up" on the prices they charge for products and services just as unions do for the wages their members receive. Today more and more suppliers are starting to document the savings they bring to the customer (see Chapter 5 for an example and methods). Unions needs to do the same.

When a company is looking to outsource an activity to a supplier, the comparison is usually of wages paid versus the supplier's price. Yet both parties bring other value-added aspects. To get a true "apple to apple" comparison or even a competitive advantage in the decision, unions need to prove the value they have added. Suppliers have learned the hard way that the customer's personnel either do not understand the value or do not know how to measure it. Naturally the union can fight any change and might even win, but why not "sell it" instead? Get the customer's management to see the added value and save the fight for those issues where management cannot see the value.

Another issue facing unions is flexibility. This lack of flexibility costs both the union and the company over the long-term. In order to protect jobs, the employee who performs specific tasks is strictly controlled by the union, yet consider what problems this leads to in the long-term. Figure 6.2 will be used to help illustrate this point. Variation in the use of any asset requires management to consider the issue of ownership compared to rental; the same is true for the employee asset. If a certain percentage of employees are not used fully, management will consider the advantages of hiring outside contractors instead of full-time employees.

The cost of layoffs and training during this fluctuating period are often too high to ignore; hence, management may want the entire proportion outsourced. The union, on the other hand, wants all supply or service needs purchased in-house.

Figure 6.2 Costs due to variations in union member utilization rates can be reduced by focusing on expanding job descriptions.

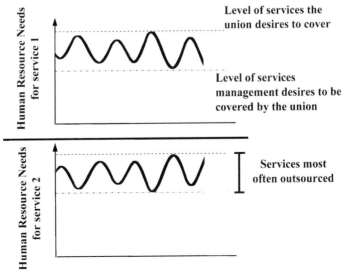

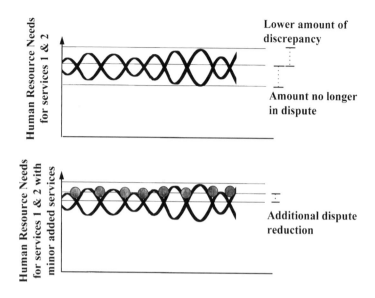

The flexibility comes to play in much the same way as in integrated supply. Different suppliers pool resources to provide value to the customer while achieving their own goals. Some unions are doing the same thing. Local 317 in Wisconsin had membership security as a union goal. This was a difficult task given the company was downsizing. It so happened that peak and low utilization times were opposite with that of another union. In order to help insure job security and minimize fluctuations for both unions, the unions exchange personnel to cover the periods of high demand. Naturally, skill levels differ so those people who are borrowed take the lower skilled jobs.

The result has been that the company pays a little more for these crossover services, but less than what it would have paid outside contractors, surplus employees on staff, or costs of layoff and retraining. The added benefit to the union has been a reduction in the number of personnel under dispute. To further this concept, additional work is being identified that can be added to the unions' responsibilities and done during non-peak periods.

Naturally, many other ideas exist by which both the union and the company can further each other's needs in non-destructive ways. This is not meant to be a "how-to" for union issues—rather it is meant to point out that the union is going to be affected by alliances in one way or another. By applying these concepts and changing with the realities of the market, the union's long-term survival may be better served.

INTEGRATED SUPPLY

Integrated supply is currently the fastest growing form of alliances in the marketplace today. It is, as discussed in Chapter 2, the concept of one-stop shopping which allows the supplier to be "integrated" into the customer's systems. Integrated supply offers some valuable alternatives for those products and services that cannot justify an alliance by themselves, but do justify an alliance when worked together, or when suppliers working together can reduce additional costs.

The focus of this discussion will not center around the customer or supplier relationship. That works the same as discussed throughout this book. The view here will center on the supplier's concerns in working with other suppliers. This discussion can give the customer helpful ideas in evaluating these integrated supply opportunities to ensure that if an integrated alliance is developed, it is a strong one.

There are two methods for creating an integrated supply. Both of these methods are illustrated in Figure 6.3. The first method is tiered. In many cases customers have forced this onto suppliers for years, getting suppliers to provide nuisance items such as in the case of an electrical supplier providing janitorial supplies. Common examples of one-stop shopping are warehouse stores such as Builders Square, Home Depot, and Wal-Mart stores, which offer large varieties of goods and services under one roof (Wal-Mart is now forming lateral alliances with companies such as McDonalds in some of their super stores). Many industrial suppliers now offer this same convenience.

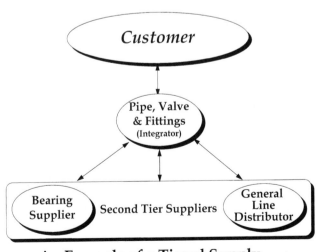

An Example of a Tiered Supply

Figure 6.3 Two methods commonly used in integrated supply.

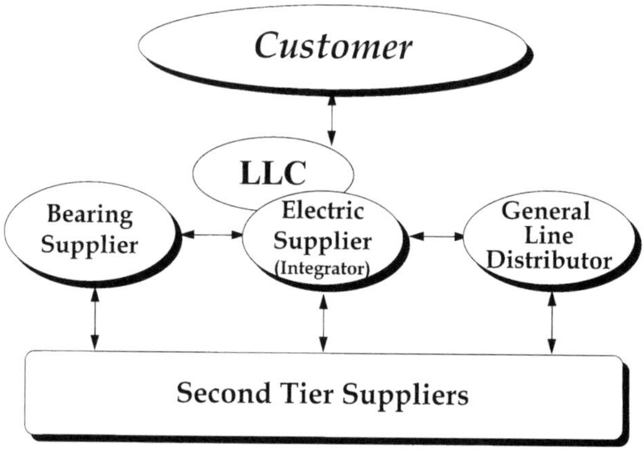

An Example of a Lateral Alliances

LLC - Limited Liability Company. Is often a legal entity with little or no assets.

The tiered supply concept contrasts with lateral integrated alliances in that laterals are more like a shopping mall. In lateral alliances multiple companies get together and still retain some unique brand name distinction. A sale at Wal-Mart is a sale for Wal-Mart. A sale at the mall shoe store does not benefit the bookstore except that it may help the mall stay in business and subsequently entice that customer to return and perhaps buy a book next time.

Both of these methods of integrated supply have benefits and costs associated with them. A brief look at these issues can help both the suppliers and the customers determine how to proceed.

Tiered Supply

Tiered supply reflects its name well. Suppliers, such as the pipe, valve, and fittings supplier in the example above, are tiered in terms of to whom and through whom they sell. The auto industry and oil and gas companies use this model often. Red Man Pipe & Supply has alliances with Mobil Oil, Exxon, Amoco, and Chevron, just to name a few. These customers buy much of their smaller quantity purchase items through Red Man. This includes janitorial, office, light construction, and safety supplies.

The downside for some suppliers is the prospect of becoming a second-tier and consequently losing direct access to the end-user. The first picture in Figure 6.3 depicts this happening to both the bearing supplier and general line distributor. This, however, is not always an unfavorable development. By selling to the first-tier supplier, the second-tier company need no longer deal with all the "hassle factors" involved with the end-user's demands. The second tier can greatly reduce its cost of doing business because the first-tier is often less demanding and deals can be worked to make the service requirements simpler. The real issue is if the integrator chooses a different second-tier. But good service to the first-tier and showing the added value eliminates much of this concern because the first-tier does not always have the time to develop new relationships for these add-on items.

The integrator brings the value of service with one-stop shopping to the end-user. The price paid is usually slightly higher than would be found in a lateral arrangement or direct purchase. The higher price is offset by reduced transactions and better service. Usually the supplier offering this form of integrated supply already makes constant trips to the customer or "lives" on their premises now, providing exceptionally high service. These add-ons (which can account for 50% of the sales) improve the profit derived from doing business through increased volume.

Other than dealing with nontraditional items, there is little difference in doing business for the first-tier integrator; it deals with all suppliers similarly. The second-tier sells in much the same manner as it always has, but adjusts its emphasis from the end-user to the first-tier supplier. On the other hand, lateral supply can offer some big changes.

Lateral Supply

The question both the integrator and the supply companies must ask revolves around the costs and benefits. For example, some stores will not do well in some malls and having the wrong stores can hurt the mall. So both entities need to look at the pros and cons. The integrator is usually the lead company that the customer contacts for purchases. As discussed earlier in this chapter, many companies form a limited liability company (LLC) for legal reasons and for minimizing risks. In Figure 6.3, the second picture, the integrator is either the electrical supplier or the LLC.

Another issue is the extent to which the relationship should be taken. Some integrated supply companies are little more than a contract, a computer and two clerks sitting in one of the owner's offices. Others are actual companies that provide real infrastructure for its members. Still others join their inventories, offices, personnel and other assets into one complete entity with one system for all members instead of one system that joins each member's own system. Naturally the risks and rewards vary by type or degree of interaction. Yet each of these methods have some of the same issues to consider.

Cost/Profit Potential. The biggest potential profit improvement comes from increased sales or *sales security*. The security aspect deals with the ability to keep the sales that the supplier currently has with a customer if that customer is leaning towards using an integrator. A number of suppliers have jumped onboard the integrated supply wagon for fear of losing a specific customer. This is not a great reason to join because the supplier may not see the same incentive as the other suppliers nor the need to provide any additional added value activities. Additionally, if the profits on that account are reduced because of the cost for integration, or the added services, performance may diminish.

Most integrated groups or entities charge some fee to join; this entrance fee can amount to over $30,000. There also may be a transaction fee charged that can amount to as much as 2% of each sale. If the customer is not willing to incur these costs, the supplier must cover them resulting in lower profits and potentially an unwillingness to perform the required services to improve profits.

The biggest benefit comes when the supplier joins the integrator as a means of increasing sales. Three suppliers with ten salespeople each now have the potential for having 30 people sell their products and services if all 30 help sell the integrated supply concept. Additionally, the suppliers gain access, through the integrated supply network, to customers with whom they currently have no sales. If the integrated supply group can develop the infrastructure to handle it, many services can be combined, such as invoicing, order taking, inventory management at the customer's location, and delivery. The result is lower costs to perform these duties together than if performed separately.

These issues always come back to the return on investments. Will the initially increased costs eventually be covered by the improvement in sales and reductions in cost? A major element of this issue is the supplier's selection for membership in the integrated supply group.

Selection. Unfortunately, a number of integrated supply groups simply have been thrown together because of new market forces. In other cases the integrator will accept anyone as long as he pays the membership fee and accepts a transaction processing fee. Both cases can have a high level of success or failure. What most suppliers really do not think about is the impact the other integrated partners have on their image and costs. Poor performance by one supplier gives every other partner a black eye. In several cases a given supplier has lost all benefits derived from the integrated association because of all the fires the supplier had to put out that were created by its partners. The integrated partner represents every other supplier in the group. Does each supplier potentially enhance or tarnish the reputation of the other members? To avoid problems consider the following points:

- Do not rush into an integrated association. If these are becoming a part of a supplier's industry, start planning now. Identify customer's buying needs and good suppliers capable of meeting those needs.
- Quality standards and performance requirements need to be set upfront. Some integrated groups are using ISO 9000 as a base, which is a good start, but set additional standards and requirements that are measurable, such as service levels.
- The responsibilities for each partner also should be set. This can include delivery schedules, billing cycles, process requirements, reports, and training.
- Methods of sharing costs and benefits will be a key point to set. Every supplier must understand the financial effects of this relationship.
- Asset ownership and how these assets can be used by the various suppliers must be determined. This includes buildings, inventories, equipment, and even people.
- The methods for termination—both in terms of one partner wishing to quit or another forcing a partner's removal—need to be spelled out. This includes the obligations that the group owes and is owed.
- The infrastructure requirements and operating processes must be laid out and agreed upon by all parties.

These issues are some of the primary concerns facing companies interested in developing lateral integrated supply groups. Companies that are interested in this should consider approaching alliances much like a merger because that is exactly what is occurring. Each company merges its strengths and weaknesses with the other suppliers' strengths and weaknesses.

There are two other factors that companies need to keep in mind. Much of the upfront value customers receive from integrated supply focuses on reduced transactions. Without a sophisticated computer system that is capable of receiving orders, splitting those orders between the suppliers, and tracking the billing issues, it becomes hard to accomplish. The system can then become labor-intensive and slow, resulting in poor customer satisfaction. Build the system before going out to customers.

The second factor is customer ownership. Who "owns" the customer, the individual suppliers, or the integrator? From an evaluation standpoint, who gets credit for the sale—the integrator or local branch office? Branch offices will be reluctant to offer the customers the integrated option if, in so doing, they lose sales and their evaluations are affected negatively. Integrated supply offers both customers and suppliers great benefits. It also offers risks and costs that need to be managed if the rewards are to be reaped.

SUPPLY CHAIN MANAGEMENT

Most of this book has focused on alliances that involve two links, the suppliers and the customer. The same concept can be used between the supplier and the subcontractor or manufacturer as well. The cost-drivers and concerns will differ but the results can be dramatic. For example, a pipeline construction company works out a deal with the manufacturer of pipe to consign it into their yard. The manufacturer has free storage space for all its customers, which it needs for production inventories during the off season and the construction company can minimize its investment in inventories. The result: everyone walks away a winner.

However, supply chain management is not an option for every company. It usually deals with products but can be adapted to services in some cases. The basic intent of supply chain management is outlined in Figure 6.4. Two links, either the customer-supplier or supplier-manufacturer can work together to reduce prices and the costs associated with working together. Yet by bringing three or more links together, there are additional benefits to be derived. (See also the illustrations in Chapter 1 concerning Amoco and the inventory example).

Figure 6.4 Supply chain management offers additional cost reduction potential.

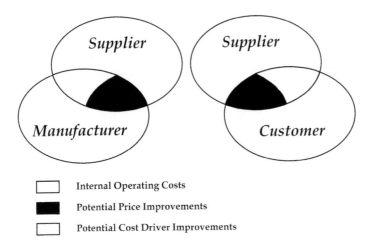

SUPPLY CHAIN COST MODEL

☐ Internal Operating Costs

■ Potential Price Improvements

☐ Potential Cost Driver Improvements

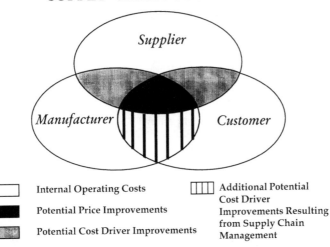

SUPPLY CHAIN COST MODEL

☐ Internal Operating Costs

■ Potential Price Improvements

▦ Potential Cost Driver Improvements

|||| Additional Potential Cost Driver Improvements Resulting from Supply Chain Management

The most common issues in supply chain management are often simply other alliance issues taken one step further. These include:

Inventory ownership. The least expensive place in the supply chain to carry inventory is with the manufacturer. Manufacturers that consign inventory to distributors and customers lock out competing brands and secure market shares.

Engineered Specifications. Many end-users are finding that the engineered specifications they give manufacturers are often either over- or under-engineered. Even when the specifications are right, the design may result in higher costs to build the parts. By working with manufacturers on design and specifications, more cost-effective systems are being built.

Planning. Retail companies such as department stores often have point-of-sale information downloaded to their manufacturers daily. By providing this information directly to manufacturers, production can be planned better, thereby minimizing lead times for both distributors and end-users.

Transactional costs. Almost any transactional cost from shipping, handling, inspection, and receiving can be minimized. Too often these actions are wasteful, repetitive, and add costs without adding value.

While there are similarities, there are also some major differences and obstacles. Many manufacturers are concerned about alliances and how they are changing the traditional channels of distribution and affecting marketing strategies. When working a supply chain alliance, the more links that are involved, the more obstacles and concerns are raised. Some of the larger concerns include:

- *Representation:* If a supplier is chosen that does not represent the manufacturer's lines or has stronger ties to other manufacturers, it may loose that end-user. Surprisingly this issue restrains many manufacturers. A better approach might be to identify key distributors and help them win the alliances. This action may result in some missed opportunities but will achieve many more hits than waiting and hoping.

- *Territories:* Some manufacturers protect a given distributor's territories. Customers may choose a distributor and in so doing disrupt the established distribution channels for a given manufacturer. In some cases manufacturers have been forced to lose the end-user in order to hold the line for the distributors. This builds loyalty and hopefully ensures that the distributor will have a vested interest in that manufacturer. In other cases a tiered approach was used to allow the sales to go through the original distributor and then on to the first-tier supplier. Still other manufacturing companies simply have allowed the territories to be bypassed for a specific end-user.

- *Leverage:* Another concern is the loss of control. If the distributor controls what product goes into the customer's location, that leverage will be used against them. And if one distributor gains too many alliances, their sales volume could allow the distributor to leverage concessions from the manufacturer that he does not want to provide.

While these concerns are real, manufacturers need to be proactive just like any other supplier. The opportunities are there; they can either work these opportunities to their advantage or be forced to accept what the market thrusts upon them. And those manufacturers that first determine how to make alliances work in their favor will achieve a competitive advantage just as other supply companies today are finding.

OUTSOURCING

The term outsourcing was originally coined to describe the decision to buy rather than make parts. The auto industry went through some major outsourcing from the point of manufacturing the majority of parts to now manufacturing well below one-half the parts used. Today outsourcing has taken on a much broader context. Outsourcing today, more often than not, refers to the decision to have processes performed by outside agencies. Numerous tasks, processes, and even entire systems and departments are now being outsourced in addition to outsourcing production.

Outsourcing is by far the most controversial form of alliance; it also can hold the greatest risk and return potential. The controversy evolves around the idea that others can perform a task or set of tasks better, faster or cheaper than can be done in-house. The controversy also concerns the effect this has on jobs. To understand this concept further and to understand better when a task should or should not be outsourced, consider Figure 6.5.

Process Hierarchy

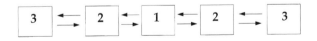

1. **Core Processes** - processes that create the goods or services for which the company is known

2. **Strategic Support Processes** - primary processes that help ensure core process objectives are achieved

3. **Support Processes** - required activities that add little direct value to the core processes

Figure 6.5 The process hierarchy determines the process outsourcing potential

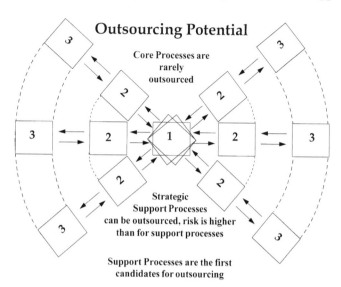

Outsourcing Potential

Core Processes are rarely outsourced

Strategic Support Processes can be outsourced, risk is higher than for support processes

Support Processes are the first candidates for outsourcing

Different processes and tasks have different levels of importance to a company's objectives. It stands to reason that the higher the degree of importance, the higher the level of competence and resources dedicated to ensuring that the task is performed well. Figure 6.5 makes distinctions between these levels of importance. In the center of the company are the *level one* processes or core processes. Core processes are those tasks that create the goods or services for which the company is known or are key to its survival.

For WEPCO, a utility company, the core processes might be the generation and distribution of electricity. For Miller it might be the processes for brewing beer. But both companies perform many tasks beyond these core processes. The next level out from these core processes are strategic support or *level two* processes, which are those tasks that directly support the core processes and help ensure that the core processes are accomplished. For example, warehousing for most companies would not be viewed as a strategic function or task. This may be true for MRO parts, but both WEPCO and Miller likely would view the storage of coal or barley as strategic support processes.

The MRO storage would be an example of a support or level three process. Support processes are those activities that are required but add little direct value to the accomplishment of the core processes. A mail room and an accounting department may be required for a company to operate, but from the standpoint of a core process they are somewhat removed.

From the standpoint of outsourcing, the further the process is from a core process the lower the risk in outsourcing and the greater the potential return. The reasoning is based on the core competencies of the companies to which the process is outsourced. WEPCO outsources the management of its fleet to Ryder Truck. Ryder Truck's core competence is fleet management; therefore, Ryder should be able to perform that task better, faster, and cheaper once it understands WEPCO's needs.

Core processes are rarely outsourced. The exception can be a lack of capacity or special needs and skills. Strategic processes are susceptible to outsourcing but incur higher risks if the outsourcing company does not perform well. For companies considering outsourcing the following includes some issues that should be considered prior to implementation:

- *Selection:* Most of the concerns for selection were discussed in general in Chapter 2. However, when outsourcing is used, the company supplying the process capabilities, should have core competencies centered on that task and not merely view it as another service it could provide. A distributor, for example, could run a warehouse since that is one of its core competencies. However, that same distributor should not be used for the outsourcing of the purchasing department, if much of what is being purchased is outside the distributor's expertise.

- *Cutover:* The more technical the operation being outsourced, the greater the need is to plan the cutover from being run in-house to being outsourced. Companies today outsource computer departments and telecommunication systems. Without careful planning and training major problems can develop. It is often a good idea to run both the old and new systems in tandem if this is possible. The initial costs are higher but the results are often worth the cost.

- *Responsibilities:* Who performs what tasks needs to be clearly established. Every system and sub-system connected to the outsourced process needs to be identified and defined as to how it will interface with the new system and the requirements involved. Too often the supplier finds additional needs and requirements surfacing only when users become upset.

- *Performance Standards:* Not surprisingly many companies

attempt to micro-manage the outsourcing company. This is a mistake. The whole reason why the process was outsourced was that the supplier could do it better. By micro-managing the company, friction and problems develop, costs go up and quality comes down. Instead, based on the responsibilities outlined, set measurable performance standards, then hold the supplier to those agreed upon measures. However, keep in mind that the customer also must have measurable performance standards for its actions as the customer's performance can greatly affect the outsourcer's performance.

- *Part of the Management Team:* In some cases the process may be turned over completely to the outsourcing company with little need for ongoing involvement. For example, credit card processing may be done by a supplier such as American Express and often is just a simple matter of processing paper. In other cases the process is so closely allied with the day-to-day business of running the company, that the outsourcer must be involved closely in management decisions. In some cases they may even help set company policies. In such cases the outsourcer must have these expectations and responsibilities spelled out and be held accountable in much the same way as other departments within the company.

- *Partial or Whole Outsourcing:* Companies also can consider the amount of activity to be outsourced; it need not be a question of all or none. The use of partial outsourcing is a good strategy for testing and planning prior to a complete switchover. Partial outsourcing is most often utilized when there is high variation in personnel requirements. The variable is handled by the outsourcer allowing for complete usage of the customer's employees.

In today's changing environments, outsourcing can make a great deal of sense. No company does everything better than all other companies. The use of outsourcers to provide specific needs or to keep up with changing technologies can provide the customer with a competitive advantage over those companies trying to do it all themselves.

CHANGING PARTNERS

The point has been made that alliances are for long-term on-going relationships. Yet eventually the relationship's continuation is bound to come into question. It may be that new savings are failing to appear and a new supplier is offering an opportunity to reduce total costs beyond the present level. Should the customer quit and start a new alliance? Or maybe one partner is simply dissatisfied; this could be either the customer or the supplier. Should the partner end the relationship?

The answer may be "yes." However, terminating an alliance should not be taken lightly. There are both risks and costs that could make the termination detrimental to one or both parties. It is hoped the alliance partners have provisions for termination that deal with each other's responsibilities built into the contract; also the contract should be amended on a continuous basis as unforeseen events result in changing terms.

To explore this issue in more detail, consider the situation where the customer is faced with diminishing returns from its alliance supplier and a new supplier promises to reduce costs beyond what the alliance partner can achieve. This situation is depicted in Figure 6.6. The customer must determine which relationship offers the best potential return. As in any investment decision, there are three factors to take into consideration that include:

- *Return*. How much is the annualized opportunity worth; that is, how much further could the new supplier potentially reduce current operating costs? Unfortunately, the most common offering is price. The new supplier usually offers to do everything the current supplier is doing plus offers a better price. This can be very tempting, particularly if there was a recent change in personnel and the customer does not remember all the other savings the current supplier provided.
- *Risk*. If any savings have been achieved, what is the risk of losing these savings because the new supplier cannot provide the same benefit? The risk is usually significantly higher than most companies realize. If the alliance supplier has worked closely with a customer for some time, there are usually hidden advantages such as familiarity with people, problems, systems, and even terminology. It is often these issues that have allowed the current reduction in operating costs to actually be achieved. Then start-up and cutover costs have to be taken into consideration as the company switches suppliers; this readjustment may never even be achieved. All this is in addition to the risk of the new supplier not being able to deliver what was promised.

- *Duration*. One of the most commonly used methods for one supplier to break into another supplier's alliance is to offer prices well below the price that any supplier can sustain for a length of time. What assurance does the customer have for the long-term that the lower operating costs promised will stay in place.

Figure 6.6 Diminishing returns can result in a reevaluation of the alliance.

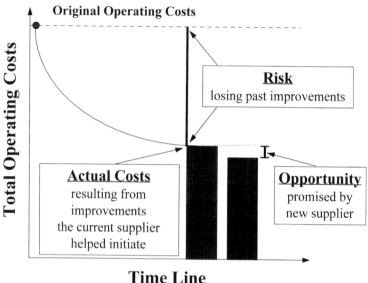

It is the comparison and weighing of these three factors against one another that determines whether the customer should switch suppliers. Some companies have decided not to risk any switches as long as the alliance supplier is performing well. While the intent is a good one, it may also prevent that customer from making advances, thereby placing it at a potential disadvantage. If the savings is worth the risk, the issue must be given some consideration.

Unfortunately any objective evaluation may be hard to actually accomplish. The reason is that most companies fail to measure the added value by the current supplier. The tendency by most customers is that if improvements were measured, a change is far less likely to occur than if the added value were not measured.

The decision to end an alliance is not always an action initiated by customers. Suppliers can find themselves in an unprofitable or unacceptable relationship and must make the decision to continue or not.

The risk can be hard feelings by the customer and a market perception by other customers of that suppliers inability to make an alliance work. Suppliers, even more than customers, need to perform an evaluation prior to starting an alliance to assess whether the relationship they are entering into is viable for the long-term.

As stated earlier, fully one-half of all alliances have at least one unhappy partner. As such, the possibility of ending an alliance is likely to exist with companies for some time to come. If the alliance does fail, it should not come as a surprise to either company. As issues or concerns are discovered, they need to be brought to the attention of the joint steering committee.

Then it becomes the steering committee's responsibility to work through the issue and to develop a solution to the problem. Sometimes a small change on the part of one partner can have a dramatic effect on the other partner. It is this willingness to make reciprocal adjustments that keeps the alliance progressing and healthy.

COMPENSATION AND INCENTIVES

A sensitive issue that must be addressed for the long-term health of an alliance is how the partners are to be rewarded in an alliance. All give and no *get* is just not acceptable. The belief that the other partner always wins goes both ways. Some customers feel all the sales, increased prices, and lower services have allowed the supplier to reap massive profits at their expense. The supplier feels that the lower prices, increased services, and shifted burdens have more than offset any gains gathered through volume sales. The reality is that both the customer and supplier can feel this way in the same alliance. Some prices may be lower and some higher, some burdens may have shifted both ways as the supplier might not provide all the services performed by all the suppliers in the past, but does perform more than it previously did.

Figure 6.7 Shifting burden, adding services, and driving down prices can result in lower net profits before tax (NPBT) for both companies, as hidden costs will increase the total cost.

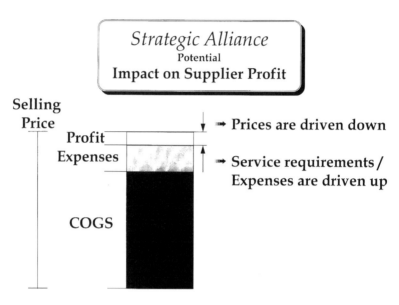

Price Focus
Can create a Win /Lose situation.
Long-term this often leads to a Lose / Lose situation.

Over time the supplier must become profitable, this is often achieved by reducing services which can result in increased inventory and operating costs for the customer.

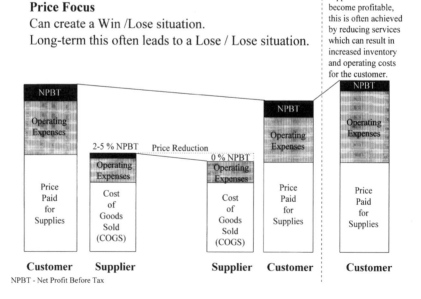

As burdens are shifted to the supplier, some operating costs for the customer may increase as the supplier attempts to minimize the cost of doing business by cutting services. In the long run it becomes more difficult to control prices and stay profitable, so prices may escalate. The result is an ending of the alliance, even when initially both partners received some front-end loaded benefits.

Figure 6.8 Reductions in total cost for one company should translate into benefits for both.

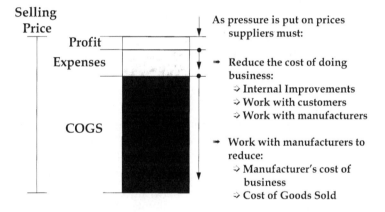

Total Cost Focus
Can create a Win / Win relationship if companies understand each others costs and work to reduce each others costs.

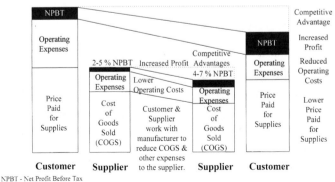

209

The alternative is to reduce costs for both companies. One of the easiest methods is to switch projects, meaning first choose a project important to the customer, and then one important to the supplier. In this manner both are ensured reduction of overall costs and winning long-term. Customers must remember that every cost driven into the supplier's cost of doing business must be paid for somehow. The most common methods are price increases or service reductions. However, the best method is to work to reduce the non-value added costs within both companies.

To ensure that each partner receives its needed improvements, many companies develop formulas for measurement, by which mutually agreed upon values can be determined. Simply put, increased costs and improved profit are weighed against each other to ensure that each partner is being benefited.

PAST, PRESENT, AND FUTURE

Alliances, although not a new concept, are still in the adolescent stage. The concept is still growing and taking on new forms and new personalities. As in almost anything, a look at its past provides insight into its future.

The past has provided companies an understanding of what to do and not to do. The three stages of alliances: discovery, implementation, and management are like sections on a map. It is far more difficult to cross a section without following the route set by others. Those blazing their own trails and taking "short cuts" through discovery find the trials of implementation far more difficult. Discovery requires a longer route but puts the traveler in a better position for implementation. As companies have followed the discovery route, it has become easier to use and complete that stage as those who traveled before have built the roads to follow.

Today the focus has shifted to implementation. This is not surprising when the traveler considers the changes occurring within the alliance. In the past most alliances focused on involving two companies. Today Integrated Supply and Supply Chain Management focus on multiple company relationships. This has lead to an increased need to learn how to work together better. Additionally, the speed of transition has been increased. This has forced companies to learn how to manage the change and build infrastructures that better support the alliance for all the companies involved. It also has created a need to measure the added value because these new alliances emphasize the total cost of doing business for each company. Some companies still ask if it is worth the effort to develop alliances. After all, forming and working alliances requires a great deal of effort. Is this just another trend? Some companies will think so, but for many others it will become a way of doing business. Yet in order to maintain and be successful, companies must move beyond the common transactional types of improvements to the more difficult. In effect, they must *raise the iceberg*.

Figure 6.9 More opportunities to reduce total cost can be found when the iceberg is raised.

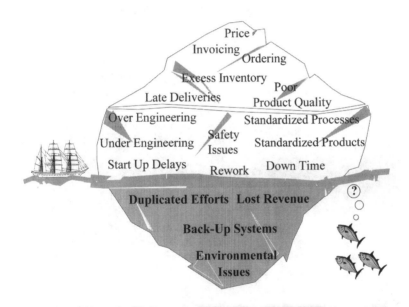

By placing emphasis on the more complex factors, the return on investment from the alliance will be greater and the probability of success will be higher. This is the future of alliances—finding new cost-drivers to work on and improving additional methods of conducting business between companies.

Additionally, new forms of alliances will be developed. For example, there are two groups currently looking at forming an integrated company comprised of some of the best-in-class companies in industry today. That in itself is not new. These groups, however, are forming to see how an integrated group of outsourcers could operate and take advantage of their joint abilities as shown in Figure 6.10.

Figure 6.10 Integrated outsourcing could be part of the alliance future.

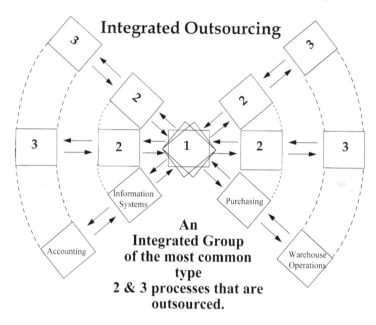

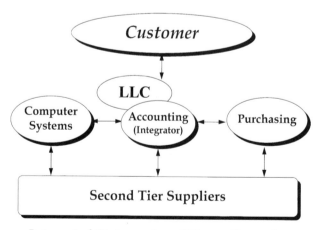

Integrated Outsourcing Alliance Example

LLC - Limited Liability Company.

While this form of alliance may or may not come to pass, alliances will continue to evolve and be a greater part of industry's future. Getting involved now could provide a distinct advantage. The future and direction of each industry will be set by those who take the lead. Companies can either have that future by companies considering alliances, shaped *by them* or *for them*, as the companies involved in alliances today will shape the look of alliances for tomorrow.

COST DRIVER
EXERCISE

To better understand the Total Cost concept, consider each cost driver opportunity. What is the risk involved in changing the cost driver? What performance issues must be addressed? What is the dollar value of each cost driver? Many of these cost drivers may not offer an opportunity for change or might be difficult to assign an appropriate dollar value. In such cases estimates should be used. Then consider how price compares against the other components of Total Cost.

Cost Categories	Cost Driver Opportunities	Performance		
		Risk	Issues	Value
Inventory	General Inventory			
	Obsolete Inventory			
	Dead Items			
	Excess / Surplus			
	Inventory Shortages			
	"Safety" Stock			
	Consignment			
	Management of Inventory			
	Multiple Locations			
	Shrinkage / Spoilage			
	Insurance			
	Taxes			
	Cost of Investment			
	Dual Storage			
	Receiving / Inspection			
	Load / Unloading			
	Delivery Paperwork			
	Handling			
	Storage			
Product	Over-Engineered			
	Under-Engineered			
	Standardization of Products			
	Substitutions			
	Failure Rates			
	Life Cycle Cost Reductions			
	Durability			
	Reliability			
	Efficiency			
	Engineering Changes			
	Operating Standards			
	Job Site Deliveries			
	Kitting / Pre-assembly			
	Lead Time			
	Billing Terms			
	New Technology			
	New Product Development			
	Revenue Enhancement Ability			

Cost Categories	Cost Driver Opportunities	Performance		
		Risk	Issues	Value
Process Costs	Accounting / Invoicing			
	- Coding			
	- Multiple			
	- Input			
	- Matching			
	- Verification			
	- Paperwork			
	Invoicing Method			
	- EDI			
	- Credit Card			
	- Summary Billing			
	- Project Billing			
	- Multiple Billings			
	Administrative			
	Too Many Transactions			
	- Deliveries			
	- Orders			
	- Invoices			
	Forecasting			
	Negotiations			
	Legal Aid			
	Invoice Payment			
	Scheduling / Rescheduling			
	Multi-Order Points/People			
	Ordering			
	- Sourcing			
	- Compile			
	- Place			
	- Compare Bids			
	- Expediting			
	- Phone Time			
	- Paperwork			
	- Input			
	- Supplier Qualification			
	Auditing			
	Duplicate Efforts			
	Complaint / Problem Solving			
	Standardized Transaction Methodology			

Cost Categories	Unnecessary / Required Tasks Cost Driver Opportunities	Risk	Performance Issues	Value
Quality Issues	Back Orders			
	Poor Working Relationship			
	Poor Service Requirements			
	Shortages			
	Mis - Billing			
	Mis - Shipment			
	Late Deliveries			
	Early Deliveries			
	Delivery to Incorrect Location			
	Waiting Around			
	Follow - up			
	Poor Product Quality			
	Product Returns			
	Response Time			
	Damaged Products			
	Rework / scrap			
	Information Inaccuracies			
Price	Price Paid			
	Quantity Discounts			
	Freight			
	Express Freight			
	Tiered Pricing			
	Plateau Pricing			
	Rebates			
	Buyouts			
	Integrated Purchases			
	Turnkey Purchases			
General	Technical / Engineering Support			
	Technical / Engineering Input			
	Planning			
	Communications			
	Training Required			
	Training Provided			
	Environmental Regulations			
	Safety			
	Shared Market Intelligence			
	Warranty			

Cost Categories	Computer Reporting Needs **Cost Driver** **Opportunities**	**Risk**	**Performance** **Issues**	**Value**
Equipment	Down Time			
	Cost of Equipment			
	Ownership (Transferred)			
	Operating Cost Impact			
	Substitutions			
	Failure Rates			
	Life Cycle Cost Reductions			
	Repair / Service Cost			
	Consumable Product Markups			
	Start-up / Installations			
	Back-ups / Spares			
	Under-utilization			
	Standard Design			
	Damage			
	Scheduling			
	Cost of Investment			
	Sale of Used			
	Training			
	Insurance			
Construction	Project cost			
	Rework			
	Safety			
	Governmental Regulations			
	Design Changes			
	Start - up / Installation			
	Methods / Standards			
	Standard Design			
	Drawing Specifications			
	Damage			
	Scheduling			
	Down Time			
	Restoration			

Cost Categories	Cost Driver Opportunities	Performance		
		Risk	Issues	Value
Maintenance / Operations	Repair Costs			
	Maintenance costs			
	Restoration			
	Down Time			
	Response to Emergency			
	Increased Capacity / Efficiency			
	Energy Costs			
	Overhead			
	Supplies			
Disposal	Cost to Remove			
	Salvage Value			
	Exchange Value			
	Environmental Regulations			

SURVEY

AUDITS/SURVEYS

Review the survey on the following pages;

    1. Identify use of the survey (pre-assessment or audit)

    2. Eliminate questions which do not apply to your needs

    3. Identify informational requirements missing and add them in

    4. Develop scoring scheme

MANAGEMENT RESPONSIBILITY			In Progress		
	5 Yes	4	3	2	1 No
1) Is there a documented Quality Policy statement(s)? Please attach copies of all available statements.	5	4	3	2	1
2) Is there a quality manual? Based on what standards (ISO, MILQ)? _____ Last updated_____ Please provide a copy.	5	4	3	2	1
3) Is there a Quality System Plan? Please provide a copy.	5	4	3	2	1
4) Is there an improvement plan(s)? Please provide a copy.	5	4	3	2	1
5) Do the plans define roles and responsibilities?	5	4	3	2	1
6) Are all functions of the organization addressed in the Quality Plans?	5	4	3	2	1

Do the quality plans address

	YES	NO
Administration		
Management		
Sales		
Order Entry		
Order Filling		
Shipping / Receiving		
Packaging		
Purchasing		
Customer Service		
Manufacturing Processes		
Stock Rotation		
Inspection		
Warehouse Operations		
Inventory Control		
Fabrication		
Training		
Accounting		
Delivery		

7) Is there a distinct management representative for insuring compliance with the quality system?	5	4	3	2	1
8) Is there a distinct quality management team (i.e,. Steering Committee)? Please provide an organizational chart for this function.	5	4	3	2	1

	In Progress				
	5	**4**	**3**	**2**	**1**
	Yes				No

9) Is this management team responsible for and involved in setting:

	Yes	No
Goals		
Plans		
Audits		
Reviews of Progress		

10) How often does the management team meet?_____

11) From the organizational chart, who has the responsibility and freedom to:

Identify and record quality problems_____

Participate in developing solutions_____

Verify the implementation of solutions_____

12) Are employees kept informed of quality levels, programs, concerns?   5 4 3 2 1

If yes, what types of communication are used? (Newsletters, charts, forums, E-mail).
_____

13) Are there employee recognition programs in place recognizing quality improvement ideas or performance?   5 4 3 2 1

Please describe briefly._____
_____
_____

14) Have the key quality measures in each department been identified and tracked?   5 4 3 2 1

Attach examples.

15) Does the company have a management reporting system that tracks the costs of poor quality in order to identify areas of quality improvement?   5 4 3 2 1

Provide a copy of a recent quality cost report.

16) Is there a regular, scheduled review of the status and adequacy of the quality improvement process?   5 4 3 2 1

If yes, how is the progress measured?_____
_____

17) Is customer feedback utilized in quality planning?   5 4 3 2 1

If yes, please describe how._____
_____

		In Progress		
5	**4**	**3**	**2**	**1**
Yes				No

18) Is employee input used to improve the process/product?

    If yes, please describe how._____

    _____

    _____

         5   4   3   2   1

19) Does a system exist to measure employee satisfaction?

         5   4   3   2   1

20) What quality milestones/standards have been achieved (i.e., ISO 9000, Baldridge Award, Deming Prize, etc.)_____

    _____

    _____

QUALITY SYSTEMS	In Progress				
	5	4	3	2	1
	Yes				No

1) Is there a documented order entry system?

    Please provide a copy

    5 4 3 2 1

2) Does the order entry system :

	Yes	No
Include a review of each order?		
Define, clarify, document requirements?		
Ensure your ability to meet contract requirements?		
Ensure that differences are resolved?		

3) Does the quality system track performance on meeting agreed upon requirements?

    5 4 3 2 1

    How? (describe)_____

    Which variable s are tracked :
- ☐ On time delivery
- ☐ Shipment Errors
- ☐ Substitute products
- ☐ Back orders
- ☐ Incorrect packing slips
- ☐ Other_____

4) Is there a documented process to respond to customer complaints?

    5 4 3 2 1

5) List three major improvements to customer service attributable to your quality improvement efforts._____

6) Is there a procedure for product identification and traceability?

    Please provide a copy.

    5 4 3 2 1

7) Are certificates of analysis, MSDS, Mill Test or other product conformance reports available upon request?

    5 4 3 2 1

8) Is there a procedure to handle returns from customers (due to defective material, overshipment, wrong material, etc.)

    5 4 3 2 1

	In Progress
	5 4 3 2 1
	Yes .... No

9) Is there a methodology for evaluation/certification of suppliers? If so, please describe._____ _____ _____	5 4 3 2 1
10) Is there an approved supplier list?	5 4 3 2 1
11) What is the selection process for approved suppliers?_____ _____ _____	
12) What criteria determine if a supplier gets the order?_____ _____ _____	
13) Is there a documented procedure for the procurement process? Please provide a copy.	5 4 3 2 1
14) Are suppliers formally encouraged to engage in quality improvement programs?	5 4 3 2 1
15) Are suppliers provided with a report on their quality performance? Please provide a copy.	5 4 3 2 1
16) How are specifications to suppliers ensured for accuracy / adequacy?_____ _____ _____	
17) How are incoming materials ensured to meet specifications?_____ _____ _____	
18) Are purchasing documents reviewed to ensure product specifications are clearly stated?	5 4 3 2 1
19) Is there a process for material inspection / rejection?	5 4 3 2 1

	In Progress				
	5	**4**	**3**	**2**	**1**
	Yes				No

	5	**4**	**3**	**2**	**1**
20) Is there a return to supplier system in place?	5	4	3	2	1

Does it include:

	Yes	No
Segregate areas for returns		
Identification of the cause for the returns		
Notification to suppliers		

21) If material does not pass inspection, does the process include:

	Yes	No
Rework options		
Scrap		
Return to supplier		
Acceptance without modification		

	5	**4**	**3**	**2**	**1**
22) Are life cycle costs on products maintained?	5	4	3	2	1
23) Where applicable, is product performance data maintained?	5	4	3	2	1

24) Are there written procedures for stock covering:

	Yes	No
Handling		
Storage		
Rotation		
Deterioration		
Packaging		
Delivery		
Receiving		
Inspection		
Replenishment		

	5	**4**	**3**	**2**	**1**
25) Is the invoice process documented?	5	4	3	2	1
Does it ensure accuracy checks to prevent billing errors?	5	4	3	2	1
26) Are processes compared (benchmarked) to "best in class" parameters?	5	4	3	2	1
27) Is there a corrective action process?	5	4	3	2	1

Does it :

	Yes	No
Identify non-conformances		
Analyze occurrences		
Track causes		
Initiate corrections		
Follow up to ensure compliance		

	In Progress			
5	**4**	**3**	**2**	**1**
Yes				No

28) Is the quality system evaluated by use of an internal audit system?

	Yes	No
Is there an audit schedule?		
Is the schedule based on importance?		

5	**4**	**3**	**2**	**1**

How is corrective action ensured? _____

_____

_____

How are findings documented? _____

_____

_____

Quality Tools and Techniques	In Progress				
	5	4	3	2	1
	Yes				No

1) Which statistical methods are used?	5	4	3	2	1

Yes   No

	Yes	No
Pareto analysis		
Histograms		
Control charts		
Cause and effect analysis		
Flow charts		
Bar charts		
Pie charts		
Line charts		

Other _____
_____
_____

2) How is proper use of statistical methods ensured?_____
_____
_____

Please provide examples of each method utilized.

3) Is the computer system capable of capturing all data necessary for statistical techniques used?	5	4	3	2	1

4) Is employee participation utilized to correct / improve systems?	5	4	3	2	1

How? (describe)_____
_____
_____

If teams are used:	Yes	No
Are multi-departmental teams utilized?		
Are departmental teams utilized?		
Do they report progress to management?		

5) Describe the problem-solving approaches used._____
_____

6) How is involvement by all employees ensured?_____
_____

7) Are individuals outside the company involved in improvement efforts (customers or suppliers)?	5	4	3	2	1

	In Progress			
5	**4**	**3**	**2**	**1**
Yes				No

8) Is inspection or testing performed within the company?

    If yes, please describe. _____

5 4 3 2 1

9) How is instrumentation measurement accuracy ensured? _____

10) Does the quality system include: Yes   No

	Yes	No
A sampling process		
An inspection / testing process		
An equipment calibration process		
A test status report		

11) Is there a formal training program in place?

Does it: Yes   No

	Yes	No
Asses training needs		
Sets a schedule for training		
Document training		

5 4 3 2 1

12) Is there a program of ongoing training in quality concepts?

Does it include: Yes   No

	Yes	No
Problem-solving techniques		
Statistical Methods		
Team Building		
Leadership		
Facilitation		

5 4 3 2 1

13) What percent of personnel have received training in quality improvement concepts and techniques?

	%
Management	
Sales (outside)	
Sales (inside)	
Purchasing	
Accounting	
Warehouse Operations	
Delivery Personnel	
Administration	
Other _____	

SUPPLIER SELECTION
INSTRUMENT

COMMODITY/SERVICE PLAN

List below the Name the systems and the people (positions) within each system which will be impacted by this alliance.

Commodity/service:

Systems   Positions

COMM0DITY/SERVICE PLAN

Describe the relationship to be developed.
Current Relationship (describe)

Alliance Relationship Desired (describe)

COMMODITY/SERVICE PLAN

List the overall objectives to be achieved.
For each objective describe —current state
　　　　　　　　　　　　—impact current state has
　　　　　　　　　　　　—desired state

COMM0DITY/SERVICE PLAN

Value to be added (Total Cost impact ideas).

COMMODITY/SERVICE PLAN

Risks to plan for if this relationship is to succeed.

Performance requirements if risks are to be minimized and the relationship successful.

Total Cost - Supplier Selection Instrument

Item Scoring Scale		Date: **6/6/95**

Item Scoring Scale

Possible Score	Definition
0	Completely unacceptable
2	Well below average- very weak
4	Below average- weak
6	Above average - acceptable
8	Well above average - outstanding
10	Far above average, no competitor is equal - exceptional

Commodity/service:
Electrical Parts & Components

Company Name:
ABC Electric

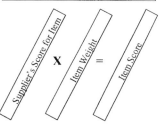

Supplier's Score for Item **X** Item Weight **=** Item Score

Cost Management

		Supplier's Score for Item	Item Weight	Item Score
1	How does the supplier's rate schedule compare compare with the companies you perceive as the top three competitors? Include supplemental pricing parameters, such as travel & set-up time, minimum hourly charges, etc..	8	.45	3.60
2	How does the supplier emphasize Total Cost rather than just price?	9	.35	3.15
3	How does the supplier's payment and/or contract terms compare with its top three competitors?	7	.20	1.40

Weights should sum to 1.00. Add all item scores together to get the score for this section.

Section Score | 8.15

Amoco Production Company

Total Cost - Supplier Selection Instrument

Item Scoring Scale		Date: **6/6/95**

Possible Score	Definition
0	Completely unacceptable
2	Well below average- very weak
4	Below average- weak
6	Above average - acceptable
8	Well above average - outstanding
10	Far above average, no competitor is equal - exceptional

Commodity/service:
Electrical Parts & Components

Company Name:
ABC Electric

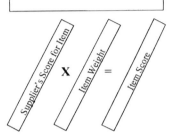

Supplier's Score for Item **X** Item Weight **=** Item Score

Financial Strength

Question	Score	Weight	Item Score
1 How does the supplier's financial strength compare with the companies you perceived to be the top three competitors?	9	.35	3.25
2 What is Hi Tech's percentage of the supplier's total sales compared to its top three competitors?	8	.30	2.40
3 Is the supplier part of a larger company? If so, rate the degree of corporate support received in terms of resources, technology, capacity, etc.. (If not part of a larger company, score the same as question 1.)	7	.25	1.75
4 Assess the supplier's history in paying for the goods and services it receives.	10	.10	1.00

Weights should sum to 1.00. Add all item scores together to get the score for this section.

Section Score | 8.40

Amoco Production Company

Total Cost - Supplier Selection Instrument

Item Scoring Scale

Possible Score	Definition
0	Completely unacceptable
2	Well below average- very weak
4	Below average- weak
6	Above average - acceptable
8	Well above average - outstanding
10	Far above average, no competitor is equal - exceptional

Date: 6/6/95

Commodity/service:
Electrical Parts & Components

Company Name:
ABC Electric

Management / Strategic

Supplier's Score for Item X Item Weight = Item Score

Item	Supplier's Score for Item	Item Weight	Item Score
1 Rate the supplier's capability to grow with increases/decreases in volume & changing business practices.	8	.25	2.0
2 How does the supplier's mission, vision and values compare with Hi Tech's values?		.20	2.0
3 Review the supplier's long-range intent as a company, strategic plans for technology, capital expenditures, location, plant capacity, etc. Compare the compatibility of the supplier's plans with Hi Tech's plans.	7	.15	1.05
4 How does the supplier's geographic presence compare to those of Hi Tech requiring the supplier's products/services?	9	.15	1.35
5 Rate the company's electronic capabilities relative to Hi Tech's (EDI, EFT, ACH, etc.)	8	.10	0.80
6 What is the company's capability of implementing and maintaining an electronic catalog reflecting its materials/services and associated costs?	8	.10	0.80
7 As compared to its competitors, does the supplier provide a diversity of materials, equipment and services which would give the supplier/Hi Tech a competitive edge?	7	.05	0.35

SAMPLE

Weights should sum to 1.00. Add all item scores together to get the score for this section.

Section Score | 8.35 |

Amoco Production Company

Total Cost - Supplier Selection Instrument

Item Scoring Scale		Date: **6/6/95**

Possible Score	Definition
0	Completely unacceptable
2	Well below average- very weak
4	Below average- weak
6	Above average - acceptable
8	Well above average - outstanding
10	Far above average, no competitor is equal - exceptional

Commodity/service:
Electrical Parts & Components

Company Name:
ABC Electric

Supplier's Score for Item **X** Item Weight **=** Item Score

Quality System / Service Performance

	Supplier's Score for Item	Item Weight	Item Score
1 To what extent does the supplier's management have a "process" to facilitate continuous improvement?	9	.20	1.80
2 To what extent does the supplier evaluate, quality and rate its own suppliers?		.20	2.0
3 To what extent does the supplier solicit regular feedback of customer satisfaction?	8	.15	1.20
4 Are there regular scheduled management reviews of elements of the quality improvement process, including feedback for corrective action?	7	.15	1.05
5 Does the supplier have a "process" to ensure early detection and notification of quality, delivery or cost concerns requiring customer approval &/or intervention?	8	.10	0.80
6 To what extent does the supplier warranty its products/services?	9	.10	0.90
7 To what extent does the supplier have an active preventive maintenance program?	9	.05	0.45
8 How does the supplier's performance/service proficiency level compare with the competition?	9	.05	0.45

Weights should sum to 1.00. Add all item scores together to get the score for this section.

Section Score | **8.65**

Amoco Production Company

Total Cost - Supplier Selection Instrument

Item Scoring Scale		Date: **6/6/95**

Item Scoring Scale

Possible Score	Definition
0	Completely unacceptable
2	Well below average- very weak
4	Below average- weak
6	Above average - acceptable
8	Well above average - outstanding
10	Far above average, no competitor is equal - exceptional

Date: **6/6/95**

Commodity/service:
Electrical Parts & Components

Company Name:
ABC Electric

Supplier's Score for Item $\times$ Item Weight = Item Score

Environmental Health & Safety

	Supplier's Score for Item	Item Weight	Item Score
1 To what extent does the supplier meet and/or exceed Hi Tech's environmental & safety requirements and liability insurance requirements?	8	.45	3.60
2 To what extent does the supplier sponsor and aid the advancement of technology in solving environmental & safety problems?	9	.30	2.70
3 Is the supplier's OSHA/EPA incident and frequency rates and worker's compensation EMR indicative of a company that emphasizes the importance of safety?	8	.15	1.20
4 Is there an EH&S department or position to identify and prevent potential liability/safety hazards?	10	.45	0.45

SAMPLE

Weights should sum to 1.00. Add all item scores together to get the score for this section.

Section Score 7.95

Amoco Production Company

Total Cost - Supplier Selection Instrument

Item Scoring Scale		Date: **6/6/95**

Possible Score	Definition
0	Completely unacceptable
2	Well below average- very weak
4	Below average- weak
6	Above average - acceptable
8	Well above average - outstanding
10	Far above average, no competitor is equal - exceptional

Commodity/service:
Electrical Parts & Components

Company Name:
ABC Electric

Supplier's Score for Item X Item Weight $=$ Item Score

Research & Development
Technology Advancements

	Supplier's Score for Item	Item Weight	Item Score
1 To what extent is the supplier an industry leader in the technology of current parts/practices required by Hi Tech?	10	.25	2.50
2 To what extent does the supplier financially support technology development?		.20	1.60
3 To what extent has the supplier strived to ensure its technology/service is not in danger of becoming obsolete?	9	.20	1.80
4 To what extent are the processes developed to minimize disruption in supplier's deliveries of goods/services as a result of factors such as labor unrest, nonavailability of critical materials, machine breakdowns, transportation problems, etc..?	9	.15	1.35
5 Is the supplier willing and capable of early involvement in design and planning (all aspects) to improve costs and quality?	8	.10	0.80
6 To what extent is the supplier capable of controlling the quality of goods/services needed by Hi Tech?	8	.05	0.40
7 Is the supplier willing and capable of providing the necessary training for its employees and customers?	8	.05	0.40

Weights should sum to 1.00. Add all item scores together to get the score for this section.

Section Score	8.85

Amoco Production Company

Total Cost - Supplier Selection Instrument

Scores from each section should be brought over to this final composite section to determine the final supplier score. A reminder: all weights for each item in each section should be the same, as should the section weights applied to this composite section.

Commodity/service:
Electrical Parts & Components

Date: **6/6/95**

Company Name: **ABC Electric**

Contact Name: **Tim Underhill**

Phone: **(918) 494-8085**

Section Score X Section Weight = Total Section Score

Composite Rating

	Section Score	Section Weight	Total Section Score
Cost Management	8.15	.30	2.45
Financial Strength	8.40	.10	0.84
Management / Strategic	8.35	.25	2.09
Quality System / Service Performance	8.65	.20	1.73
Environmental Health & Safety	8.00	.10	0.80
Research & Development - Tech. Advancement	8.85	.05	0.44

SAMPLE

Weights should sum to 1.00. Add all section scores together to get the total score for this supplier.

Total Supplier Score | 8.35

Amoco Production Company

242

Exercise Instructions

Use the Section pages to complete the following questions

1. Determine primary criteria upon which to evaluate the commodity / service needs. For each criteria create a new section (page).

2. Determine the questions which will need to be answered in order to determine if the supplier can meet the expectations for the relationship sought.

3. Determine the weight for each item of information sought. Note: weights should sum to 1.00.

4. Using the scoring scale of 0 - 10, provide a definition for the possible scores.

NOTE: You are not expected to come up with supplier scores during this exercise.

Use the Item Source pages to complete the following questions

5. Determine the source(s) where the information sought can be found.

6. For each source, determine the specific information to be gathered.

Use the Composite Rating sheet to complete this exercise

7. For each primary criteria identified (section), list it in the boxes provided.

8. Weight each criteria (section) and place weight in section box. NOTE: weights should sum to 1.00.

Note: Use the "SAMPLE" sheets to review what to do.

Total Cost - Supplier Selection Instrument

Item Scoring Scale

Possible Score	Definition
0	
2	
4	
6	
8	
10	

Date:

Commodity/service:

Company Name:

Supplier's Score for Item **X** Item Weight **=** Item Score

1

2

3

4

Section Score

Amoco Production Company

Item Source

How and where to get the information needed to answer the questions.

Example: Dunn & Bradstreet - credit rating, sales, profit
Financial statements/records - Profit/loss, COGS, expenses, inventory, debt write-offs
Annual reports - (same as above), detail on expenditures, strategies, direction, R&D
Site visits - systems, inventories, personnel, facilities, capabilities, improvement processes
Surveys - primary systems evaluation, improvement systems, subcontractor evaluations
References - cost improvements, service provided, innovative ideas

Section & question:

Source:

Information sought:

Section & question:

Source:

Information sought:

Total Cost - Supplier Selection Instrument

Scores from each section should be brought over to this final composite section to determine the final supplier score. A reminder: all weights for each item in each section should be the same, as should the section weights applied to this composite section.

Commodity/service:

Date:

Company Name:

Contact Name:

Phone:

Composite Rating

Section Score X Section Weight = Total Section Score

Weights should sum to 1.00. Add all section scores together to get the total score for this supplier.

Total Supplier Score

Amoco Production Company

TOTAL COST
WORKSHEETS

The following pages are examples of forms alliance partners have use to gather the impact on total lost from their improvement efforts.

Revenue Enhancement

Processes Improved	(A) Past Process Cost	(B) Past Frequency of Use	(C) Current Process Cost	Savings = (A*B) -(C*D)

Note: Process savings should be annualized to reflect the savings for one year.

Total Process Savings

Price Improvement Worksheet

Items	(A) Annual Purchase Quantities	(B) Price Differences	Annual Savings (A*B)

Total Price Savings

Inventory Improvement Worksheet

Inventory Items	(A) Average Quantities in Inventory	(B) Average Value of the Item	Dollars Freed (A*B)	Savings = (A*B)*K Cost

Note: "K Cost" is used to denote carrying costs:
Interest, taxes, insurance and shrinking spoilage.

Total Dollars Freed	Total Carrying Cost Savings

Tier Pricing Worksheet

Date	Invoice Number	Amount of Invoice	Discount Received

Total Price Savings

Plateau Pricing Worksheet

	1st Quarter	2nd Quarter	3rd Quarter	4th Quarter	Total
Total Purchases					
Purchases Needed to Reach Plateau					
Plateau Savings					

Price Protection Worksheet

Items	(A) Quantity Purchased During Protection	(B) Price Increase Not Passed On	Savings = (A*B)

Price Protection Savings

Like Material Exchange Worksheet

Material to be Exchanged	(A) Market Value	(B) Book Value	(C) Investment Tax Impact (A-B)*Tax Rate	(D) Value After Tax (A-C)	(E) Exchange Value	Savings = (E-D)

Note: Investment tax can vary year-to-year based on the tax code.

Total Material Exchange Savings

One-Time Savings Worksheet

Date	Description of Event	(A) Process Savings	(B) Price Savings	(C) Man Hour Savings	(D) Equipment Savings	(E) Other Savings	Savings = (A+B+C+D+E)

One-Time Savings

Lead Time Impact Worksheet

Project/Items	(A) Amount Paid	(B) Amount Could Have Paid with Better Planning	Lost Savings = (A-B)

Total Lost Savings

New Product Technology Worksheet

New Product	(A) Output Improvement Value	(B) Process Improvement	(C) Price Savings	(D) Life Cycle Cost Improvements	Savings = (A*B) -(C*D)

Total New Technology Savings

Value Added Services Worksheet

Service Provided	(A) Fair Market Value of the Service (or Training)	(B) Time Spent on Service (or People Trained)	Value Added = (A*B)

	Total Value Added	

Life Cycle Worksheet

Comparable Products	(A) Number of Units Purchased	(B) Number of Failures	(C) Price of Units	(D) Average Cost to Correct Failure	Unit Life Cycle Cost = [(A*C)+(B*D)]/A

Note: This is a very rough estimate given that various products may have been in service for various lengths of time. Collect data on an ongoing basis and use data from at least two years.

AMOCO/RED MAN PIPE & SUPPLY JOINT NEWSLETTERS

Amoco / Red Man

Alliance Newsletter

January, 1995   Volume 1 Issue 1

Supply Chain Management Training

By Mickey McClure, Amoco, Odessa

Red Man and Amoco employees' training was held at South Plains College in Levelland, Texas, October 26th and 27th. Approximately 25 employees attended. The group at the training session expressed some understandable concerns about the alliance initially, but left as a motivated and committed team. Upon completion of this training the group had a better understanding of Amoco's relationship with its suppliers and the base we are trying to build through, which includes:
  ◆ Alliances
  ◆ Total System Cost
  ◆ Supply Chain Mgnt.
  ◆ Field Improvement Teams
  ◆ Quality System Review
  ◆ Communication
  ◆ Trust

Hats off to Tim Underhill on the job he did in putting on this training.

> *Every great achievement was once considered impossible.*

Red Man Field Improvement Team

By Don Sides, Amoco, Houston

Total dollar savings for Amoco at the Longview Operation Center, as depicted in the graph below, has amounted to $116,283.

The Red Man Field Improvement Team (F.I.T.) in Longview reported a savings of $16,000 associated with the purchase of valves for the meter runs for the Cotton Valley Drilling program. The specifications from Amoco required two [manufacturer A] valves for each hookup. One of the valves is in a critical service, while the other valve is blind flanged.

The Red Man store manager recommended that a cheaper valve be used on the non-critical application. The [Manufacturer B] valves for the non-critical application are $400 less than the [Manufacturer A] valves. The savings on the purchase of 40 of these valves was $16,000.

If we were doing business the "old" way, our supplier would have sold us the higher priced valve and never made the recommendation to change our specifications. *Working together really does work!!*

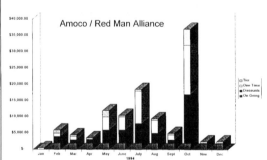

Mid Continent Business Unit

By Ted Hendryx, Amoco, Denver

The Red Man / Amoco partnership continues to enjoy successes throughout the Mid-Continent Business Unit.

At Ulysses, an aggressive 65 infill well program is planned for 1995. Ulysses operations personnel have targeted as a goal 30 days from rig release to first gas. Red Man is working with Amoco to meet this goal in defining lead time required for materials to be on location, while also allowing Amoco to take advantage of tier pricing discounts when material for more than one well can be ordered at one time. Amoco is projecting additional savings of $16,000 due to tier discounts from pre-planning, while invoicing by Red Man will be reduced significantly.

Ulysses operations have also reduced buy-outs to roughly 10% of total sales, and attributes the reduction in this category due to the mutual review by Amoco and Red Man of historical and current store purchases.

With the Amoco/Williams settlement announced last month, significant spending on the gas gathering system is anticipated. Both Amoco and Red Man currently are looking at packaging material purchases for the system where warranted.

Red Man's purchase of stock trailers is having favorable results at Watonga in Western Oklahoma. Remoteness of locations for this area has often necessitated multiple runs for new installation hookups. Red Man's stock trailer innovation has greatly reduced, and in several installations eliminated, multiple runs for both parties.

A final note at Wilburton-- where Red Man and Flint Engineering are members of a newly formed Amoco completion team. The team has been charged with defining general hookups for well completion while ensuring what has been designed is what is actually needed. Red Man's contribution will aid in developing completion standards for Amoco in Eastern Oklahoma.

Going the extra mile puts you miles ahead of your competition.

NGLBU ALLIANCE TEAM

By Craig Ketchum, Red Man, Tulsa

With the commitment of Amoco Production Co. and the NGLBU to strategic renewal and the Amoco Supplier Alliance Program (ASAP 2000), a cooperative relationship has been formed between ABB Randall, Flint Construction, Red Man Pipe & Supply, and Amoco.

The vision of the alliance is that the particular strengths of the companies involved, being properly evaluated and utilized, can collectively meet the challenges and opportunities in materials management, general maintenance, and project planning and execution through the NGLBU'S 13 plants.

A Steering Committee, made up of representatives from each company, has been formed to strive towards this alliance vision. The committee is focusing on developing a comprehensive management approach that streamlines engineering design, material procurement, spare parts inventory, and construction coordination efforts. This major objective utilizes the collective strength of the companies to ensure timely execution and application of strategic plans.

Initially, only the plants in the West Texas area will be included. The implementation phase has included a managers' meeting in Tulsa on October 20, 1994, a role-out of this alliance concept to all NGLBU plant asset managers in early November, followed by a role-out to all plant employees in West Texas, and two Steering Committee meetings. As this alliance implementation becomes established, the Steering Committee will develop a plan to achieve the same partnering relationship with other plants within this business unit.

Supply Chain Mgmt. Training

By Tim Brown, Amoco, Levelland

Over the past two months, the PBBU has taken a total of 43 Red Man alliance personnel (Amoco, Red Man, Flint and Randall) through the introduction to Supply Chain Mgnt. and Total System Cost training. The training was well received by most everyone, and we received some very positive comments on the training evaluation forms. The beer game turned out to be the most popular element of the training. Some of the groups really got into it with "beer" being ordered by the truckloads. It proved to be a very graphic demonstration of what can happen when communication is lacking, and you have to guess what the other people will do.

A special thanks to Katie Smith, Robert Travis and Tim Underhill for their efforts. They did an excellent job conducting the training.

Permian Basin Wins

By Dave Dillon, Red Man, Midland

The following is an update on the Amoco / Red Man alliance wins for the Permian Basin.

Amoco's Empire Abo Gas Plant, working with Red Man in Artesia, N.M. has Identified pressure gauges as an item that can be provided by Red Man, and save Amoco eight to ten dollars a gauge. With the purchase of 15 gauges per month there will be a savings of $1800 per year. The specifications fit the bill, and both Amoco and Red Man win.

In Andrews, TX., Amoco and Red Man have combined their efforts to integrate [*Manufacturer*] into the materials list which Red Man can provide. The Midland Farms OC purchases approximately 60 per year at a savings of $20 a tool. That is an annual savings to Amoco of $1,200. The Andrews store has also added value by cleaning, rearranging and stocking the production and plant warehouses at Midland Farms. In addition, they have coordinated another vendor in placing bolt bins at this facility, helping Amoco in getting the job done.

In Denver City, TX., Amoco and Red Man have worked together and made several improvements, starting with Amoco's two-way radios being installed in two Red Man vehicles, helping communications for both companies.

Schedule order and delivery times have been set up at the Wasson Field, establishing better planning and savings for both companies. A standardization program came out of the local F.I.T. team that establishes manufacturers quality and cost differences. With a little team-work, these types of deals will bring substantial savings. Amoco has also included Red Man in their morning meetings covering improving, planning, and deliveries.

At the North Cowden OC, Amoco and Red Man have won together by using Red Man's buying power on internal plastic coating. We're talking $5600 in a year's time on this one. Red Man will save Amoco 20% on their plastic coating needs. They have also saved freight charges of $110 on a special valve order being added to a Red Man stock order.

The Odessa store also found a better deal on cotton gloves that saved Amoco $1561 compared to the gloves they were previously buying.

All of these cases are documented and prove that working together, Amoco and Red Man can substantially improve both companies' bottom line.

Permian Basin Kickoff

By Tim Brown, Amoco, Levelland

The Field Improvement Teams (F.I.T.) in the PBBU & NGLBU have been making good progress in the past two months and have started attacking the "quick hits" for both companies. The teams all deserve high marks for their efforts to date. Although these teams have not been in place for long, here are some of the items they are attacking:

1. Evaluating items that have not been purchased through Red Man in the past. The general consensus is that savings through the elimination of processes and some price improvements will have a beneficial impact on the bottom line for both companies. (Next time we will have data to support this).
2. Scheduling deliveries to reduce costs.
3. Moving towards standardization within some product groups.
4. Combining plant and field inventories. This consolidation could significantly reduce the investment costs to Amoco.
5. Buyout review so Red Man can stock better, and Amoco can receive a better price.
6. Amoco provided Red Man with radios and field maps to improve delivery accuracy.
7. Red Man is operating an Amoco warehouse facility.
8. Joint efforts to work material needs have resulted in a 25% savings for Amoco in the purchase of fiberglass rodstrings ($100 per item).

Thanks!!

By Tim Brown, Amoco, Levelland

Overall, we believe that the Permian Basin portion of this alliance is off to a great start! In commencing this alliance effort, we recognized that it could be very difficult to successfully implement this alliance because of the massive cultural change required to get away from "three bids a buy" in MRO supplies, the existing infrastructure and historical relationships with various suppliers, and the large number of individuals within Amoco who order MRO supplies on a daily basis (virtually every field or plant employee). The information in this newsletter is just an overview of some of the early accomplishments of this alliance. The key to our success to date is the commitment and motivation of Red Man and Amoco employees on our F.I.T. teams, and the buy-in from all our plant and field employees. Please thank your coworkers who are working on our F.I.T. teams, and continue to bring up any ideas or concerns you might have about the alliance.

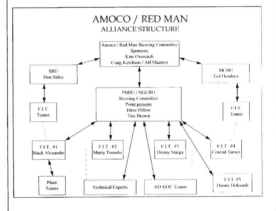

This chart shows a Joint Alliance between Amoco / Red Man depicting relationships between Field Improvement Teams, Steering Committee, various business units and resource people to be involved. If you have any questions please contact Tim Brown, (806)894-8307 or Tim Underhill, (918)494-8085.

Amoco / Red Man
Alliance Newsletter

April 1995   Volume 1 Issue 2

Alliance Training

By Ted Hendryx, Amoco, Denver, CO

Amoco and Red Man personnel attended a two day seminar in Oklahoma City that addressed alliance principles in general and more specific, progress of our MRO partnership.

Amoco representation included individuals from all MCBU operations centers as well as Jim Binegar from the Denver drilling team and Don Sides of the SEBU Longview Operation. Store managers for all Red Man locations in Oklahoma and Kansas were present as was upper management from Tulsa. Two contractors, L&L Backhoe and McLaughlin Electric of Western Oklahoma also contributed to the session.

Tim Underhill defined alliance concepts, types and desired goals and objectives. Although most of our folks have been introduced to these theories, it was a first for this group to really discuss face to face and see what was and was not working throughout the business unit. Price versus total cost in the supply chain was discussed and the analogy of single sourcing equating to price and that of partnering to total cost seemed to be understood by all.
It was noted, however, price still takes precedence in the field and the idea of total cost may still be viewed as somewhat subjective by many.

A brainstorming session was held to determine where big hits could be made in the alliance regarding reducing costs to both sides. Reduced inventories, planning, number of deliveries, standardization, etc. were discussed. Individuals were assigned to four groups and asked to forward their respective groups' ideas to Denver for summarization that were subsequently mailed to all attendees.

The session not only looked at cost improvement opportunities, but also how to capture cost savings and value-added activities. Several scorecards were introduced, many of which we now use; however, the groups were asked to review these cards for utility in their areas. Red Man did agree that most data captured would have to come from their joint efforts as Amoco did not have access to all the information needed. All agreed, however, that communicating this data capture was the responsibility of both partners. *Continued on page 4, Alliance...*

Red Man Acquisition

By Lew Ketchum, Red Man, Tulsa, OK

Red Man has purchased the inventory and certain fixed assets of the Vinson Supply Co. and has merged this into our operation

Cheniere Field Project

By Don Sides, Amoco, Houston, TX

The Amoco / Red Man team has been successful in reducing the cost of materials for a major project in the Cheniere Field just outside West Monroe, Louisiana. In an effort to increase the natural gas production rates, Amoco identified a project to loop the lines in the gas gathering system. The A.F.E. authorization for this project included pipe, fittings, valves, materials, inspections and construction labor. Because of a job well done, a substantial amount of money was saved on this project. All the companies involved in the project helped to accomplish these outstanding savings through improved planning and coordination.

Dennis Evans, with Amoco, and Kevin Matthews, with Red Man Pipe & Supply Company's store in Marshall, TX, worked together to drastically impact the total system cost for the materials. Through advanced planning, Red Man Pipe & Supply was able to provide a project trailer for the majority of the needs associated with the construction. Utilization of the trailer drastically reduced the number of trips required by Red Man. The 280 mile round trip to the construction project made the reduction in the number of trips critical for cost control for Red Man.

Another substantial savings came from the recommendation from Red Man to substitute the new [Manufacturer A] full port floating valves for the specified [Manufacturer B] valves. Through good communication and planning, the Amoco

team was able to realize savings of $8,996. on valves for the project.

There were additional savings on pipe prices, tier discounts and savings on other materials such as silk fencing and rye grass seed. The total savings attributed to the Red Man Alliance was $11,539. including the savings mentioned above on the valves.

Alliances do create competitive advantages. Red Man increased their sales volumes and Amoco gained full advantage of Red Man's expertise and favorable pricing terms. The improved pricing scenario enhanced economic pay-out of the project and increased cash flow by increasing daily production rates from the Cheniere Field. The daily rates have increased from 20/mmcfd to 32/mmcfd through this project.

> *Do it! Move it!*
> *Make it happen!*
> *No one ever sat their*
> *way to success.*

Score Carding Wins!

So far Amoco and Red Man, working together have been able to find a number of improvement opportunities which have allowed us to reduce the cost of doing business for the benefit of both our companies. These improvements can be found at both the corporate and field level. In some areas the pace of improvements has been so fast and furious we have failed to capture just what the benefit was.

This is unfortunate. All of us need to take the time to write down the wins we make happen. This need not be an awful task. It can be fairly easy. Working together, we have developed a number of score cards to help capture this information. The primary score cards we are asking people to use are:

1) *Alliance Price Savings* - being done through the alliance steering committee

2) *Tier Price Usage* - being done through the alliance steering committee

3) *Integrated sales* - needs to be done at each field, requires a joint effort

4) *One Time Savings* - needs to be done at the field level, can be done by either company

5) *Inventory Buy Backs / Outsourcing* - needs to be done at the field level, requires a joint effort

6) *Inventory Consignment* - needs to be done at the field level, requires a joint effort.

Most of Red Man's field personnel have been trained in their use and a number of Amoco personnel have as well. We do have other score cards (21 others in fact), but are only asking that these 6 be used at all locations and with all F.I.T.s. We know it is often hard to find the time to do this, but I think you will find it beneficial for several reasons:

1) The more information you can supply about the alliance the better we can show the impact to your specific location

2) With this information you can better show the effects of the alliance to others in your area

3) This is great evidence of the cost improvement efforts you are making to show to management to get the recognition you deserve for your efforts.

Additionally, if your F.I.T. team has a particularly "neat" win, write a short story about what you did and how much you saved and we will try to get it into this newsletter. Send your stories to:
Tim Underhill
c/o Red Man Pipe & Supply Co.
8023 E. 63rd Place
Tulsa, OK 74133

One popular idea with Amoco employees is to have Red Man stock and operate an on-site warehouse. This concept is currently being piloted at the North Cowden Unit / North Gas Plant. Red Man and NGLBU representatives are also discussing a pilot location for the Slaughter / Mallet complex as well. Although there can and will be circumstances where a Red Man operated warehouse makes sense from a total cost standpoint, there will likely be a very limited number of locations where this is a win-win arrangement. In order for Red Man to "break even" on the personnel costs involved with a warehouse, the total business must exceed $90,000. monthly. This break-even situation in itself does not represent a win for Red Man (since the sales volume should be a result of our alliance, not contingent on operating a warehouse). Long term, the best way to look at a warehouse is from a total cost standpoint. Pros and cons of a warehouse are:

PROS:

✎ Quick turnaround time for customers -- reduce or eliminate cost of delays

✎ Reduced mileage and "trip time" for Red Man

✎ Reduce or eliminate Amoco time spent managing inventory

CONS:

✎ Duplicate inventory -- between Red Man store and Amoco warehouse

✎ Cost of dedicated warehouse personnel

From the total cost standpoint, the preferred method is to improve planning and retain a **small** stock

of those few items on site that make economic sense. One example of a high "total cost" item would be polish rods, where the cost of keeping a unit waiting while a polish rod is delivered results in a very high total cost. However, many of our polish rod replacements could be better planned.

The North Cowden warehouse was established as a pilot and will be evaluated in the future to understand how effective it is from a total cost standpoint. North Cowden is a large facility with a high sales volume, which helps to justify Red Man personnel costs.

The main reason for considering the Slaughter / Mallet pilot is that Red Man has not historically done much work with the unique requirements of processing plants. Managing the warehouse for a large facility will give Red Man the chance to learn these material requirements first hand by being responsible for all purchases. Red Man's recent acquisition of Vinson Supply is a big step in setting up to service the "downstream" processing and chemical industries. In current discussions, Red Man and the NGLBU are considering splitting costs of a warehouse person if sales volumes are not sufficient to cover costs.

We will publish updates of these pilot efforts in future newsletters. In the meantime, we all need to continue to improve our planning process and communication to cut down total costs by reducing on-site equipment inventories and eliminating frequent and/ or rush deliveries.

Red Man Warehouses
By Tim Brown, Amoco, Levelland OC, TX

Pricing Issues

By Dave Dillon, Red Man, Midland, TX

One of the recurring Issues that continues to cause some concerns is price per item. There are ways to evaluate price in an Alliance agreement.

Are we talking apples to apples? Does that valve in question have the same trim, seats and seals? Is it 1500#, 2000#, or 2500# working pressure? If so, and everything is equal, can the other supplier offer a sustained price for that item? Is it a one time sale with special pricing? Are they selling this at a loss, hoping to get their foot in the door? If all the answers to the previous questions are the right answers, and there is still a discrepancy, what do we do?

The first step would be to weigh the expenditures on that particular item. If there are substantial dollars involved, what is the difference? Take this information to the Field Improvement Team. Look at alternatives if possible. Let Red Man go to work with the manufacturer and see if they can establish a better price. In a lot of cases your answers will be favorable. There will be times

Red Man cannot get there. You then must factor in the tier and plateau pricing if applicable. This could put you over the hurdle. It will take some planning and scheduling, but big cost gains have been proven in several cases. Cutting cost by vendor reductions, invoice reductions, and many other process costs will out-weigh the price difference in most cases.

Amoco has already seen substantial gains in price reduction due to forming the alliance with Red Man. These MRO market basket savings have been calculated out through joint efforts from Amoco and Red Man. Based on current spending levels, expected savings to Amoco for the 1995 year on stock sales from Red Man are over $700,000.00.

We are making good progress. Working together to reduce the total cost of ownership is where we want to go, and by following through with these types of procedures, we will get there.

Alliance Training
Continued from Page 1......

Stages of alliances such as discovery, implementation and maintenance were outlined to the group. A good point for everyone was identifying the maintenance stage, where most alliances fail due to structure and barriers encountered. A good communication exercise was performed at this point, where Amoco and Red Man were asked to identify both positive and negative perceptions currently held of each other. A summary of these perceptions was also forwarded to all attendees the following week.

Communicating was stressed several times as to where both parties can improve. Data and scorecarding from Red Man for Amoco's information will be filtered and communicated to the field by Denver. MRO and market change information needs to continue at the field level by both Amoco and Red Man. F.I.T. teams were addressed, and all agreed to pursue where warranted for their areas. Finally, as the opportunity existed, individuals were identified to act as contacts between management, the steering committee and field.

By all accounts the meeting was viewed as highly productive to our ongoing alliance.

Working Together To Reduce Total Cost
By Mickey McClure, Amoco, Odessa, TX

Two primary concerns in the PBBU and NGLBU have been buyouts and surplus material. In the short term, we've made a couple of improvements. First, in the area of buyouts the PBBU & NGLBU Field Improvement Teams are reviewing buyout reports monthly (furnished by Red Man) and items identified as normal used material, are placed in Red Man stock. Amoco should see a reduction in spending of $7,000. per month from this process. Second, the Red Man store manager at the Odessa store has agreed to help the PBBU & NGLBU lower their inventories and cut waste by utilizing Amoco's surplus material. We are going to identify surplus material, classify as good or as junk, clean up the good material, inventory, and use this material throughout the Business Units. There should be some large savings from this process.

Amoco / Red Man
Alliance Newsletter

July 1995   Volume 1 Issue 3

6 S's of an Alliance
By Mickey McClure, Amoco, Odessa

As Amoco develops relationships with suppliers and contractors, it is critical to measure the success of each relationship. There are six areas that will help identify and quantify the progress of the alliance. They are:
1. Scorecards
2. Standardization
3. Simplification
4. Sharing
5. Solutions
6. Savings

Each of these areas has special importance in an alliance. First, **scorecards** are used to measure the progress in cycle time, cost improvements, etc. It is impossible to improve what cannot be measured. **Standardization** has varied forms. There are efficiencies to gain from standardizing materials and processes. **Simplification** of a process improves the relationship through better utilization of manpower for both partners. **Sharing** information improves lead-time and material requirements. As the relationship develops, this shared information builds trust. Finding **solutions** for problems becomes the focus of the alliance, rather than placing blame. Finally, through the improved relationship, **savings** are realized by both Amoco and our partner. Through these 6 S's, we have a competitive advantage and are truly successful!

A Successful Year Together
By Mickey McClure, Amoco, Odessa

What can happen in a year! Well, it's been about that long since beginning our Alliance together. Through the efforts of many individuals, the Alliance has had many successes. Several of these successes are listed below:

➡ There are three business units in the alliance (Mid-Continent, Southeast, and Permian)

➡ Communication (between Red Man and Amoco's three business units that are in the Alliance)

➡ Organization (The forming of Field Improvement Teams)

➡ Establishment (of a standardized process)

➡ Reduced cost (It is estimated that Amoco E&P will save approximately $850,000 through the alliance)

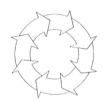

➡ Buy in from employees (Approximately 85 to 90 percent of all MRO spending is with Red Man in these business units)

➡ Joint succession planning (Red Man employees are beginning to attend Team Meetings)

➡ Establishment of champions

The Alliance would like to recognize Tim Brown, Don Sides, Ted Hendryx, Dave Dillon, Craig Ketchum and Dennis Niver for their efforts to make this Alliance such a success.

Success is best measured by how far you've come with the talents you've been given.

Product Saves $$
By Dan Kinnett, Red Man, Carthage

John Conway, field technician for Amoco's Longview Operations Center's Carthage Field, asked Dan Kinnett, manager of Red Man's Carthage Texas store, to check sources for liquid soap to foam high water to gas ratio wells. Conway wanted to find a more cost effective product than what he had been using.

The product recommended was a liquid foamer made by [*Manufacturer*] that is available in 55-gallon drums. Amoco's cost for a single drum of the product previously used was $479.00. The cost of the [*Manufacturer*] soap would be $336.00 for a single drum, or a savings of $143.00 per drum.

After talking with the [*Manufacturer*] representative, Conway decided to try a drum of the [*Manufacturer's*] soap on the Burnett Bros. #12 in the Carthage Field. Conway's goal was to get a 75MCF to 100MCF per day increase in production. Before using soap injection, production of the Burnett Bros. #12 was 150MCF per day. After soap injection, production was 240MCF per day. For an increase of 90MCF per day, it cost $14.69 per day after set-up expense. The total revenue increase at $1.80 per thousand, less expenses, will be $147.31 per day, or added revenue of $4,419.30 per month. These results led to an inquiry about buying the [*Manufacturer's*] liquid soap in bulk quantities. In working with [*Manufacturer*], an agreement was reached to purchase this product in ten-drum lots for additional savings of $62.00 per drum to Amoco, or a total

savings of $205.00 per drum over the previously used product. The Carthage Red Man store is stocking this product and will deliver it to Amoco locations as it is needed.

The results of the Burnett Bros #12 well, prompted Conway to set up a pump installation at the Carthage Gas Unit #15-5 to inject soap. Before soap injection, CGU #15-5 produced 75 MCF per day, after injection production increased to 223MCF per day. For an increase of 148MCF per day, cost totals are $8.24 per day. At $1.80 per thousand, less the cost, the increased revenue is $258.16 per day; for an increase in monthly revenue of $7,744.80.

The F.I.T. team had some concern about whether the soap treatment would cause problems with the well formation. Conway consulted with Mike Wells, Amoco engineer in Tulsa, who assured him the soap treatment would cause no problems.

The [*Manufacturer*] product has performed as well as the product previously used, but at a substantial savings. For the first month Amoco realized a savings of $1,168.00 by purchasing liquid soap from Red Man. In addition, Amoco has realized better gas production. In time, additional wells may be candidates for using this product.

Red Man Pipe and Supply Company continues to strive to strengthen the Amoco / Red Man Alliance.

Amoco / Red Man Alliance Wins

Our Alliance progress has been very rapid, and we continue to improve our operations with win/win solutions. We currently are installing an Amoco computer in this store to allow E-Mail and placing orders. We consider this one step in the direction of merging our systems.

Standardization has proven to benefit both parties by reducing mistakes on orders and lowering inventory levels. Integrated sales have resulted in new business for Red Man and fewer vendors and invoices for Amoco. This has occurred without increasing cost and has actually effected a reduction in some material. Amoco people advise this has relieved pressure on their time that allows them to take care of other business.

A new order/delivery process was developed which has been highly successful. Using Amoco's warehouses, we make scheduled deliveries every Monday and Wednesday (Friday if needed). We have also found a market for used sheaves that would have been scrapped. Amoco will make $1500.00 and in return purchase this amount of useable material from Red Man.

We continue to look every day at ways to improve this Alliance and head into the future.

Alliance Benefits

Red Man Positive Feedback

By Mike Killion, Red Man, Woodward

We had a lot of positive feedback on our yearly review. We met with Amoco and L & L Backhoe, and they each listed three positive and three negative responses. As a result of this meeting we were able to come up with improvements in several areas of development.

We switched Amoco from using [*Manufacturer A*] Acuators to [*Manufacturer B*] Acuators. This resulted in the savings of money and the time it took to get the acuators, from three months to two weeks.

Midland Farms Unit is preparing to reconstruct one of the unit's satellites to reduce leaks, improve well testing, etc. The vic connections are to be coated. Frank Florez, Red Man Sales Representative, advised that he could pick up our used material that he collected for this project. He would transport it to Odessa, have the material cleaned and coated and returned to MFOC. Red Man would invoice us only for the cost of the service from the coating company (no 10% surcharge). This expenditure would also count toward plateau pricing.

Also, Frank is picking up some of our excess surplus vic connections and transporting them to the Fullerton area for their use in some reconstruction efforts. Result --- Red Man, in these two instances, is helping Amoco to really cut operation costs. *PR+ to Frank for his help.*

Field Improvement Team; Watonga Area

By Jimmy Luke, Red Man, Lindsay
Larry Ross, Amoco
Ringo Thompson, Flint Construction
Randy Easter, Radar Construction

Working together in F.I.T.
(Field Improvement Teams)

A team, consisting of Amoco, Flint Construction, Radar Construction, and Red Man Pipe & Supply, worked on one trip tier savings and standardization of new well hook-ups. Through the meeting we have managed to save Red Man an estimated $2,500.00. Amoco had a one trip tier savings of $3,070.33 on hook-ups at five locations and $1,380.33 on East Niles Field Flo line project.

Working Together

By Lynn Terry, Red Man, Artesia and Fred Torrez, Amoco, Artesia

We have worked together in organizing the warehouse by keeping the warehouse stocked according to minimum and maximum requirements on bar coding. Together we have updated the prices and descriptions of all material. This prepared us to be ready for the shut-down. Amoco had given us plenty of lead time on material that we did not have.

Amoco thanks Red Man for the fast and excellent service they received during the shut-down.

Amoco/Red Man Win / Win!!

By Dan Andersen, Red Man, Andrews

Through our growing relationship with the different fields, we (Red Man) know we can continually reduce operating cost for our customers. In certain situations we have given Amoco credit on new surplus material then resold it to one of our other alliance customers, constituting a win/win/win for all involved. Sharing information along with the knowledge of each field's needs, concerns, and requirements are vital in bringing down cost.

Red Man Pipe & Supply Co. Amoco Mid-Continent

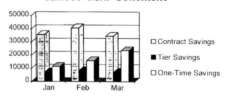

1 9 9 5

Red Man's MRO Alliance Generates $112M Savings for 1st Quarter of 1995

By Ted Hendryx, Amoco, Denver

Both volume discounting and tier pricing levels established when formalizing our alliance for MRO purchases with Red Man have collectively reduced expenditures in this category for the Mid-Continent by $112M during the first quarter. MRO sales throughout Mid-Continent for this period totaled $653M. Applying our 14 percent discount against these sales, (pre-alliance discount to Amoco was 6 percent), $91M in savings was realized. Tier discounts were taken advantage of at all OC locations, and totaled $21M.

Red Man store managers are committed to ensuring that Amoco is aware when requisitions do not quite meet the tier thresholds. Red Man's commitment and our personnel's planning efforts are paying off as Red Man advised; Mid- Continent did not miss a single discount during the first quarter.

On April 26, a full 11 days ahead of the predetermined timeline, Amoco Production Co. in Perryton, TX, completed a 6 month, 1.5M automation install on 140 wells. Amoco also came in under budget by $200,000.

Red Man assisted greatly with the timeline and the budget in several ways. At the beginning of the project, Dan Clinkingbeard, (Field Foreman) and Richard Schmidt (Automation Tech), got together with Tommy Carroll, (Store Manager, Red Man), to let him know what the project was all about and to see what kinds of materials that Red Man could supply them, lead times, deliverability, and the timeline constraints that Amoco was under. Tommy, in turn, informed and educated Dan and Richard on what he could supply them. He explained how Red Man could save Amoco money by using the quantity purchasing tool and what it could do for Red Man and Amoco as far as tier discounts.

Some of the biggest savings were incurred with the [Manufacturer A] valves and [Manufacturer B] actuators. Tommy gave the [Manufacturer A] valve personnel the entire order for the valves and let them know Amoco's timeline. By allowing them to fit the order into their production schedule, Amoco received a 12% discount on the *Manufacturer A]* valves. This was a $7,761.00 savings benefit. Tommy assisted Amoco greatly in their timeline when he stayed in almost constant communications with [Manufacturer B] and the sales representative, [Salesman's name]. It was known that the actuators would be a long lead item

and [Manufacturer B] nearly dropped

the ball, but Tommy persisted and Amoco did not ever take a loss on time due to actuators. The total benefit to Amoco, as far as tier discounts on the automation project, totaled to $7,238.73.

The [Manufacturer B] actuators were becoming a concern for all the Amoco Anadarko JOMT because of the apparent lack of interest on [Manufacturer B's] part for supplying them in a timely fashion. Tommy, along with Mike Killion, (Red Man, Woodward), also took charge in this area and found a different supplier. He researched and found a *Manufacturer C]* actuator and provided Larry Moody (Automation Tech, Woodward), to test. These are very similar in price and have a much better lead time. The lead time goes from about 3 months to 3 weeks. Richard Schmidt and Larry Moody both use these actuators in the field now.

One other area where Red Man and Amoco worked well together was at the half-way point on the install. Amoco's contractors in charge of the install warned Richard of some piping supplies that were running low. Marvin Borthwick, (contractor, Amoco alliance partner in Ulysses), used some of Richard's copies of receipts from his initial purchase from Red Man and made another quantity purchase so that Amoco could benefit from the tier discount structure.

Tommy and Richard believe that constant communication, during the automation project kept Amoco's project on time, and the benefits were felt by all involved.

Amoco's Timeline Project

By Tommy Carroll, Red Man, Perryton and Richard Schmidt, Amoco, Perryton

Amoco / Red Man
Alliance Newsletter

October 1995   Volume 1 Issue 4

Dear Friends,

My mother, my brothers and I all very much appreciate your prayers, thoughts and expressions of sympathy. They have been a comfort and assistance in our grief.

*During this most difficult time we feel it important to share with you our plan for the future of Red Man. Since January, 1991, controlling stock ownership of Red Man Pipe & Supply Company has been held in the trust of Lewis B. Ketchum with the beneficiaries of the stock ownership being the Ketchum family. Our plan and the plan of the Board of Directors is to proceed with my father's vision to continue to grow as **"The Supplier of Choice."***

My father had complete faith in the Red Man team, and I too share in that confidence. Dad will be greatly missed, and though he can never be replaced, we will carry on the legacy.

Sincerely,

Craig Ketchum

NGLBU Material Management Team
By *Dave Dillon,, Red Man, Midland*

The Material Management Team was formed in late April of this year by joint Amoco and Red Man Management. The sponsors are Neal Spencer, Amoco NGLBU Operations Manager, and Craig Ketchum, President of Red Man Pipe & Supply. The core team members are Mack Alexander, Amoco Asset Managers Representative, Tony Cooper, Amoco Project Focus, Dave McElhaney, Amoco Co-Leader, and Dave Dillon, Red Man Co-Leader.

The mission of the MMT is to develop, recommend and facilitate the implementation of innovative, cost effective materials management processes that satisfy the NGLBU's critical business requirements and optimize the utilization of the skill sets of Amoco's key Allied Contractors.

The goals of this team are to reduce the cost of inventory, reduce the amount of surplus material and equipment, reduce the cost of overall materials management processes, reduce the cost of overall warehouse processes, and to recognize the additional potential benefits available from the production (field) side of Amoco's business. The team has put together an eight phase work plan that will guide us through this project. Each individual phase gives the process, goals, expected deliverables and completion date of the phase. If you would like to see a detailed copy, please feel free to contact any of the four core team members.

We are currently in completion of the third phase, and moving to the fourth. We want to thank all the Amoco and Red Man personnel that have helped us get to where we are today, and look forward to working with the rest of you.

A special thank you goes out to Charlie Connell from Amoco E & C Shared Services who was an original core member and co-team lead. Charlie has recently moved on to another project.
Good Luck Charlie!

> Use life to provide
> something that outlasts it.

Red Man's MRO Alliance Generates $112M Savings for 1st Quarter of 1995

By Ted Hendryx, Amoco, Denver

Both volume discounting and tier pricing levels established when formalizing our alliance for MRO purchases with Red Man have collectively reduced expenditures in this category for the Mid-Continent by $112M during the first quarter. MRO sales throughout Mid-Continent for this period totaled $653M. Applying our 14 percent discount against these sales, (pre-alliance discount to Amoco was 6 percent), $91M in savings was realized. Tier discounts were taken advantage of at all OC locations, and totaled $21M.

Red Man store managers are committed to ensuring that Amoco is aware when requisitions do not quite meet the tier thresholds. Red Man's commitment and our personnel's planning efforts are paying off as Red Man advised, Mid- Continent did not miss a single discount during the first quarter.

On April 26, a full 11 days ahead of the predetermined timeline, Amoco Production Co. in Perryton, TX, completed a 6 month, 1.5M automation install on 140 wells. Amoco also came in under budget by $200,000.

Red Man assisted greatly with the timeline and the budget in several ways. At the beginning of the project, Dan Clinkingbeard, (Field Foreman) and Richard Schmidt (Automation Tech), got together with Tommy Carroll, (Store Manager, Red Man), to let him know what the project was all about and to see what kinds of materials that Red Man could supply them, lead times, deliverability, and the timeline constraints that Amoco was under. Tommy, in turn, informed and educated Dan and Richard on what he could supply them. He explained how Red Man could save Amoco money by using the quantity purchasing tool and what it could do for Red Man and Amoco as far as tier discounts.

Some of the biggest savings were incurred with the [Manufacturer A] valves and [Manufacturer B] actuators. Tommy gave the [Manufacturer A] valve personnel the entire order for the valves and let them know Amoco's timeline. By allowing them to fit the order into their production schedule, Amoco received a 12% discount on the [Manufacturer A] valves. This was a $7,761.00 savings benefit. Tommy assisted Amoco greatly in their timeline when he stayed in almost constant communications with [Manufacturer B] and the sales representative, [Salesman's name]. It was known that the actuators would be a long lead item

and [Manufacturer B] nearly dropped

the ball, but Tommy persisted and Amoco did not ever take a loss on time due to actuators. The total benefit to Amoco, as far as tier discounts on the automation project, totaled to $7,238.73.

The [Manufacturer B] actuators were becoming a concern for all the Amoco Anadarko JOMT because of the apparent lack of interest on [Manufacturer B's] part for supplying them in a timely fashion. Tommy, along with Mike Killion, (Red Man, Woodward), also took charge in this area and found a different supplier. He researched and found a Manufacturer C] actuator and provided Larry Moody, (Automation Tech, Woodward), to test. These are very similar in price and have a much better lead time. The lead time goes from about 3 months to 3 weeks. Richard Schmidt and Larry Moody both use these actuators in the field now.

One other area where Red Man and Amoco worked well together was at the half-way point on the install. Amoco's contractors in charge of the install warned Richard of some piping supplies that were running low. Marvin Borthwick, (contractor, Amoco alliance partner in Ulysses), used some of Richard's copies of receipts from his initial purchase from Red Man and made another quantity purchase so that Amoco could benefit from the tier discount structure.

Tommy and Richard believe that constant communication, during the automation project kept Amoco's project on time, and the benefits were felt by all involved.

Amoco's Timeline Project

By Tommy Carroll, Red Man, Perryton and Richard Schmidt, Amoco, Perryton

Amoco / Red Man

Alliance Newsletter

April 1996

Volume 2 Issue 2

Win--Win!!!

By D. Dillon, Red Man, Midland

During the month of February, Amoco, North Cowden, discovered a leak in their 4" pipe that was costing them 100 barrels of oil per day, which is approximately $18.00 per barrel. Red Man contacted the fiberglass manufacturers and could not get delivery for at least six weeks. Red Man contacted Coastal Management with a request to borrow the required pipe from their surplus. Coastal Management Corporation agreed that this could be done and saved Amoco four weeks of downtime and $55,800.

Also during February, Amoco, North Cowden, was to receive fiberglass pipe from the Bravo Dome area but they would not release the pipe when needed. This put North Cowden in a bind. Red man once again checked delivery dates on the requested fiberglass with no luck. Dana Gillit, Odessa, with the assistance of Dan Andersen, Andrews, located the pipe in stock with Exxon's consignment in Ratliff City, OK. They released the required pipe on short notice which in turn saved Amoco approximately $10,000.

This is not only a saving for Amoco and Red Man but also proves that the Alliance concept is a definite "win-win" situation. This also proves that TEAMWORK is not just for one, but is beneficial for the entire oil industry.

Alliance Training Held at Wilburton, Woodward, and Ulysses

By T. Hendryx, Amoco, Denver

In response to various team meeting requests for additional training in the alliance arena, a generalized course addressing this subject was developed and presented in January at the Wilburton, Woodward, and Ulysses OC's. The course was co-facilitated by Tim Underhill, Quality Coordinator for Red Man Pipe & Supply, and Jack Aulick, VAMSM supervisor.

Although the course was designed as a guide to an alliance initiative, essentially defining various types of partnerships, their desired outcomes, and identifying obstacles that may be encountered, the training was also 'individualized' to meet the needs and concerns of those attending at each location. Principals of supply chain management were reviewed with emphasis on today's changing relationship with both suppliers and competitors, Amoco's requirements and expectations, as well as understanding cost drivers in our day-to-day business. Challenging our 'old ways' of doing business and promoting the Amoco/Supplier team concept were also stressed throughout the course.

Each OC had the opportunity to communicate successes and concerns they have had with the alliance process. Everyone agreed most issues could be resolved through better communication with their partners, and where we enjoy success, these initiatives should be moved to the next level.

The course concluded with a review of Amoco's 1995 spending with alliances. Currently, the Amoco's Mid-Continent Business Unit has formed some 54 partnerships that account for more than 60% of total vendor spending.

> **The Next**
> **Amoco/Red Man Newsletter:**
> **July 1, 1996**

Soap Stick Savings

By M. Killion, Red Man, Woodward

Red Man, Woodward store, went to Amoco to discuss different types of soap sticks and the amount they would save by changing products. Amoco was using [*Manufacturer A*] soap sticks that were soft and came in cardboard boxes. Greg Gerdes tested over six different soap sticks and Amoco settled on [*Manufacturer B*] soap sticks that are hard and come in drum quantity. Next we went to Amoco, Watonga, and let them repeat the test. They also settled on[*Manufacturer B*] soap sticks. Production increased using [*Manufacturer B*], and Amoco saved $1.05 per stick from what they were previously using. This was a win for both Amoco and Red Man.

Red Man also saved Amoco $2000 per well by changing well hook-ups from a two tank battery to a one tank battery.

Amoco / Red Man
Material Management Team

By K. Holland, Red Man, NM
By M. Alexander, Amoco, Materials Coordinator

The NGLBU'S first material activity centers (MAC) are currently being established at the Mallet/Slaughter Complex. We will no longer have a warehouse as it is now known. The backbone of our MAC's will be our alliance partners who will help manage the material that will consist of vendor consignment, Amoco- owned critical items and surplus that will be kept to the minimum. Red Man will play the role of director and is a key player in setting up the MAC's.

A very important step is to ensure our surplus does not expand, but is continually reduced. We are working on our process to prevent this from happening. Teamwork, between not only Amoco and its alliance partners will be essential, but also teamwork between alliance partners themselves will help reduce our overall costs. April 15, 1996, is our target date to have our MAC's up and running at Mallet/ Slaughter. We will then expand to the Permian Basin South Plants through the last half of 1996.

Alliance vendors are helping reduce surplus by utilizing material throughout Amoco and other markets. Several *Clearinghouses* have been set up with companies like [*Company A and Company B*] to repair relief and other valves. We hope to have several more soon with other alliances.

The Material Management Team's presentation was well received at the Amoco progress fair held in Houston. It was good to see our work was in line with the other seven teams working towards a single goal.

Consigned Stock
By R. Blocker, Red Man, Sundown--Graph by L. Main, Red Man, Midland

The Sundown store and David Stegall, Levelland area drilling and workover foreman, have continued in our efforts to reduce the "total cost" of doing business in one area. We set up a consigned stock of polished rods and polished rod liners in Levelland (15 miles from the Sundown store) which has reduced our deliveries considerably. This has also reduced the time crews had to wait for us.

We reduced our deliveries from 31 in November to 10 in January. This is just another way we can work together to reduce "total costs".

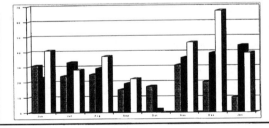

INDEX

FORMS

Revenue Enhancement

Date	Event	(A) Annual Unit Improvement	(B) Unit Value	(C) Increased Cost	Profit Improvement= (A*B)-C

Note: Process savings should be annualized to reflect the savings for one year.

Total Profit Improvement

Process Improvement Worksheet

Processes Improved	(A) Past Process Cost	(B) Past Frequency of Use	(C) Current Process Cost	(D) Current Frequency of Use	Savings = (A*B) -(C*D)

Note: Process savings should be annualized to reflect the savings for one year.

Total Profit Savings

Price Improvement Worksheet

Items	(A) Annual Purchase Quantities	(B) Price Differences	Annual Savings (A*B)

Total Price Savings

Inventory Improvement Worksheet
(Consignment Buy Backs Surplus Outsourcing)

Inventory Item	(A) Average Quantities in Inventory	(B) Average Value of the Item	Dollars Freed (A*B)	Savings = (A*B) * K Cost

Note: "K Cost" is used to denote Carrying Costs;
Interest, taxes, insurance and shrinkage/spoilage.

Total Dollars Freed   Total Carrying Cost Savings

Tier Pricing Worksheet

Date	Invoice Number	Amount of Invoice	Discount Received

Tier Price Savings

Plateau Pricing Worksheet

	1st Quarter	2nd Quarter	3rd Quarter	4th Quarter	Total
Total Purchases					
Purchases Needed to Reach Plateau					
Plateau Savings					

Price Protection Worksheet

Items	(A) Quantity Purchased During Protection	(B) Price Increase Not Passed On	Savings = (A*B)

Price Protection Savings [ ]

Like Material Exchange Worksheet

Material to be Exchanged	(A) Market Value	(B) Book Value	(C) Investment Tax Impact (A-B)*Tax Rate	(D) Value After Tax (A-C)	(E) Exchange Value	Savings = (E-D)

Note: Investment tax can vary year-to-year based on the tax code.

Total Material Exchange Savings [ ]

One-Time Savings Worksheet

Date	Description of Event	(A) Process Savings	(B) Price Savings	(C) Man Hour Savings	(D) Equipment Savings	(E) Other Savings	Savings = (A+B+C+D+E)

One-Time Savings

Lead Time Impact Worksheet

Project/Items	(A) Amount Paid	(B) Amount Could Have Paid with Better Planning	Lost Savings = (A-B)

Total Material Exchange Savings

New Product Technology Worksheet

New Product	(A) Output Improvement Value	(B) Process Improvement	(C) Price Savings	(D) Life Cycle Cost Improvements	Savings = (A+B+C+D)

Total New Technology Savings

Value Added Services Worksheet

Service Provided	(A) Fair Market Value of the Service (or Training)	(B) Time Spent on Service (or People Trained)	Value Added = (A*B)

Total Value Added

Life Cycle Worksheet

Comparable Products	(A) Number of Units Purchased	(B) Number of Failures	(C) Price of Units	(D) Average Cost to Correct Failure	Unit Life Cycle Cost = [(A*C)+(B*D)]/A

Total New Technology Savings

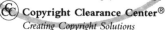